A DUTERTE READER

A DUTERTE READER

CRITICAL ESSAYS ON RODRIGO DUTERTE'S EARLY PRESIDENCY

Nicole Curato
EDITOR

SEAP Publications
an imprint of
Cornell University Press
Ithaca, New York

Contents

PREFACE

When this book went to press, *Time* magazine had just released its list of 100 most influential people. No surprise that Rodrigo Duterte, as well as his political archrival Senator Leila de Lima, made it to the list. Since Duterte had joined the presidential race in 2015, the world, it seems, has looked on the Philippines differently.

From the perspective of some international observers, the Philippines appears to be this exotic tropical island run by a strongman who hit it off with Vladimir Putin and used Hitler as reference in his bloody approach to the war on drugs. From the perspective of overseas Filipino workers, Duterte is a rock star, welcomed by loud applause and the warmest of cheers, from Laos to Saudi Arabia. Here is a leader who enlivens the self-esteem of people who have felt beaten down for decades.

This book is an attempt to make sense of these different portrayals, not only of the president but also of the nation that is emerging alongside the rise of Dutertismo. Hundreds of think pieces have been written on this subject. Lots of heated discussions have been exchanged over Facebook. In an era of fast politics, there is the pressure to come up with quick commentaries before the next spectacle takes over our conversations.

A Duterte Reader hopes to contribute to these conversations by taking a step back to carefully examine the social conditions and historical processes that shape the trajectory of Philippine democracy. To do this, a line-up of contributors was put together to provide considered yet critical perspectives on a range of issues—from elite democracy to human rights to celebrity politics to online trolling.

Many people have made this edited collection possible. Foremost is Karina Bolasco of the Ateneo de Manila University Press, whose immense persuasive powers encouraged me to work on this volume, do it well, and complete it on time. Then there are the contributors to this collection. It is inspiring to hear nineteen yeses when I approached nineteen authors to write a piece for the Reader. Even more inspiring is when everything stays on schedule, proving that there are still things that work in this very confusing time. I am also grateful to Vicente L. Rafael for providing critical comments on the earlier draft of the manuscript.

I worked on this collection as part of my Discovery Early Career Research Fellowship awarded by the Australian Research Council (DE150101866). My ethnographic work on Duterte's political supporters was conducted as part of this fellowship, where I examined the "politics of misery" in communities affected by Typhoon Haiyan. Also instrumental to the completion of this project is a research grant from the Australian National University's Philippines Project.

Some chapters in this edited collection are abridged and revised versions of pieces published in academic journals. Julio C. Teehankee's chapter is based on an earlier publication entitled "Weak State, Strong Presidents: Situating the Duterte Presidency in Philippine Political Time" in the *Journal of Developing Societies*, volume 32, issue 3. Walden Bello's chapter was originally submitted as "The Spider Spins His Web: Rodrigo Duterte's Ascent to Power" in the *Philippine Sociological Review*, volume 65.

The topics covered in *A Duterte Reader* are by no means complete. Indeed, there are more issues that warrant close investigation and critical scrutiny. May the era of Dutertismo be a fruitful time for scholars and citizens to think of creative ways to fight repressive and abusive power, support emancipatory projects, and imagine a democracy that will work for all.

Nicole Curato
Canberra, April 2017

WE NEED TO TALK ABOUT RODY

Nicole Curato

W e need to talk about Rody. Rodrigo Duterte—the "self-confessed mass murderer" who vowed to kill in the thousands, an
unapologetic womanizer who saw no wrong in making a rape joke
about a dead Australian missionary, the "bastard child of Philippine
democracy" whose popularity is built on his "dark charisma," the
"dictator-in-waiting" threatening to shut down Congress—was
elected president of the Republic of the Philippines in May 2016.
He cursed the Pope, called President Barack Obama the "son of a
whore," and hailed Vladimir Putin as the paragon of leadership.
He was called many names—Trump of the East, The Punisher, and
Duterte Harry—all seemingly disparaging and exotic portrayals of
the tropical island leader. Indeed, we need to talk about Rody.

But we need to talk about him differently. A lot has been said
about the president's eccentricities and character flaws, but more
can be said about the broader context that gives rise to such a
controversial personality to take power. *A Duterte Reader* hopes
to take part in this conversation by bringing together a line-up of
Philippine studies scholars from different generations, geographic

locations, and disciplinary backgrounds. Each of the authors was tasked to take a long view of the factors that gave rise to Duterte's phenomenal electoral victory and reflect on the kind of society that emerges from the era of Dutertismo.

The views presented in this collection are diverse, and, in several instances, in opposition to each other. This is inevitable, for Duterte's politics is one of the most polarizing issues today. But there is one thread that runs through all the chapters in this edited collection: that Dutertismo both disrupts and perpetuates the Philippines' elite democracy, marked by stark inequalities in political power, economic resources, and social esteem. His rise to power forces a rethinking of the nation's aspirations, what it means to be a democratic country amidst the global crisis of liberal democracy, and what freedoms citizens are willing to sacrifice for the common good.

The book is written six months into Duterte's presidency—six months being Duterte's self-imposed deadline to transform the country from a "narco-state" to a "peace-and-order" paradise. By that point, the regime has started, canceled, and restarted peace talks with the communist rebels. The president has met with Moro revolutionary leaders to pave the way for a comprehensive peace agreement. The Supreme Court has decided in favor of burying the late dictator Ferdinand Marcos's remains at the Heroes' Cemetery. The House of Representatives overwhelmingly voted in favor of restoring the death penalty. Former members of the Davao Death Squad publicly testified to Duterte's involvement in summary executions during his tenure as city mayor. The Philippine National Police has reported a drop in property crime but recorded thousands of drug-related killings. One of Duterte's staunchest critics, Senator Leila de Lima, has been arrested for drug-related charges. Duterte met with world leaders, visited China, and declared the country's "separation" from the United States. As these political developments were unfolding, the World Bank projected faster growth rates driven by high infrastructure spending and sound macroeconomic fundamentals. Duterte continues to enjoy widespread popularity, with an 83 percent trust rating six months into his presidency. This book hopes to make sense of these complex times.

The Phenomenal Rodrigo Duterte

There is little disagreement in using the term "phenomenal" to describe Duterte's landslide electoral victory. The seventy-one-year-old firebrand became the sixteenth president of the republic after serving as mayor of Davao City for more than two decades. For the first time in Philippine history, a son of Mindanao made it to Malacañang.

Few would have imagined this a year before the elections. In President Benigno S. Aquino's valedictory State of the Nation Address, he provided a narrative of the country's remarkable growth story, from being the "sick man of Asia" to becoming "Asia's bright spot." As he talked about the stakes of the forthcoming elections, live pictures of Vice President Jejomar Binay, Senator Grace Poe, and Secretary of Interior and Local Government Manuel Roxas seated in the audience were flashed on split-screen giant monitors. Without the president having to say anything more, this choreographed image framed the elections as a three-way race between these national officials, elegantly dressed in formal Filipino attire, comfortable under the national spotlight. Duterte, meanwhile, was not part of this annual gathering of the political elite. He watched Aquino's address at a public screening in Davao's People's Park, sitting on a plastic chair, wearing his signature plaid polo and poorly tapered trousers. The contrast could not be more evident. As Manila's political class geared up for the elections, Duterte kept his cards close to his chest. Very few, at that point, would have predicted Duterte to claim the presidential seat ten months hence.

Duterte snatched the lead from Senator Grace Poe five weeks before the elections. Before his presidential run, he was mostly invisible in the national conversation, except for urban legends about this mayor who made a tourist eat a cigarette for violating the city's smoking ban and praised his daughter for punching a sheriff. But momentum was on Duterte's side. There were mumblings among middle class and urban poor communities about the appeal of a certain Mayor Duterte who could get things done. These conversations are most pronounced in Mindanao, as Duterte's Davao City is a stark demonstration of how strong leadership transformed the

Philippines' murder capital into one of the most progressive cities in the country.

As talks of a possible Duterte run began to gain traction, the mayor categorically rejected calls for his candidacy. "Too old, too tired, and too poor" was Duterte's response when asked about a possible presidential run. At the same time, he was spotted going around the country, engaging in "listening tours," and talking about his advocacy of shifting to a federal system of government. Many interpreted this as a tease—a way to intensify public clamor for the mayor to throw his hat into the ring. After a will-he-will-he-not-run saga—playfully called #Duterteserye in social media—Duterte declared his presidential bid.

Duterte's rise to power confounded observers of Philippine politics. He seems to have an uncanny ability to gain supporters even as his catalogue of gaffe grows. His long, off-the-cuff, expletive-ridden speeches constantly find a mammoth audience in town plazas and social media. While Roxas's Liberal Party and Binay's United Nationalist Alliance expected their local machinery to deliver votes on election day, Duterte took pride in his ragtag army of volunteers. "Not a single congressman supported me," he often says as part of the narrative of his come-from-behind win. News reports belie this claim. For example, the Nograleses from Davao—once political rivals of the Dutertes—threw their support behind Duterte's presidential bid.

Duterte won by a commanding lead of six million votes. Hours after the polls closed, his competitors conceded defeat in one of the most bitterly fought elections in the Philippines.

How can one make sense of Duterte's phenomenal rise to power? What does his popularity say about the emerging character of Philippine democracy?

The subsequent chapters in this book illustrate how Duterte simultaneously disrupts and perpetuates elite democracy in the Philippines. There are three aspects to this claim.

1. Electoral insurgency and inevitable rise. Duterte's ascendancy is both a product of an electoral insurgency and an inevitable rise of a populist leader. While he disrupted the

typical expectations of presidential contenders, Duterte's electoral victory, when viewed through a historical lens, is not surprising, for his win conforms to the populist-reformist pattern of presidential victories that has marked post-authoritarian politics in the Philippines. Duterte may have ushered in a new era for Philippine democracy, but early indications suggest that his governance style remains partial to elite rule.

2. Liberal ideals and illiberal fantasies. Winning a campaign based on a promise of a bloody war on drugs challenges the liberal ideals of human rights and due process. Duterte unsettled dominant assumptions about the extent to which liberal virtues are rooted among the citizenry thirty years after the People Power Revolution that ousted the dictator Ferdinand Marcos. Duterte's illiberal fantasy, however, has an ironic character. While it rejects the liberals' approach to crime and human rights, his illiberal project is also built on, and perpetuates, the same imperfections that discredited the Philippines' liberal democracy: a corrupt and unprofessional coercive apparatus of the state, on which he relies to carry out his war on drugs.

3. Crass politics and spectacle-driven publics. A major part of Duterte's controversial character has to do with his language. His crass politics has shed light on the citizens' anxieties, exposed powerful institutions' hypocrisies, and provided the vocabulary to capture the public's brewing anger against the unfulfilled promise of elite democracy. Duterte's crass politics, however, is ultimately rooted in, rather than transformative of, the character of political communication in contemporary times. Crass politics works well in today's mediatized cultures of reality television, digital disruption, and spectacle-driven news cycles, as well as broader cultures of violence and sexism. Duterte's crass politics comfortably fits in, rather than disrupts, today's communication architecture that shapes the character of conversations in the public sphere.

This introductory chapter discusses each of these claims. Foregrounding the tensions between the politics of disruption and continuity is crucial to capture the nuances of the Duterte regime, as well as examine the negotiated and contingent character of emerging political and social realities today.

Electoral Insurgency and Inevitable Rise

Elections in the Philippines are often viewed using the lens of machine politics—a context where local factions or alliances of political families form a coalition with candidates running for national position, who, in turn, provide resources in exchange for these local actors' "brokerage network" (Aspinall, Davidson, Hicken, and Weiss 2016). In popular parlance, this practice is described as a showdown of candidates' guns, goons, gold, and belatedly, gigabytes. Whoever musters the most resources for vote buying and intimidation wins the seat of power.

The 2016 race was thought to be defined by machine politics. Weeks before the polls, once-frontrunner Jejomar Binay expected his local network of mayors and barangay captains to deliver votes on election day. For years, Binay has cultivated these networks, which propelled him to his unexpected victory in the vice-presidential race in 2010. The same is true of Roxas. As he had spent the past few years going around the country as the Interior Secretary, the Liberal Party counted on governors and mayors to return the favor to the party that gave them roads, bridges, and airports. Senator Grace Poe, on the other hand, relied on star power. She had the weakest political machinery as a neophyte in the political scene but her strong brand as the compassionate daughter of one of the legends of Philippine cinema carried her to the top of the polls until Duterte took over the race.

Disrupting Elite Rule?

But 2016, as Maureen Dowd (2017) puts it, is "the year of voting dangerously." The public placed their bets on an odd city mayor with an alluring record of accomplishments. "Electoral insurgency" is the term Walden Bello uses to describe this phenomenon. Duterte anchored his campaign on "citizen-led political action that disrupts traditional campaign practices" (Curato 2017, 104). Small-scale entrepreneurs provided minivans, sound systems, truck ads, and even catering for Duterte's campaign sorties. The excitement is also palpable among overseas Filipino workers. An ethnographic study of Duterte's campaign reveals how funding sources were "democratized" through modest remittances from places like Jeddah and Kuwait that funded printing banners, wristbands, and t-shirts in support of Duterte. Even more moving is the enthusiasm for Duterte's campaign among impoverished communities, where his supporters pulled together what meagre resources they had to buy a Duterte t-shirt and find ways to pay their jeepney fare to get to the plaza to witness the candidate's speech. This is not an insignificant achievement. Elections are typically viewed as an, if not the, occasion for redistributive politics, where politicians reach out to the constituencies whom they have ignored outside the campaign period in exchange for their votes. Instead of getting material rewards in exchange for supporting a candidate, this time it was voters who spent their own resources to support Duterte. Bello witnessed this first hand as he ran for the Senate in 2016. In his field diary, he describes the affective and spontaneous foundations of Duterte's candidacy:

> Spontaneity and improvisation and grassroots momentum have been the hallmarks of the Duterte campaign. Believe me, I saw this bubbling up from below as I traveled the length of the archipelago in my own campaign for the Senate. Duterte, more by instinct rather than plan, simply set fire to emotions that were already just below the surface. I think we should avoid accounts that promote the understanding of this movement as one created by manipulation from above. I am disturbed by the Duterte movement and fear a Duterte presidency, but we risk gross misunderstanding of its dynamics and direction if we attribute its emergence to mass manipulation. It is, simply put, a largely spontaneous electoral insurgency. (Bello, forthcoming)

This, however, is not to say that big money did not figure

in Duterte's campaign. The Philippine Center for Investigative Journalism challenged the narrative that Duterte ran on a shoestring budget. Duterte's Statement of Contributions and Expenditures—a requirement by the Commission on Elections—reveals that he raised PhP 375 million (USD 7.5 million), with almost 90 percent of his funds coming from thirteen individuals. Among Duterte's prominent campaign contributors are businessmen from Davao, including Davao del Norte Representative Antonio Floirendo and personalities who have bagged government contracts. Meanwhile, less than 1 percent of the president's total campaign fund came from small donations amounting to less than PhP 10,000 (Ilagan and Mangahas 2016). Duterte himself has been vocal in identifying the deposed dictator's daughter and Ilocos Norte Governor Imee Marcos as one of his first supporters.

There are various interpretations when it comes to Duterte's relationship with elites. For some observers, Duterte stood out as someone with no clear link to national and traditional landowning elite, unlike his competitors (Casiple 2016; Desker 2016). While not necessarily a counter-elite, Duterte has portrayed himself as an outsider-elite: he is connected to the elites but not part of them (Mudde 2004, 560). After all, Duterte was the son of Davao's former governor, his roots can be traced to some of the most influential political clans of Cebu, and he himself developed his own political dynasty in Davao, with his daughter and son concurrently sitting as mayor and vice mayor. For Bello (chapter 4), however, Duterte cannot be reduced to another puppet of the elites. He has a power base of his own, and is "beholden to no one." Elites who threw their support behind Duterte did so for their own protection, "like small merchants paying protection money to the mafia." Lisandro Claudio and Patricio Abinales (chapter 5), on the other hand, make a distinction between Duterte's disdain for the old feudal elites and his congenial relations with new elites that emerged after the war, such as the Marcoses. They argue that Duterte is an "heir to elite attempts to centralize a system of a multi-polar oligarchic democracy," and his pronouncements against the *coños* (cunts) of Manila's gated communities do not stem from his desire for social levelling. Instead, it is an attempt "to demonize the oligarchs so that he may reign over them."

The discussion of Duterte's relationship with the elites is sure to develop in the coming months. Whether he would expend his political capital to implement policies that go against elite interest is worth observing, particularly which elite interests he is ready to challenge. Elites in the Philippines do not form a monolithic block. Each segment has its own competing interests. While Duterte already singled out oligarchs such as Roberto Ongpin and Lucio Tan for unscrupulous business practices, his cabinet is also full of them.

Disrupting Imperial Manila?

Data suggesting that Duterte's campaign was bankrolled by big donors puts him in broadly the same category as other presidential candidates as far as money politics is concerned. What then sets Duterte apart from the others? One explanation has to do with his strategy and political message.

It is not the first time that Duterte blindsided his political opponents. In an interview with *The Journal of Social Transformation, MindaNews* co-founder Jowel Canuday narrated how Duterte beat Corazon Aquino's anointed candidate Zafiro Respicio in the 1987 mayoral race. "In Davao, nobody understood how he won the mayor's office," he said. "He was kind of an oddity: Who is this government prosecutor who joined the anti-Marcos parliament of the streets? And yet he became mayor" (Canuday 2017, 134). Knowing that Respicio is popular in the city, Duterte opted to focus his campaign on the countryside with a large rural population and informal settlements near the industrial zone. This same strategy, for Canuday, worked in the national race. Employing "the Davao strategy," Duterte focused on winning the votes of specific regions such as Ilocos and most of the Visayas, and consolidated the Mindanao vote (135). "It tells you something about the way his mind works," Canuday adds, "he can see political opportunity from a mile away" (135).

One of the major opportunities Duterte spotted is to consolidate the Mindanao vote. For Jesse Angelo L. Altez and Kloyde A. Caday (chapter 6), winning a "solid south vote" is a "rarity in a region marked by ethnolinguistic, economic, and socio-political divide." Duterte's landslide victory in Mindanao cannot be reduced to regionalism or relying on bailiwicks. For Altez and Caday, Duterte's appeal runs deeper than electing a president who came from Mindanao. For them, Duterte masterfully articulated the language of inclusion among the diverse peoples of the South.

> His triumph is the unison of voices of the Mindanaoans to associate themselves with him, with the progress of Davao City as the microcosm of the Mindanao dream where the tri-people of Mindanao live side by side despite their differences. (Altez and Caday, chapter 6)

Duterte's promise of leaving a Mindanao governed in peace is understood as "a commitment forged in blood—a kin's word vouched to be fulfilled" (Altez and Caday, chapter 6). In his campaign speeches, Duterte always emphasizes his Maranao heritage from his mother, Soledad Roa, and his link to indigenous peoples, through his daughter-in-law, a Tausug-Maranao woman. While leaders from the Autonomous Region in Muslim Mindanao are members of the Liberal Party, Duterte's sorties were warmly received, with thunderous chorus of "Allahu Akbar" from an enthusiastic audience. Duterte, for his part, would cheer "Long live the Moro! Allahu Akbar!" as he did in his final campaign sortie. For Altez and Caday, the people saw in Duterte "an opportunity bound by familial commonality: a space for negotiation where the Mindanao orthodoxy of Christian-Muslim divide can meet through a rightful compromise."

Having an entire region marginalized for decades to shape the course of the elections is a symbolic feat. Mindanao is often the site of electoral fraud, as in the case of the contentious 2004 elections, where 58 percent of Filipinos in Mindanao believed that President Arroyo cheated in the elections. The credibility of elections in Mindanao hit a record low, with 70 percent believing that there was cheating in the elections (Pulse Asia 2008). Duterte's entry into the political race changed the view that the Mindanao vote is dispensable—that the war-torn region can easily be used as staging ground for cheating. Instead, the neglected South regained its esteem in 2016 and became the game-changer in what started as a tightly contested race.

Duterte's rise to power shifted the center of politics from Manila to Mindanao. Even though Duterte has taken official residence in the Malacañang Palace, he regularly travels to Davao. The presidential guest house in Panacan, in Davao City, which earned the moniker Panacañang, has become the site of key meetings—from hosting Australia's Foreign Secretary Julie Bishop to discussing the prospects of "just and lasting peace" with the Moro National Liberation Front's founding chairman, Nur Misuari. Among Duterte's key appointments are some of his closest allies in Mindanao, including Leoncio "Jun" Evasco Jr. (Secretary to the Cabinet) and Carlos Dominguez III (Finance Secretary). It is also the first time in history that the president, Senate President, and Speaker of the House all hail from Mindanao. For Barry Desker (2016), Duterte's election signals "a shift away from Manila-centered politics" and an effort to place the south in the center of his administration. Duterte disrupted Imperial Manila's privilege, and started building a nation with a gaze coming from the south.

Disrupting the EDSA System?

Duterte's convincing win did not find traction only in Mindanao. A few weeks before elections, he secured support across different geographies, age groups, and socio-economic classes. A bigger narrative is taking shape beyond the South's revolt against Imperial Manila. Following the trend of global discontent against "mainstream politics," Duterte's victory is viewed as a protest vote against the ruling EDSA regime (Casiple 2016).

The Philippines' path to democratization since the EDSA People Power Revolution in 1986 has been an uneven one. While liberal rights were restored and a vibrant public sphere flourished, elections continued to be a system for shifting clan alliances to compete for political power. The EDSA system's failure created conditions for Duterte's success. As Bello puts it:

> What destroyed the EDSA project and paved the way for Duterte was the deadly combination of elite monopoly of the electoral system, the continuing concentration of wealth, and neoliberal economic policies and the priority placed on foreign debt

repayment imposed by Washington. By 2016, there was a yawning gap between the EDSA Republic's promise of popular empowerment and wealth redistribution and the reality of massive poverty, scandalous inequality, and pervasive corruption. (Bello, chapter 4)

Duterte's electoral victory represents a "major rupture" from the EDSA regime (Teehankee and Thompson 2016, 125). He is the first post-authoritarian president that brazenly talks about declaring martial law, or shutting down Congress should there be obstacles to the pursuit of his agenda (Claudio and Abinales, chapter 5). In Cleve Kevin Robert V. Arguelles's essay on the politics of memory (chapter 14), he characterizes Duterte's "subversive attempts" to redefine the victors of the revolution and renegotiate its centrality to national memory. This is manifest not only in his campaign promise of allowing the burial of the deposed dictator Marcos in the Heroes' Cemetery but also in his lack of enthusiasm in performing rituals that commemorate the People Power Revolution. For Arguelles, Duterte is mobilizing state resources to promote "public amnesia" to set the new terms for a post-EDSA regime. Julio C. Teehankee (chapter 2) describes this as Duterte being "a repudiator reconstructing the Philippine presidency." Duterte is changing the EDSA regime's storyline from an elite-led crusade for good governance to a "counter elite nationalist-populist law and order developmentalism." This is manifest in Duterte's key priorities, including changing the constitution to shift to a federal-parliamentary-semi-presidential system of government, and his pursuit of an "independent foreign policy" that is less reliant on the United States.

Duterte, it seems, is resolved to dismantle the insidious legacies of the EDSA system—from its symbolic rituals to its institutional arrangements. What about economic policy? A key part of the EDSA system is its export-orientation, reliance on foreign investments, and crony capitalism. Is Duterte also disrupting the nation's political economy that created one of the most unequal societies in the region?

Duterte self-identifies as a socialist. He has expressed admiration for the Communist Party of the Philippines' (CPP) founder Jose Maria Sison and given key cabinet positions to nominees of the

CPP, including the Department of Social Welfare and Development, the Department of Agrarian Reform, and the National Anti-Poverty Commission. At the same time, his picks for the economic team do not show indications of departing from previous regimes' prudent macroeconomic policies. Despite his nationalist rhetoric, Duterte's economic ministers have shown:

> no intention of nationalizing strategic industries, distributing lands to small farmers, or increasing substantially both the fiscal deficit and national debt of the government, as did the most recent socialist governments of Greece, Venezuela, Brazil and up to recently Argentina. (Villegas and Manzano 2016, 198)

Duterte also supports removing restrictive economic provisions in the 1987 constitution to attract foreign direct investments. Dutertenomics, as his economic ministers envision, is driven by large infrastructure spending (5 percent of GDP) to usher in the Philippines' "golden age of infrastructure," and a revamp of the tax system to make the Philippines competitive with the region.

Duterte's economic policies have been one of the earliest sticking points in his alliance with the Left. As Emerson Sanchez (chapter 15) explains, nationalist think tanks have called out Duterte for continuing to privilege foreign firms and big businesses while neglecting issues like wage increase and developing local industries that can spur nationalist development. Instead of dismantling elite structures that defined the EDSA regime, Duterte put together what Teehankee refers to as an "insurgent counter elite coalition to neutralize the strategic interests that constitute the EDSA ruling elite." Part of this coalition are

> the traditional politicians marginalized by the EDSA forces (i.e., the Marcos, Estrada, and Arroyo forces); the non-Manila business elites (i.e., former Marcos crony and banana magnate Antonio Floirendo, former Cory Aquino cabinet member Carlos Dominguez, Filipino-Chinese Lorenzo Te, Dennis Uy, and Samuel Uy); the new middle class (i.e., call center agents, Uber drivers, overseas Filipino workers); the communist national democrats; and the national police. (Teehankee, chapter 2)

If the Davao model of economic development were any indicator, one could surmise that Duterte's economic agenda will be defined by lessening red tape and corruption to ensure ease in doing business anchored on a strong-handed peace and order agenda. As for the pro-people and nationalist policies that the Left demands, there seems to be few indications that Duterte is headed in that direction. The question remains whether the EDSA regime's elite-centered political economy will remain intact, albeit run by different actors.

Disruptive but Inevitable

Thus far, this section has described the ways in which Duterte has both disrupted and extended practices of elite democracy as he ushers in a new phase of the post-EDSA regime. Was Duterte's ascent to power inevitable? The answer, for some observers, is yes. Duterte's rise is as surprising as it is inevitable.

Take the case of what Mark Thompson (2010) refers to as the pattern of reformist-populist swing in Philippine politics. Thompson observes that presidencies in the Philippines tend to swing from electing a populist to a reformist leader, beginning with Corazon Aquino's emergence in a popular uprising that gave birth to the EDSA regime. Since then, the swing has been consistent, except in the 2004 elections smeared with electoral fraud, where populist action star Fernando Poe Jr. was widely believed to have beaten the incumbent reformist Gloria Macapagal-Arroyo. The year 2016, it appears, is the turn for another populist to take power. Initially, the race was thought to be in the bag for Vice President Binay—a man who has mastered the art of winning the hearts of poor constituencies—and, later on, with Fernando Poe Jr.'s daughter Grace, who promised to form a compassionate government. But Duterte offered a different form of populist discourse that resonated with the brewing public discontent with Aquino's administration. The reformist Roxas, meanwhile, never took the lead in any credible poll. Thompson's observation of the populist-reformist swing continues to hold in 2016.

In chapter 2, Teehankee provides an explanation for Duterte's inevitable rise. He situates Duterte's electoral victory in cycles of presidential regimes in the Philippines. Drawing on Stephen Skowronek's work, he examines how political leaders transform narratives into governance scripts that give shape to political regimes. Teehankee locates Duterte's rise "in between structural regimes and agential choices." The combination of background conditions of economic resentment and Duterte's fierce rhetoric created favorable conditions for Duterte's rise. He successfully tapped "into the 'politics of anger' fueled by the general sense of frustration among the voters and the growing desire for a strong leader to restore law and order" (Teehankee, chapter 2).

Duterte's seemingly simplistic solutions to complex problems often lead to the impression that his supporters are, for the most part, from the "masa" voters—the poor, uneducated constituency vulnerable to demagoguery. Data, however, does not support this observation. In chapter 3, one of the Philippines' top pollsters, Ronald Holmes, presents survey data illustrating Duterte's multi-class base, although it is among the elites and middle classes where his campaign first gained traction. This leads Teehankee to argue that

> the Duterte phenomenon was not a revolt of the poor but was a protest of the new middle class who suffered from lack of public service, endured the horrendous land and air traffic, feared the breakdown of peace and order, and silently witnessed their tax money siphoned by corruption despite promises of improved governance [from the Aquino regime]. (Teehankee, chapter 2)

As poor families received social safety nets in the form of conditional cash transfer programs and expanded healthcare benefits, it is the middle classes in urban centers that experience the inconveniences that cause resentment against a booming economy with no impact on the middle classes. For sociologist Randy David, this kind of discontent is an inevitable part of modernity, for those who have relatively more in life react to complex problems "with great impatience" (David 2016). Problem-solvers like Duterte respond well to this context. While years of the Aquino regime have focused on long-term investments in human capital through reproductive health, educational reform, and the institutionalization of good governance mechanisms, these often come at the expense of responsiveness to issues that make an impact on people's everyday lives.

Duterte's rise to power is a disruption of the EDSA regime, but it is important to qualify which parts of the political system it has challenged. Duterte's presidency may have ushered in a post-EDSA regime, but one that is marked not by dismantling exclusionary political and economic structures but by the formation of a counter-elite that has been marginalized in the EDSA regime, particularly during Aquino's time. The excitement Duterte brought to his constituencies in the South, however, must not be ignored. The resentment against Imperial Manila is real, and the way in which he played the Mindanao card has provided inspiration for voices that have been in the margins of the nation's narrative for decades. One could only hope that bringing peace in the South is as inevitable as Duterte's rise.

Liberal Ideals and Illiberal Fantasies

In the first six months of Duterte's presidency, the Philippine National Police reported that it has conducted 41,155 anti-drug operations, arrested 44,334 drug suspects, knocked on the doors of over six million households, made over a million drug users surrender, and seized over PhP 3.7 billion (USD 74 million) worth of illegal drugs. Casualties in drug-related operations hit a total of 2,217, although human rights groups and journalists' estimates reach up to over 6,000 deaths. That leaves over a thousand people killed in each month of Duterte's term. Indeed, the president was both serious and literal when he declared that his regime would be bloody.

The Philippines' bloody war on drugs hinges on an illiberal fantasy. It is *illiberal* in the sense that human rights are viewed as particular, not universal. No less than the Justice Secretary considered "criminals, the drug lords, drug pushers," as "not [part of] humanity," in response to criticisms from watchdogs that the spate of killings constitutes crimes against humanity under international law. Palace spokespersons invoke the language of Asian values and national sovereignty to justify carnage as part of "cleaning up society." As spokesperson Ernesto Abella puts it, the "liberal Western values being imposed upon an Asian nation that places common good is both insensitive and displays a lack of appreciation for the diversity of global culture."

While the war on drugs has been the subject of intense criticism by the international community, it has gained traction locally for it offers a compelling *fantasy*: a vision of national development where fighting criminality is a prerequisite for prosperity. It is, as Lowell Bautista (2017) puts it, a "quixotic war" that "rides on a colossal crest of political capital by his loyal supporters who sincerely believe in his utopian vision of a Philippines free from drugs and crime." Fantasies, whether they are hinged on the liberal ideal or on an illiberal vision, are political constructs. Who benefits from these fantasies? How are they created, contested, and sustained?

The chapters in this edited collection suggest that Duterte's illiberal fantasies are built on five components: (1) the scaling up of the Davao model; (2) the securitization of the drug menace; (3) the mobilization of the state's coercive apparatus; (4) the projection of public support; and (5) weak mechanisms for accountability in the drug war. Empirical observations suggest that these components are anchored on the very same issues that deterred the realization of the liberal ideal: a criminal justice system that benefits from the failures of the peace and order agenda. Without solving systemic issues of corruption, reforming an unprofessional police force, and rectifying a culture of impunity, the illiberal fantasy will end up as murky as the liberal ideal.

Scaling-Up of the Davao Model

Some observers argue that to understand Duterte, one has to understand the region that shaped him. It is easy to dismiss the president as an odd political figure, but it is important to recognize that his behavior is "in keeping with the politics of his home island where violence is commonplace" (Tidwell 2016). Historian Vicente Rafael (2016) describes this context as a "Hobbesian world."

It's this Hobbesian world that was the Davao of the 1990s—with its Alsa Masa death squads, its New People's Army sparrow units,

its ex-NPA [New People's Army] private armies, its rogue military protecting miners and loggers, its drug lords, and its corrupt journalists—that shaped Duterte and that he brings with him to every press conference. It's a world where human rights are translated into highly particularized notions of honor and revenge where my freedom depends on my right to take yours away. (Rafael 2016)

Duterte's strategy of transforming Davao City into what it is today uses a combination of brute force and astute political skills. Much of the focus has been on the Davao Death Squad—a vigilante group composed of "local thugs, former rebels, and ex-soldiers and policemen" (Coronel 2016). Death squad members, according to the testimony of former hitman Edgar Matobato, were on the city's payroll, and were made to kill suspected drug dealers, muggers, rapists, and street children.

As a journalist in Davao in the 1990s, Canuday recalls the "template" of the killings at that time. They are comparable to the slayings attributed to the New People's Army's sparrow units, where messages claiming to kill enemies of the people were made public. Motorcycle-riding assassins shoot victims point blank, a method commonly referred to today as "riding-in-tandem." The killings, based on Canuday's narration, started with "small time street pushers," but "they were known to be prolific drug sellers" of *shabu* (crystal methamphetamine). He continues:

It began with suspected illegal drug dealers. But sometime in the late '90s, a few suspected snatchers and hold-uppers were also gunned down. Their ages didn't matter; some were minors. Some of these people were recidivists, people who went in and out of jail. They were also targeted. What is interesting is that, when we started reporting about the killings, people initially referred to them as vigilantes. And then someone from radio, for some reason, called them a "death squad." And since this was happening in Davao, the media started calling the killers the "Davao Death Squad." The term [was] lifted from the language of earlier reports about the Philippines. I think there was this report by Ramsey Clark—the American human rights lawyer and former US attorney general—on "death squads" during the Cory Aquino period. So the term "death squad" was already familiar in Davao. (Canuday 2017, 128)

Unlike death squads of the anti-communist vigilante group Alsa Masa, however, the Davao Death Squad (DDS) did not have a clear ideology. Neither were they comparable to the "salvaging" or summary executions that happened in the Marcos era where bodies were kidnapped, killed, and dumped in the fields. Instead, the DDS killings were "pointblank, done in front of crowds, sometimes in daylight" (Canuday 2017, 129). For Nathan Quimpo (chapter 8), it is surprising that the DDS has not been considered a private armed group.

> With its alleged 1,400 killings, the DDS may well be the country's most murderous private army in the post-Marcos era, rivalling that of the infamous Ampatuan political clan. Whether or not direct links between Duterte and the DDS can be proven, he has long served as its inspirational beacon, as well as its virtual godfather, whose mere word is equivalent to a command. (Quimpo, chapter 8)

Duterte has never been formally charged in relation to the killings. He has taunted his critics, admitting "I am the death squad" on television, to challenge them to find evidence and file cases against him.

Davao's narrative, however, cannot be reduced to the story of death squads. Beyond the use of brute force are Duterte's astute political skills of arbitration and accommodation. One cannot rule by force alone in a city divided by communists and anti-communist vigilantes, religious formations, indigenous identities, and violent kin-based conflicts. Political capital and institutional structures are necessary to mediate these divisions. One governance innovation that Duterte maximized is the appointment of "deputy mayors" from various ethnic groups who can represent the mayor in kin-based conflicts. This model has been proven effective, and has been replicated in various parts of Mindanao (Canuday 2017; see Gonzales 2005). In other instances, he had to use tactics of intimidation against recalcitrants to drive them out of the city. He had to buy off others by giving them jobs in government (Coronel 2016). All these strategies can only work because Duterte, as Canuday puts it, "understood the various sources of polarization in the city. He knew if it was an ethnic conflict, a political conflict, and he knew when these conflicts intersected with each other" (Canuday 2017, 126). As a result,

> he won the backing of the Davao elite, as improved peace and order allowed their businesses to thrive. He was conciliatory toward Muslim separatists and got the support of NGOs for programs that provided services for the city's poor. Today, Davao is a peaceful and booming commercial and tourist hub. (Coronel 2016)

During the presidential campaign, Duterte used Davao City as his "Exhibit A"—a vision of what the Philippines can become under his leadership. While it is not the first time that presidential contenders promised an ironfisted approach to governance, Duterte is the first to offer a compelling track record of delivering his promise of change using Davao as exemplar.

Duterte's claims about Davao gained credibility from the vocal support of Davao residents. Posts in social media clarify the exoticized depictions of Davao as a city governed by fear and instead offered portrayals of a vibrant and livable city. One can walk in the city late at night without getting mugged, get a business permit in three days, or expect taxi drivers to give exact change. These are some practical, relatable testimonials from Davao's residents that lent credibility to Duterte's claims. Davao has come far from what it once was, and this was achieved through a social contract in which citizens were willing to give up some of their liberties for the sake of the collective good, from accepting a curfew for minors and a city-wide smoking ban, to turning a blind eye on reports of summary executions.

Today, it appears that the Davao model is being used as a template—in terms of both brute force and the politics of accommodation. From the bloody war on drugs to the president's use of his own political capital to engage in peace talks with communist and Moro insurgents, what worked for two million people is being scaled up to a country of more than a hundred million.

Securitization of the Drug Menace

Scaling up the Davao model to the national level is a challenging task. How exactly can this be done considering there are many competing interests and issues on a national scale?

In chapter 8, Nathan Quimpo uses the language of securitization to make sense of Duterte's strategy. For Quimpo, Duterte has "shrewdly picked on an issue of popular concern—drug trafficking"—and "hyperbolized" the menace to justify the deadly war on drugs. Part of Duterte's rhetorical strategy is to tell stories of brutal cases of murder committed by drug addicts, such as children being raped or grandmothers being stabbed to death. His supporters extend these conversations online by disseminating news reports of heinous crimes, provoking human rights advocates to justify why murderers deserve human rights when they have dehumanized others. During the campaign, Duterte claimed that the Philippines has turned into a narco-state. "This is a clear national security threat," he said. "This is an invasion of a new kind. Drug lords, domestic and foreign, have declared a war against our families and children."

Telling a story of an impending crisis is essential to the strategy of securitization. Duterte is able to legitimize his drug war by describing the nation as being on the brink of fragmentation. The government's own data does not bear out Duterte's claims. His estimate of 3.7 million drug addicts, for example, is inconsistent with the Dangerous Drugs Board's recorded 1.8 million drug users. The United Nations Office on Drugs and Crime also places drug use in the Philippines at the rate of 1.69 percent, which is below the global rate of 5.2 percent. Nevertheless, Duterte's framing of the impending drug crisis gained traction, as evidenced by a poll that identifies illegal drugs as well as low wages as top concerns among voters (Pulse Asia 2016). This is a departure from typical issues respondents identify outside election season, where jobs, poverty, and inflation are among their top concerns, while illegal drugs are not part of the list.

It is important to underscore, however, that securitization is not a matter of demagogues manipulating citizens to believe in an impending crisis. If there is one lesson to be learned from the global rise of populism, it is that populists are able to tap brewing discontent among large segments of the population and give voice to these frustrations. For populists to be effective speakers, they are first strategic listeners who can spot simmering public discontent. In the Philippines' case, Duterte was able to give voice to the "latent anxiety" the drug menace caused. Stories of drug busts and petty thieves high on crystal meth are part of the nation's popular imagination. These are regular features of primetime newscasts and tabloids, and folded into the daily lives of citizens living in gated communities or urban slums. Whether it is teenagers in private schools inviting their friends to try out party drugs or gangs harassing women in street corners, the issue of illegal drugs has become direct experiences that make life uncomfortable to many. These anxieties are "mundane but still worrisome, publicized but not politicized" (Curato 2016, 99).

It is this latent anxiety that the securitization of the drug menace was able to surface. As Carmel Veloso Abao suggests in chapter 16, Duterte's form of populism may have thin ideological underpinnings but it derives its power from the presentation of "'the people' as fighting back against some enemy." Identifying criminals as the enemy, as Abao suggests, is a logical choice. Going back to the Davao story, Duterte can make a case that it is the outcome, not the process, of solving the drug menace that matters. The citizens of Davao are safe but this comes at a cost. The Philippines is effectively "at war" and exceptional methods are necessary to win.

Mobilization of Coercive Apparatus

The Philippine National Police is at the frontlines of this war. "Operation Plan Double Barrel" is the war's operating framework, which seeks to target both high-value and street-level personalities. Part of this plan is the application of the "tokhang" (knock and plead) technique, where policemen visit the homes of drug addicts and street-level dealers, ask them to surrender, and keep them under close surveillance.

Six months into Duterte's regime, "tokhang" has become

synonymous with the spate of killings. "Na-tokhang" has become part of the everyday vernacular, this time referring to the bodies of the slain in the drug war. The escalating death counts begin to make a discernible pattern, which Sheila Coronel describes in chapter 9:

> "Legitimate" police actions accounted for about a third of the casualties, most of them slain in the course of drug busts or supposedly while resisting arrest. The death rate in these operations was unusually high. Reuters reported a 97 percent kill ratio in the 51 drug-related police shootings it examined, indicating, it said, that drug suspects were being summarily gunned down. The PNP attributed the rest of the killings—almost 4,000 of them—to gang rivalries, vigilantes, and rogue or "ninja" policemen coddling or extorting from drug dealers. Human rights groups, however, saw the police's hand in these so-called death squad or vigilante killings. Both police and vigilante slayings, said Human Rights Watch, used the same modus operandi: Suspected drug offenders were warned by the police or barangay officials. Before long, hooded or masked men working in groups of two, four, or a dozen barged into their houses without warrants and gunned them down. Often, uniformed policemen were nearby, securing the crime scene, and special crime scene investigators arrived within minutes of the kill.

These scenes have been the subject of numerous news features from both the local and the international press. From *New York Times*'s Daniel Berehulak's prizewinning coverage, "They are Slaughtering Us Like Animals" (2016), to Patricia Evangelista and Carlo Gabuco's (2016) "Impunity" series, Duterte's drug war has been portrayed through images of weeping widows and orphans, packed jail cells, and bloodied corpses in the streets of Manila. Meanwhile, the police reported a drop in crime rate by 32 percent. Murder, however, is up by 50 percent.

The spate of killings is not unique to Duterte's regime. The Philippines has long suffered from a culture of violence. Over the past decades, there have been numerous summary executions of human rights defenders, indigenous rights leaders, land reform advocates, left-wing activists and journalists. As Coronel argues:

Duterte is not the first president of the republic to wield the police as a blunt instrument. His bloody purge of drug offenders was possible only because the PNP was a ready, willing, and able killing machine. A template for police killings already existed. For decades, policemen as well as vigilantes, death squads, and contract killers linked to the police have murdered criminals, journalists, lawyers, and activists. It's therefore not surprising that the modes of killing employed in the anti-drug campaign—shooting by hooded gunmen riding on motorcycles or strangulation by cords or wires—are reminiscent of executions past. (Coronel, chapter 9)

In chapter 10, human rights lawyer Jayson Lamchek observes that drawing up "watch lists" of drug addicts is similar to the notorious "order of battle lists" in both the Arroyo and the Aquino administrations. "In theory," Lamchek argues, "individuals who make it to the list are encouraged to 'surrender,'" but in practice, "they often end up abducted and/or killed, often in broad daylight." These lists have a chilling effect, in that community members who do not "cooperate" in reporting suspected members of communist movements are threatened to suffer the same fate. "Depending on who is counting and how, the total number of such execution ranges from 100 to over 800," declares UN Special Rapporteur Philip Alston (Alston 2008, 2). "The military," he continues, "is in the state of denial concerning the numerous extrajudicial executions in which soldiers are implicated" (Alston 2008, 2).

State-sponsored violence is not unique to Duterte's regime but what makes the drug war distinct is the sheer numbers. "Not in recent memory have so many members of a target group been killed in so short a span of time," argues Coronel (chapter 9). For Quimpo, while Duterte is indeed a product of the Hobbesian world in which he lived, he is also transforming the "national police machinery into his power base and into a quasi-private army with some Davao Death Squad features" (chapter 8). Quimpo warns that Duterte's use of the state's coercive apparatus is a way of bringing back "national boss rule" without having to declare martial law (see also Kreuzer 2016).

Public Support

How has the public reacted to Duterte's bloody war? The data is mixed. In a survey conducted by the Social Weather Stations (2016) six months into Duterte's presidency, the majority of Filipinos registered satisfaction with the president's campaign against illegal drugs. Fifty-three percent are "very satisfied," while 32 percent were "somewhat satisfied." Eighty-eight percent also agree with the statement "from the time when Rody Duterte became president, there has been a decrease in the drug problem in my area." To a certain extent, this confirms the police's claims that streets are now safer because of the campaign.

There have been various interpretations of these numbers. For Bello (chapter 4), public support for the war on drugs reflects EDSA republic's failed discourse of democracy, where human rights and rule of law "had become a suffocating straitjacket for a majority of Filipinos who could not simply relate to it." For *The New York Times*'s Amanda Taub (2016), the drug war's popularity indicates public loss of confidence in state institutions, particularly the judicial system. "Frustration with the government's inability to provide basic security," she writes, "led to rising public demand for new leaders who would take more decisive action to provide security."

It is, however, more challenging to interpret these numbers when read in conjunction with other items in the Social Weather Stations survey. Data also suggests that 94 percent of respondents think that it is important to keep suspects alive while 78 percent are worried that someone from their families will be a victim of extra-judicial killings. Sixty-nine percent also think that the problem of extra-judicial killings is a serious issue.

What stories do these numbers tell? One can only make cautious inferences. One possibility is that while the public supports serious efforts to put an end to drug-related crimes, it is averse to its illiberal character. It is possible that the public still maintains the liberal aspiration of reforming the justice system, instead of getting content with summary executions as a central part of the anti-drug campaign. Some suggest that the issue of human rights is a distant ideal or a western imposition that means little to impoverished Filipinos. But if one were to listen to the pleas of drug suspects' widows who demand to be treated with dignity or the aspirations of residents in slum communities to be treated like human beings, then these claims lie right in the heart of the human rights discourse, only that they are articulated differently. To say that Filipinos no longer care about human rights because they support the war on drugs warrants rethinking.

Another possibility highlights the contingent and complex character of public support for Duterte's war. One must not conflate public support for Duterte, who enjoys majority satisfaction ratings, with support for the war and support for the killings. Instead, public opinion is more complex, nuanced, and negotiated. When the public weighs support for Duterte, for example, one may give premium to his compassion for disaster survivors, distressed overseas Filipino workers, or his authenticity over the way his regime handles the mounting body count. What is worth monitoring is whether preferences to keep drug suspects alive translates to collectively articulated discontent where citizens demand a shift in the government's murderous approach, or whether uneasiness of the killings stays on the level of tacit concern and, by extension, complicity in the bloody war.

System of Accountability

When South Korean national Jee Ick Joo was brutally murdered by police officers, the president imposed a moratorium on his drug war. Joo is the first high-profile victim of "tokhang-for-ransom," an extortionate plot of rogue cops who use tokhang as pretense to raid homes and kidnap victims in exchange for money. His murder exposed the police force's vulnerability to "the underground economy of extortion, theft, abduction, and murder in which the police are both enforcers of the law and its worst offenders" (Coronel, chapter 9).

A few weeks later, "Double Barrel Reloaded" was relaunched. Police Chief Ronald "Bato" ("The Rock") Dela Rosa assured the public that only police officers with unquestionable integrity would be deployed as part of the drug war. This was the first test of the Duterte administration's resolve to hold the police accountable for its excesses.

The drug war exposes how the police force adapts to a new policy regime as well as the resilience of the institution's "bad habits" in spite of Duterte's presidency. In chapter 9, Coronel illustrates how the drug war opened new opportunities for entrepreneurial policemen to make profits, whether through extortion rackets as in the case of Joo, or by securing financial rewards after suspected drug users have been killed. Coronel argues that "far from being passive followers," police officers "are entrepreneurs on the lookout for moneymaking opportunities," as well as personalities who continually weigh the "shifting balance of incentives and risks as they seek to deter crime, advance their careers, please their political patrons, and make money while also evading exposure and protection."

Patterns of police behavior remain consistent in spite of the new policy regime. One, for example, may ask why the police resort to excessive use of force in tokhang operations. One explanation is they are emboldened by Duterte's rhetoric, particularly his assurance that police officers do not need to worry about the Commission on Human Rights should they kill in the line of duty. Another reason, as Coronel suggests, is that "this is the only type of policing they know." Poor training and resources, coupled with a dysfunctional criminal justice system, make it difficult, if not impossible, for policemen to carefully gather forensic evidence, obtain eyewitness testimonies, and file criminal charges. For a police force under pressure to report the progress of the drug war in their own locales, officers are left with little choice but to resort to "morally and legally questionable workarounds," including sting operations where drug suspects end up getting shot. "The reality is that illegal behavior is embedded in the way the police operate" argues Coronel.

> The police routinely violate procedures and just as routinely get away with it. In their pursuit of criminals, policemen resort to criminal methods, justifying this as the only way they can realistically curb criminality in the face of a broken justice system. (Coronel, chapter 9)

The problem with Dela Rosa and Duterte's view of the police, therefore, is it assumes "that there is a clear line that separates scalawags in uniform from all the rest." This is inconsistent with realities on the ground. The police "operate in the grey zone" where rules are negotiated given the limitations of the context.

These issues of accountability place Duterte's illiberal fantasy in the same fate as that of the failed realization of liberal ideals under the EDSA regime. There is something more powerful than Duterte, and that is the deeply embedded institutional culture of the police force, a flawed justice system that perpetuates impunity, and the autonomy of police officers who continue to weigh their own interests against other competing demands. As the future of Duterte's illiberal fantasy remains uncertain, the death counts will continue to mount and deeper problems will remain unsolved if broader institutional reforms are not made.

Crass Politics and Spectacle-Driven Publics

The "coarsening of political discourse" has become a key feature of contemporary populism (Moffit and Tormey 2014, 392). Gravitas, seriousness, and statesmanlike speech have now been taken over by brutal frankness and sensational language as prime rhetorical qualities. A populist, as Benjamin Arditi puts it, is like a drunken guest at a dinner party. He "can disrupt table manners and the tacit rules of sociability by speaking loudly, interrupting the conversations of others, and perhaps flirting with them beyond what passes for acceptable cheekiness" (Arditi 2007, 78).

Duterte fits this description of a populist leader. He offers the spectacle of a strong leader ready to expose the uncomfortable realities of Philippine politics using the most vulgar vocabulary. He speaks in the vernacular of a five-year-old, identifying enemies and friends, calling for revenge upon people who have bruised his ego. Duterte's crass politics was effective in serving three political purposes. It (1) exposes the hypocrisies of powerful institutions; (2) gives voice to citizens' deep-seated injuries; and (3) sets the tone necessary for his style of governance.

As populists break the rules of polite conversations, they

render society's hypocrisies visible, and call attention to realities that others do not talk about because they are too polite, too conservative, or just plain spineless. Duterte has not held back in picking fights with powerful institutions. The Roman Catholic Church is one of his regular targets, reminding the public that this is the same institution that coddled priests who molested children, accepted bribes from corrupt politicians, and, just like him, maintained two wives. By reprimanding the Church, Duterte discredits the institution most vocal against his drug war, by casting doubt on its moral legitimacy. He uses the same logic with the United States. In chapter 7, Adele Webb explains why Duterte's confrontational approach to the United States resonated with his supporters. "In telling Obama to mind his own business, Duterte behaved badly," she argues, "but it is in this very subversion that his appeal lies." Duterte stood up for the people, disrupted the imaginary of Filipinos as subordinated subjects, and refused to continue the indignity of the past. In this chapter, Webb takes a historical view of the construction of the American legacy of constructing the Filipino as subordinate people incapable of self-rule. Duterte's exposure of American hypocrisy, therefore, goes deeper than merely telling off a superpower. It also means reclaiming the esteem of once-subservient subjects by creating a confident nationalist vocabulary that can stand up to the powerful.

Duterte's crass language gained traction in the 2016 race for it lent an authentic *characterization of citizens' deep-seated injuries*. Dutertismo, as David puts it, "is pure theatre—a sensual experience rather than a rational application of ideas to society's problems" (David 2016b). Rafael shares a similar observation. Duterte is a "consummate story-teller," who shares with the crowd "not any sort of policy proposal or political vision, but the residues of an injured pride and a frayed ego" (Rafael 2016b). As Duterte's competitors put forward policy proposals during the series of presidential debates, Duterte showed no interest in engaging in a conversation on conditional cash transfer programs and tax reform. What he offered, instead, is a voice that captured the voters' pent-up resentments. Discernible from Duterte's vulgar speech is a frustrated tone, an exasperated voice that is familiar to anyone who has endured the daily inhumanity of living in the city. It is the tone that Manila's commuters have in their heads, every morning, when they queue up for hours for underserviced trains. It is the tone that overseas Filipino workers keep to themselves as Philippine government employees tell them to come back tomorrow because their documents have not yet been processed. It is the tone that taxi drivers have when the release of their licenses has been delayed for months. Duterte may be offending the norms of respectful communication when he prefaces his remarks with "mother fucker," but he brings to the surface the collective frustration many feel. He may not offer the clearest policy, but he puts forward the sincerest discourse of sympathy.

Finally, Duterte's crass politics is crucial in *establishing his governance style*. It is not the first time that a charismatic leader tried to capture the popular imagination by using colloquial language. Joseph Estrada did this successfully in his presidential bid; so did Vice President Binay. Both politicians' rhetoric is built on class, by speaking against elites who have looked down on the poor. But Duterte is different. While he did make references to oligarchs and corrupt cops, his rhetoric comes from his "dark charisma" and a dystopian interpretation of a country in crisis. Duterte's gutter language establishes the urgency of saving the republic. Including "kill" and "death" is essential to the president's vocabulary for the country is at war, and his politics of "I will" demands quick, albeit painful, solutions.

Embeddedness of Rhetoric

While Duterte's crass vocabulary set a new tone for political rhetoric, his style is firmly anchored on enduring visual cultures and political economy of mass communication in the Philippines.

In chapter 11, Anna Cristina Pertierra argues that Duterte is a beneficiary of a political culture where the glitz of showbusiness and personal charisma outweigh the persuasive power of policy ideas. Duterte's popularity hinges on the "convergence of entertainment and politics as it is experienced in the Philippines (and in other parts of the world) through emotional connections with audiences." By making this observation, Pertierra does not offer a pejorative judgment of the Philippines' treatment of politics as tele-visual melodrama. She instead takes a sympathetic view, suggesting that in a context where very few politicians have improved the lives of their constituencies through actual policies, it is the emotional dimensions of political dramas that offer connections between politics and citizens in their capacities as viewers. Pertierra's chapter prompts reflection on the democratic potential of celebrity politics. It challenges the dichotomy between "rational policy debates" as a superior form of doing politics in the public sphere and the power of storytelling in forging connections with an increasingly impatient public. This observation raises the question: what kind of connection has Duterte forged with the public?

For some observers, Duterte has unleashed a vitriolic culture that inspired his supporters to also engage in crass politics. *Dutertard* is the derogatory term used to describe the unthinking, die-hard "retards" unable to make coherent arguments online. In chapter 12, Jason Vincent A. Cabañes and Jayeel S. Cornelio examine the politics of using such a term, particularly in equating Dutertards with political trolling. Cabañes and Cornelio make critical interventions in this chapter. First, they argue that such politics of labelling shrinks the space for political discourse, for the label "Dutertard" disparages some citizens as unworthy of engagement. The same can be said when Duterte's supporters label critics as *dilawan* or yellow—a shorthand for supporters of the previous Aquino administration that uses yellow as campaign color.

Second, this chapter unpacks the concept of political trolling, and draws a spectrum to distinguish "trolls" who are paid to infiltrate online conversations and those who sincerely believe in their arguments. Their discussion of paid trolls is particularly revealing, for they draw on primary interview data with personalities who admit to making a living out of professional trolling. This analysis exposes the underlying political economy of vitriolic discourse not only under Duterte's regime but also in the broader context of a digital public sphere where influencing public discourse has become a commodity that can be bought and sold. This chapter challenges readers to further ask critical questions about the character of political trolling in the Philippines. Who makes money from political trolling? And what cultures enable such toxic political practice to take root?

For Cabañes and Cornelio, the vitriolic message of trolls only gained traction because they "speak to the felt experiences of many people that were being neglected in broader public discourses." In the same way that Duterte was able to give voice to citizens' frustrations, professional trolls' dummy accounts gain credibility because they provide relatable messages, in contrast to mainstream media's elite-driven reportage. John Andrew Evangelista puts forward a similar observation in chapter 13, where he examines vitriolic discourse in the context of Duterte's sexist commentary. For Evangelista, Duterte's misogynistic and homophobic comments elicit laughter and support because his discourse is both disruptive yet familiar. Crass politics may put some people off, but it is also undeniable that Duterte's language is not as repulsive to people who hear his sexist banter in everyday conversations. As a feminist senator and Duterte ally put it, even her male colleagues in the Senate talk like Duterte in the back room, because "they are just a bunch of boys." "Duterte's masculinity has always been known to us," Evangelista suggests. Like the crass politics of trolling, the crass politics of sexism also hinges on deeply embedded discursive cultures. The only difference now is that this language is spoken by the head of state.

Discourse in the Public Sphere

Many have already spoken against Duterte's performance in his first few months in office. Duterte was a "huge disappointment and letdown," according to former president and Duterte supporter Fidel Ramos. "President Duterte is repeating my mistakes," said former Colombian President César Gaviria in his *New York Times* commentary about Duterte's bloody war. UN rapporteur for extrajudicial killings Agnes Callamard strongly appealed to Duterte, "You cannot deny people the right to life." While several high-profile personalities have already registered critique against the controversial president, there seems to be a huge void in the usually vibrant oppositional politics in the Philippines. Who is championing the powerful practice of no-saying and speaking truth to power?

In chapter 15, Sanchez suggests that the Left continues to be a space for oppositional politics to take root. In spite of its alliance with the Duterte regime, the Left continues to articulate dissent and hold protest action. Ferdinand Marcos's burial at the Heroes' Cemetery, for Sanchez, is a critical turning point, for this reshaped the terms of the Left's support for the president. This development led to a series of major protests throughout the country, where some of the president's most vocal allies also became his most vocal critics in supporting the Marcoses' capricious wish.

Bello (chapter 4) and Abao (chapter 16), on the other hand, discard the Left as a possible force for opposition. Abao has measured expectations when it comes to forging a credible opposition that can stand against Duterte's murderous regime. "Because no other group aside from the Left has traditionally occupied the anti-authoritarian, anti-elite space, it will probably take a while for the current vacuum to be named, much less filled." She draws hope not from the emergence of a new –ism but from the shared issues on which various publics can converge, such as security of tenure, rehabilitation, or federalism without dynasties. This prescription is both a modest and a transformative project, for she imagines the space where the most meaningful and productive intervention can take root, which lies at the intersection of Duterte's populism and liberalism's pluralism.

Possibilities for the Post-EDSA Regime

"Change is coming" was Duterte's winning campaign slogan. One can only speculate about the trajectory of this change as the Philippines ushers in an era of post-EDSA regime. Duterte has been successful in interrupting politics-as-usual. He inspired an electoral insurgency that challenged the elitist EDSA regime. He placed crass politics at the center of democratic life to give voice to silenced frustrations. He shifted the gaze of governance from Imperial Manila to the forgotten South. He promoted a murderous approach to nation building without apologies.

But Duterte's interruption also hinges on the perpetuation of the very same social structures that led to the failures of the

Philippines' thirty years of democratic experimentation. While Duterte spoke against oligarchs who benefitted from the People Power Revolution, his regime is reliant on a counter-elite who also have sins against the nation. On the front lines of his bloody war on drugs is a police force with a deeply flawed institutional culture. On the sidelines is a seemingly complicit, if not increasingly cruel, public who opts to turn a blind eye to the growing number of widows and orphans of the drug war. While pockets of protests have emerged in Duterte's first months in office, an escalating body count is not compelling enough to generate widespread discontent.

Throughout this book, various scholars offer a prognosis of the kind of regime that the Philippines now faces. Bello calls Duterte a fascist. Abao refers to him as a populist. Quimpo thinks he is consolidating forces to become a national boss. For Claudio and Abinales, Duterte represents a "dangerous, extremist past . . . folding into the Philippine present." For Altez and Caday, he is Mindanao's best shot at a peaceful future. Duterte evokes different reactions from different people. Underlying the value judgments about Duterte are debates about the nation's aspirations, prospects for the future, and the price citizens are willing to pay to achieve those collective dreams. One can only hope that in the Philippines' great interregnum, democracy does not surrender to its monsters.

References

Alston, Philip. 2008. "Report on the Special Rapporteur on extrajudicial, summary or arbitrary executions. Mission to the Philippines." *United Nations General Assembly Human Rights Council.* Eighth Session. 16 April. Available at http://www.karapatan.org/files/English_Alston_Report_Mission_to_the_Philippines_HRC8.pdf.

Arditi, Benjamin. 2007. *Politics on the Edges of Liberalism: Difference, Populism, Revolution, Agitation.* Edinburgh: Edinburgh University Press.

Aspinall, Edward, Michael W. Davidson, Allen Hicken, and Meredith L. Weiss. 2016. "Local Machines and Vote Brokerage in the Philippines." *Contemporary Southeast Asia: A Journal of International and Strategic Affairs* 38 (2):191–96.

Bautista, Lowell B. 2017. "Duterte and His Quixotic War on Drugs." 20 *Thinking ASEAN 2–5.*

Bello, Walden. Forthcoming. "The Spider Spins His Web: Rodrigo Duterte's Ascent to Power." *Philippine Sociological Review* 65 (1).

Berehulak, Daniel. 2016. "They Are Slaughtering Us Like Animals." *New York Times*, 7 December. https://www.nytimes.com/interactive/2016/12/07/world/asia/rodrigo-duterte-philippines-drugs-killings.html.

Canuday, Jose Jowel. 2017. "Locating Duterte in Davao: Conversations on the Global South." *Journal of Social Transformations* 5 (1):121–36.

Casiple, Ramon C. 2016. "The Duterte Presidency as a Phenomenon." *Contemporary Southeast Asia: A Journal of International and Strategic Affairs* 38 (2):179–84.

Coronel, Sheila. 2016. "'I Will Kill All the Drug Lords.'" The Atlantic, 10 September. https://www.theatlantic.com/international/archive/2016/09/rodrigo-duterte-philippines-manila-drugs-davao/500756/

Curato, Nicole. 2017. "Politics of Anxiety, Politics of Hope: Penal Populism and Duterte's Rise to Power." *Journal of Current Southeast Asian Affairs* 35 (3):91–109.

David, Randy. 2016. "'Dutertismo' or Clearheaded Patriotism?" *Philippine Daily Inquirer*, 8 May. http://opinion.inquirer.net/94649/dutertismo-or-clearheaded-patriotism.

David, Randy. 2016b. "Dutertismo." *Philippine Daily Inquirer*, 1 May. http://opinion.inquirer.net/94530/dutertismo.

Desker, Barry. 2016. "President Duterte: A Different Philippine Leader." *RSIS Commentary*, no. 145. 14 June.

Dowd, Maureen. 2016. *The Year of Voting Dangerously: The Derangement of American Politics*. New York: Twelve.

Evangelista, Patricia, and Carlo Gabuco. 2016. "Impunity: In the Name of the Father." *Rappler*. http://www.rappler.com/newsbreak/in-depth/duterte-drug-war-name-of-the-father-impunity.

Gonzales, Daisy. 2005. "The Rise and Rise of Rodrigo Duterte." *Bulatlat*, 13 November. http://www.bulatlat.com/news/5-40/5-40-duterte.htm.

Ilagan, Karol, and Malou Mangahas. 2016. "P334M from only 13 Donors Funded Duterte's Presidency." *Philippine Center for Investigative Journalism*, 5 December. http://pcij.org/stories/p334m-from-only-13-donors-funded-dutertes-presidency/.

Kreuzer, Peter. 2017. "'If They Resist, Kill Them All': Police Vigilantism in the Philippines." PRIF Report No. 142. Frankfurt, Germany.

Moffitt, Benjamin, and Simon Tormey. 2014. "Rethinking Populism: Politics, Mediatisation and Political Style." *Political Studies* 62 (2):381–97.

Mudde, Cas. 2004. "The Populist Zeitgeist." *Government and Opposition* 39 (4):542–63.

Pulse Asia Research Inc. 2007. "Cheating During the 2004 Presidential Elections." Commissioned Survey.

Pulse Asia Research, Inc. 2016. "Pulse Asia Research's January 2016 Nationwide Survey on Urgent National Concerns to be Addressed by Presidential Candidates and Most Important Consideration in Choosing a Presidential Candidate." 19 February.

Rafael, Vicente L. 2016a. "Duterte's Hobbesian World." *Philippine Daily Inquirer*, 13 June. http://opinion.inquirer.net/95185/dutertes-hobbesian-world.

Rafael, Vicente L. 2016b. "Digong the Story-teller." *Rappler*, 5 June. http://www.rappler.com/thought-leaders/135378-rodrigo-duterte-digong-story-teller.

Schaffer, Frederic Charles. 2005. "Clean Elections and the Great Unwashed: Vote Buying and Voter Education in the Philippines." *Institute for Advanced Study, School of Social Sciences, Occasional Paper No. 21.* https://www.sss.ias.edu/files/papers/paper21.pdf.

Social Weather Stations. 2016. "Fourth Quarter 2016 Social Weather Survey." 21 December. http://www.sws.org.ph/swsmain/artcldisppage/?artcsyscode=ART-20161219110734.

Taub, Amanda. 2016. "How Countries Like the Philippines Fall Into Vigilante Violence." *The New York Times*, 11 September. https://www.nytimes.com/2016/09/12/world/asia/the-philippines-rodrigo-duterte-vigilante-violence.html.

Teehankee, Julio C., and Mark R. Thompson. 2016. "Electing a Strongman." *Journal of Democracy* 27 (4):125–34.

Thompson, Mark R. 2010. "Reformism vs. Populism in the Philippines." *Journal of Democracy* 21 (4):154–68.

Tidwell, Alan. 2016. "Duterte, Mindanao, and Political Culture." *Asia Pacific Bulletin*, no. 362, 9 November.

Villegas, Bernardo, and George N. Manzano. 2016. "Prospects for the Philippine Economy under the Duterte Presidency." *Contemporary Southeast Asia: A Journal of International and Strategic Affairs* 38(2):197–201.

Was Duterte's Rise Inevitable?

Julio C. Teehankee

At the beginning of President Rodrigo "Rody" Duterte's term in 2016, it was hoped that the institution of the presidency would change him. Yet, after his first year in power, it has become apparent that it was Duterte who was changing the presidency. Through his controversial actions such as the deadly "war on drugs," the hero's burial for the ousted dictator Ferdinand E. Marcos, and the reimposition of the death penalty, one can surmise that he is repudiating the reformist, albeit elitist, narrative of the liberal democratic regime established three decades ago with the ouster of the Marcos dictatorship.

Duterte's electoral victory is a major rupture in the post-Marcos "EDSA regime" founded by Corazon "Cory" C. Aquino in 1986. It came in the aftermath of six years of high growth and political stability under the administration of her son, President Benigno "Noynoy" Aquino. Duterte's phenomenal victory can be understood within the context of what the second Aquino administration has failed to do. Despite his personal popularity due to his clean image and lack of personal political scandals, Aquino failed to institutionalize the reform agenda of Daang Matuwid (Straight Path).

One can also argue that this was emblematic of Philippine governance under the so-called "EDSA regime." A number of scholars have explained how the narrative of the 1986 People Power uprising at Epifanio de los Santos Avenue (EDSA) has been appropriated by the Aquinos, the Catholic Church, and their "yellow" elite supporters into a semi-religious national myth of "good" defeating "evil" and bringing back "righteous" democracy to the land (Bello 1986; Anderson 1988; Tancangco and Mendoza 1988; Coronel 1991; Ileto 1993; Velasco 1997; Thompson 1996, 2007, 2010; Rivera 2002; Quimpo 2008; Claudio 2013; Casiple 2016; Arguelles 2016). The rise of Duterte exposes the inherent weakness of a democracy that is impervious to the demands of the public. Philippine democracy has been rendered inutile by a strong-willed populist president acting on the people's frustrations by any means possible (Arguelles 2016). Thirty years since the EDSA People Power uprising, Philippine democracy still hobbles with significant dysfunctionality in which resistant political and business elites refuse to undertake much needed reforms to realize genuine socioeconomic and political transformations (Timberman 2016, 143). Hence, the return of democracy in 1986 did not necessarily guarantee the emergence of genuine emancipatory politics, but only an effective way for elite consolidation and their concentration of state power—an elite-oriented state capture (Regilme 2016, 239–40).

This chapter situates the rise of Duterte within the cycle of presidential regimes in the Philippines. It adopts Stephen Skowronek's concept of presidential leadership in political time to analyze how crafted narratives are transformed into governance scripts that bind together a coalition of interests within a particular institutional setting. Moreover, it will analyze the cycle of presidential challenges within the context of strategic moments that lie between structural regimes and agential choices.

Cycle of Presidential Regimes

Stephen Skowronek situates the presidency not according to

personal traits and attributes but on structural patterns of regime change and cycles within the presidency. In his two books, *The Politics Presidents Make* (1997) and *Presidential Leadership in Political Time* (2008), Skowronek explores the recurring regime pattern in the American presidency. He places presidents within the context of regimes or "the commitment of ideology and interest embodied in preexisting institutional arrangements" (Skowronek 1997, 34). Presidential performance is shaped by a president's relationship to a dominant "regime"—a prevailing set of interests, ideologies, and institutions. A regime-based approach takes into account the constraints set by presidential regimes (Lieberman 2000, 274).

The First Philippine Republic (1899–1901) refers to the short-lived revolutionary government established by President Emilio Aguinaldo after the Filipino declaration of independence from Spanish colonial rule. However, the American colonial rule inter-rupted the Filipino march to national independence (1898–1943, 1945–1946). The institutional foundations of the modern Filipino nation-state were largely shaped by the American colonial expe-rience (Paredes 1989; Cullinane 2003; Castañeda Anastacio 2016). American political tutelage also resulted in the rise of two Commonwealth presidents: Manuel L. Quezon and Sergio Osmeña. During World War II, the Japanese occupation of the Philippines ushered in the Second Republic (1943–1945) which saw the selec-tion of Jose P. Laurel as the president of the Japanese-sponsored government.

While the first three short-lived regimes can be considered "proto-regimes," the Third Philippine Republic can be considered the "foundational regime" in the development of the Filipino nation-state (see Table 1). The Third Philippine Republic (1946–1972) can be characterized as an elite democracy or "a constitutional democ-racy dominated by an oligarchy that was buttressed by patronage, coupled with continued dependence on the former colonial power" (Wurfel 1988, 325). Moreover, the landed families that formed the national oligarchy dominated electoral competitions and maximized their linkage with the state apparatus in order to access the lucra-tive American markets. Thus, oligarchic rent-seeking and control of government have thwarted the state's capacity to pursue national development goals and social equity (Doronila 1992; Rivera 1994; Velasco 1997). Five postwar Philippine presidents, Manuel Roxas, Elpidio Quirino, Ramon Magsaysay, Carlos P. Garcia, and Diosdado Macapagal, committed themselves to a national economic development plan premised on close ties with the United States. All faced the challenge of local insurgencies fueled by agrarian unrest in the countryside. All promised to institute the agrarian reform but failed to dismantle the powerful landed elites (Putzel 1992; Abinales and Amoroso 2005).

Table 1. Philippine Presidential Regimes

Regime	Republic	President	Date
Proto-regimes	First Philippine Republic	Emilio Aguinaldo	23 January 1899–1 April 1901
	Philippine Commonwealth	Manuel L. Quezon	15 November 1935–1 August 1944
		Sergio Osmeña	1 August 1944–28 May 1946
	Second Philippine Republic	Jose P. Laurel	14 October 1943–19 August 1945
Neo-colonial regime	Third Philippine Republic	Manuel Roxas	28 May 1946–15 April 1948
		Elpido Quirino	17 April 1948–30 December 1953
		Ramon Magsaysay	30 December 1953–17 March 1957
		Carlos P. Garcia	18 March 1957–30 December 1961

Regime	Republic	President	Date
		Diosdado Macapagal	30 December 1961–30 December 1965
		Ferdinand Marcos	30 December 1965–21 September 1972
Authoritarian regime	Fourth Philippine Republic	Ferdinand Marcos	21 September 1972–25 February 1986
Reformist regime	Fifth Philippine Republic	Corazon C. Aquino	25 February 1986–30 June 1992
		Fidel V. Ramos	30 June 1992–30 June 1998
		Joseph Estrada	30 June 1998–21 January 2001
		Gloria Macapagal-Arroyo	21 January 2001–30 June 2010
		Benigno Aquino III	30 June 2010–30 June 2016
		Rodrigo Duterte	30 June 2016

Source: Collated by the author

Elite democracy has sustained the long-running revolutionary challenge from below. The intensification of intra-elite competition for wealth and power further added strain to the postwar regime. Demands for change were echoed by an emerging middle class—composed of students, professionals, and small entrepreneurs who were exposed to the rise of radicalism around the world in the 1960s and 1970s. Inspired by the writings of Filipino nationalists, students and workers' groups launched mass protests against the corrupt, elitist, and US-dependent government. Ferdinand E. Marcos, who was first elected as president in 1965 and was reelected in 1969, seized the opportunity amidst the social unrest to declare martial

law in 1972 and dismantled the formal institutions of elite democracy. Marcos justified the imposition of an authoritarian regime as a
"revolution from the center" against the forces of the extreme right
represented by the oligarchs and the extreme left represented by
the radicals and communists (Velasco 1997, 84).

The Marcos authoritarian regime (1972–1986) repudiated the
institution, ideas, and interests of the previous postwar democratic regime. Marcos replaced the *ancien régime* with a new order
he labeled the "New Society." Operating under the Orwellian rubric
of "constitutional authoritarianism," Marcos used his martial law
powers under the 1935 Constitution and manipulated the passage of
the 1973 Constitution to provide himself extraordinary powers. He
then assembled a coalition of interests that were formerly marginalized in the previous regime—the technocrats, his cronies, and
the military. These sectors became the three pillars of the authoritarian regime. Through his control of the military and the coercive apparatus of the state, Marcos consolidated his regime and
adopted an export-led growth policy managed by the technocrats.
He attempted to dismantle the economic and political base of the
traditional agricultural elite and established his own stranglehold
on the export of sugar and coconut through his cronies. He also
centralized the distribution of political patronage to local political
clans through the state-based political machinery (i.e., the Ministry
of Local Governments) and the centrally directed and monolithic
party machinery (i.e., the Kilusang Bagong Lipunan, KBL) (Wurfel
1983–1984). Ultimately, the Marcos regime can be classified in
Weberian terms as "sultanistic" since he "pursued not ideological
but personal goals, and his regime was organized around family and
friends, not strong state institutions" (Thompson 1996, 4–5). Soon
after, the Marcos regime collapsed under the weight of its own
corruption and was overthrown in the first people power uprising
in Asia in 1986.

Filipino Presidents in Political Time

According to Skowronek (2011, 18), political time "is the medium
through which presidents encounter received commitments of

ideology and interest and claim authority to intervene in their development." Comparing presidents in different historical periods according to parallel moments of political time would yield more similarities in leadership challenges than those presidents compared according to the regular sequential period of secular time. From the perspective of political time, the Filipino presidents can be categorized into great repudiators, preemptive leaders, orthodox innovators, and disjunctive leaders (see Table 2). Skowronek observes: "Presidents bid for authority by reckoning with the work of their predecessors, locating their rise to power within the recent course of political events, and addressing the political expectations that attend their intervention in these affairs" (Skowronek 2011, 18).

Table 2: Post-Marcos Philippine Presidency in Political Time

	Affiliated	Opposed
Vulnerable	Disjunctive Leaders	Great Repudiators
	Macapagal-Arroyo, Noynoy Aquino	Cory Aquino, Rodrigo Duterte
Resilient	Orthodox Innovators	Preemptive Leaders
	Fidel Ramos	Joseph Estrada

Source: Adopted from Skowronek 1997

The political identity of an incumbent president is either as someone affiliated with or opposed to the prevailing regime. Moreover, the political opportunity (i.e., for the "success" or "failure" of presidential leadership) available to the incumbent president hinges on how resilient or vulnerable a prevailing regime has become: a regime that remains strong is good for affiliated presidents, but harsh on would-be preemptors to it; the opposite holds true for a weakened regime. Thus, presidential leadership is defined more by one's relationship to the prevailing regime than by personal style or character in facing down challenges. Except for rare opportunities in which the regime becomes ripe for repudiation, a president ascends to power within a prevailing regime that largely shapes the nature of the administration. Skowronek cross-tabulates these general considerations of political identity and opportunity to yield a typology of four structures of political authority: (a) politics of reconstruction—when the president emerges from the opposition at a time when the prevailing regime is ripe for repudiation; (b) politics of disjunction—when a president is affiliated with a regime that has been put into question as failed or irrelevant to the problems of the day; (c) politics of articulation—when a president is affiliated with a resilient regime; and (d) politics of preemption—when an opposed president ascends to power within a resilient regime (Skowronek 1997, 34–44).

A "foundationalist" president usurps the pre-existing political order. In the context of the United States, for example, Skowronek asserts that the presidency of Ronald Reagan established the current political regime of "small government," which repudiated the "liberal" New Deal-style regime started by Franklin Roosevelt in the 1930s (Skowronek 2008, 19). In the Philippines, Cory Aquino "repudiated" Marcos's failed "developmentalist" authoritarian regime and installed a "reformist" presidentialist democratic regime in its place. "Reformism" in this context has involved a discursive narrative committed to democracy and combatting corruption in the name of "good governance" that binds together key elite strategic groups (big business, the Catholic Church hierarchy, civil society activists, and the military brass) within the context of generally weak state institutions (Thompson 2010, 2013, 2014).

By battling the "evils" of corruption, reformists often make claims of the "good" in their crusade for "good governance." This story line is attractive to the middle class who often decries government inefficiency and wasted economic resources brought about by institutionalized corruption. By enduring personal sacrifices at the hands of "corrupt" officials, reformists are worthy of the public's trust. Hence, the reformist narrative flows from the political promise, "I will help you . . . because I am (morally) good." "Honesty" and "sincerity" are often used as the code words for the reformist narrative. On the other hand, populism (from the Latin word *populis*), refers to "a movement, a regime, a leader, or even a state which claims close affinity with the people" (De Castro 2001, 2). Populists usually make class appeals and claim to champion the poor minus the ideology. They decry the hypocrisy of the elites.

Corruption is a non-issue for them since their archetypical image is Robin Hood who would steal from the rich to give to the poor. The populist narrative is "I will fight for you . . . because I am one of you." Populists often stoke the embers of class warfare with code words like *mahirap* (poor) and *masa* (masses) (Thompson 2010).

Presidential leadership in the Philippines can be analyzed within the context of the post-Marcos "reformist" regime. Specifically, it can be used to delineate the series of discrete political choices made by post-Marcos presidents: Corazon C. Aquino, Fidel V. Ramos, Joseph E. Estrada, Gloria Macapagal-Arroyo, Benigno S. Aquino III, and Rodrigo R. Duterte. By adopting a relational approach of situating a president's "sequencing" within an existing regime, the agency of presidential choices can be contextualized within the structural constraints under which they are forced to make decisions (Thompson 2014). Thus, in the Philippines, a presidency can be a prequel or a sequel to an ongoing regime narrative. Given the underdeveloped ideological articulation in Philippine politics, presidential regimes consist of quasi-programmatic, emotive narratives in election campaigns and/or a governance script that binds together a coalition of interests within a particular institutional context.

Applying Skowronek's terminology, Cory was the "great repudiator" of the Marcos authoritarian regime. Ramos, the "anointed" successor of Cory, became an "orthodox innovator" of the reformist regime. Estrada attempted to "preempt" the reformist regime with his own populist narrative but was ousted for it. Arroyo was initially affiliated with the reformist regime but was rebuked for allegedly committing electoral fraud to defeat a strong populist challenger. Noynoy Aquino was first hailed as another "orthodox innovator" who will bring balance back to the reformist regime but turned out to be "disjunctive" in the wake of controversies that further weakened the reformist narrative.

EDSA and Its Discontents

The peaceful military-backed people power uprising at the historic EDSA saw the birth of the Fifth Philippine Republic (from 1986 to the present). Cory Aquino, who was installed president after the ouster of Marcos, presided over the initial phase of the post-Marcos democratic transition or the "EDSA regime," which was devoted to the dismantling of the centralized authoritarian power structure and restoration of pre-martial law democratic institutions. In effect, the EDSA regime is a "reconstructionist regime" premised on two complementary objectives: de-Marcosification and democratization (Velasco 1997, 91). The institutional foundations for the EDSA regime were laid down in the 1987 Constitution drafted to replace the 1973 Marcos Constitution.

Marcos was a firm believer in destiny and greatness. He had carefully interwoven his rise to power with greatness and the destiny of the Filipino nation. But he also represented the "original sin" of Philippine postwar politics—patronage politics inherited from the American colonizers coupled with the warlordism generated by the violence of the Japanese occupation during the Second World War. Marcos "played dirty from the beginning, but his victories had been spectacular, and that was what counted for voters, who prized courage and cunning above all qualities" (Burton 1989, 37). In the end, he repudiated the very same postwar political regime that spawned him and established a dictatorial regime in pursuit of his destiny and personal greatness.

Aquino, on the other hand, was the anti-thesis to Marcos's approach to power. The Aquinos and their "yellow" elite supporters draw their legitimacy from the so-called "EDSA miracle"—a divinely sanctioned people power that overthrew Marcos's "evil" dictatorship in order to reestablish a "righteous" democracy (Claudio 2013, 11). Hence, the "EDSA miracle" (also known as the "EDSA spirit") became the "foundationalist" narrative of the post-Marcos liberal reformist regime that began with Cory Aquino and continued with her son Benigno "Noynoy" S. Aquino III. Cory and the anti-Marcos political elite framed this narrative in quasi-religious terms and immortalized it in the EDSA Shrine, a Roman Catholic Church located at the center of Epifanio de los Santos Avenue. The church is unique for the huge statue of the Virgin Mary on top of it and the mix of religious and political icons inside it celebrating the so-called "miracle" of people power (Claudio 2013, 27).

Ironically, this miracle will be repeated in the form of a divisive elitist discourse that justified the elite-led overthrow of the populist president Joseph Estrada in 2001 in what was dubbed "EDSA Dos" or "People Power II." When Estrada's supporters mounted their own "Poor People Power" or "EDSA Tres" in front of the shrine, they were violently dispersed and their leaders arrested. The yellow forces derided the vandalism, garbage, and foul smell left by the poor protesters.

Four extra-electoral strategic groups have played critical roles in the Philippine context: big business, the Catholic Church, civil society activists, and the military. Each is comprised by large organizations that enable it to mobilize supporters for or against a sitting president, either through nonviolent demonstrations or demonstration of force through military intervention. They have been united against Erap and divided under Arroyo, but have generally supported reformist presidents and have often turned against those whom they consider to have challenged or betrayed the reformist narrative (Thompson 2014, 447). Cory Aquino survived her term of office with the support of big business represented by the Makati Business Club, the Catholic Church led by Jaime Cardinal Sin, an assortment of civil society organizations representing the social democratic left, and a dominant faction of the military led by General Fidel Ramos.

The second and third post-Marcos presidents represented political opposites. Ramos cloaked his presidency with the mantle of reformism—promising good governance through policy change and more honest and efficient administration—the dominant narrative in the post-Marcos regime. He became its most successful "orthodox innovator," as he subscribed to, and attempted to improve the implementation of, the governing reformism philosophy of the "foundationalist" president Corazon C. Aquino. On the other hand, Estrada attempted to preempt the reformist narrative with his populist narrative. However, the two also shared some similarities as well. Both served in the Marcos regime—Ramos (a Marcos cousin) as chief of the Philippine Constabulary that served as primary martial law enforcer, and Estrada as a loyal small-town mayor of San Juan. Both were also unconventional political outsiders: Ramos the first protestant president and Estrada the movie actor. Both did not get the support of the Catholic Church.

Ramos the minority president won the election by a narrow plurality and managed to build a majority political coalition through the astute distribution of pork barrel while Estrada was a majority president who won one of the largest margins in post-Marcos elections but gradually dissipated his political support by not distributing enough. In the end, Ramos's presidency was deemed successful because he managed to establish a *modus vivendi* with key strategic interests—the Church, business, military, and civil society. In contrast Estrada's presidency ended in tragedy because he antagonized all of these interests with his corruption and bad governance.

The election of populist movie actor Joseph "Erap" Estrada to the presidency followed the economic turmoil of the Asian financial crisis. Through his populist narrative of *Erap para sa mahirap* (Erap is pro-poor), he attempted to preempt the reformist, albeit elitist, narrative of the EDSA regime. In turn, Estrada was plagued by allegations of abuse of power, a lavish lifestyle, incompetence, and corruption. This led to his impeachment and subsequent ouster in a second people power uprising in 2001. Estrada's Vice President, Gloria Macapagal-Arroyo, was then installed as president. Hence, the EDSA forces led by Cory Aquino, Fidel Ramos, and Cardinal Sin, through extra-constitutional means, ousted a democratically elected president in the name of "good governance" (Thompson 2007).

Arroyo's first term was marked by serious challenges to the legitimacy of her government, which began with a failed attempt at a popular uprising by Estrada's supporters and ended with a mutiny led by junior military officers in July 2003. Arroyo stood for re-election in the 2004 presidential election despite claiming numerous times she would not. Amidst serious charges of electoral fraud, Arroyo narrowly defeated the populist challenge of movie actor and close Estrada-ally Fernando Poe Jr. (popularly known as FPJ). The allegation of massive fraud was only substantiated in June 2005 with the release of recordings of wiretapped conversations between the president and a high-ranking election official.

The controversy threatened the Arroyo presidency when the EDSA forces, again led by Cory Aquino, withdrew their support for her. Ironically, the EDSA forces, composed of big business, the Catholic Church, and segments of civil society, tacitly supported or turned a blind eye to these election irregularities, and justified it with the need to defeat the populist challenge of FPJ. For the latter half of her term in office, she faced a wave of massive street protests, four successive impeachment charges in Congress, and one more failed military coup attempt. She managed to survive by dispensing pork barrel and patronage to key allies in Congress and the local governments. She also adeptly curried favors with the military, big business, the Catholic Church, and segments of civil society.

Arroyo can be classified as disjunctive in the Skowronekian sense, not because the reformist narrative has been exhausted but due to the perception that she has betrayed the so-called "EDSA spirit." Hence, Cory Aquino preserved her image as the *bida*, or heroine, of the EDSA regime, as confirmed by the massive outpouring of grief after her death from cancer in 2009. On the other hand, despite Arroyo's solid economic performance, she was portrayed as the *kontrabida*, or villainess, in the political telenovela.

Unlike his scandal-plagued and unpopular predecessor, it long seemed that Benigno S. "Noynoy" Aquino III could do no wrong. Aquino promised to take a "straight path" to clean up corruption, which he also claimed would eradicate poverty. The EDSA forces rallied around him and implicated his closest rival in the 2010 presidential elections, Senator Manuel Villar, in corruption scandals and portrayed him as a traditional politician (*trapo*). Villar, a "rags-to-riches" billionaire, offered a compelling populist narrative to the Filipino electorate that rivaled Estrada's *masa* appeal.

Noynoy Aquino was the reluctant candidate thrust into the presidency upon the outpouring of national grief over the death of his mother, Cory Aquino. This was not the first time that death propelled an Aquino into the presidency. Cory ascended to the presidency after the brutal assassination of Noynoy's father, Benigno "Ninoy" Aquino Jr. Noynoy's presidency is a testament to the potency of the Aquino narrative, a particular variant of the reformist storyline that harks back to the presidency of Ramon Magsaysay.

Moreover, the second Aquino administration, through its allies in the Senate, also exerted great efforts in persecuting Vice President Jejomar Binay for alleged corruption. Binay served as mayor of Makati City for close to three decades by dispensing patronage and building extensive webs of clientelism. He has taken up the mantle of traditional populism to challenge the "yellow" reformist forces in the 2016 election. Consistent with the reformist governance script, Binay was portrayed as a "bad" and "corrupt" populist not worthy of the people's trust. In their virulent attack against populist candidates like Binay, and later, Duterte, the EDSA forces only accentuated the growing perception that they are anti-poor.

Drawing parallelisms with Thailand in which the "yellow-shirt" elites have repeatedly overthrown pro-poor Thaksin-linked governments, the Philippine yellows have overthrown a sitting president (Estrada in 2001), cheated a leading presidential candidate (Poe in 2004), and discredited presidential frontrunners (Villar in 2010 and Binay in 2016) in their effort to defeat pro-poor populism. In successfully undermining the pro-poor populist narrative, the reformist elite inadvertently provided the impetus for the emergence of a darker shade of populism, once their "good governance" narrative faltered (Thompson 2016b, 46).

Rise of the Post-EDSA Regime

Duterte's victory in 2016 signifies the revival of a nationalist-populist narrative first articulated by Estrada in 1998. Duterte's unorthodox campaign style has captured the imagination of the Filipino voters. His political back story runs parallel to the archetypical Filipino populist, ousted President Estrada. Both come from middle-class families with minor political connections who found affinity with the poor at an early age. Both were expelled from Jesuit-run schools and both started their careers as successful mayors: Estrada during the Marcos era, Duterte during the post-Marcos era. Both projected a *siga* (tough guy) image, with Estrada magnifying this persona in the movies and in the town of San Juan and Duterte crafting this image in the communist-infiltrated and crime-infested city of Davao.

Unlike Estrada, however, who has successfully parlayed his

working man and underdog movie roles into his ascent to the presidency, Duterte's unorthodox and unfiltered style was tailor-fitted for reality TV and the social media. For years, he hosted a local television show in Davao *Gikan sa Masa, Para sa Masa* (From the Masses, to the Masses) where he called out and cursed the names of inefficient local and national bureaucrats, suspected criminals, and other erring government officials. Thus, Duterte (and Donald Trump in the United States) has embodied "performative populism"—a style of populism in the age of television and digital media that draws on a "repertoire of performance" and builds a relationship between the leader as performer and the follower as the audience (Moffitt 2016; 2017; Magcamit and Arugay 2017).

Duterte first rose to national prominence by turning Davao— once a hotbed for crime and the communist insurgency—into a disciplined and developed city that has attracted a significant amount of investments. But this transformation came at a heavy price, as the mayor has earned the reputation (seldom denied) of using heavy-handed tactics and (alleged) extra-judicial killings to fight criminality, especially narcotics and drug trafficking. After some initial indecisiveness, Duterte plunged into the presidential race with two basic campaign narratives: he would push for federalism to bring peace to Mindanao and he would restore peace and order in the Philippines through any means possible. When Duterte was first elected mayor in 1988, the citizens of Davao "entered into a Hobbesian social contract with Duterte, which allowed him to rule with an iron-fist in exchange for social peace and personal security" (Isaac and Aceron 2016).

Duterte was not the first to contest the presidency on a "law and order" narrative. In 1998, EDSA icon Cory Aquino, together with the Liberal Party, supported the presidential run of former police general and Manila mayor Alfredo Lim (also known as "Robocop"), who, just like Duterte, was suspected of committing human rights violations and extra-judicial killings in his own anti-drug campaign (Rufo 1998). In 2004, former chief of the Philippine National Police, Estrada protégé, and senator Panfilo "Ping" Lacson (also implicated in extra-judicial killings) ran for president with the slogan "kamay na bakal" (iron fist); and, in 2010 former Marikina mayor Bayani

Fernando, known for his tough disciplinarian style, contested the Lakas Party presidential primaries by invoking "political will" (Curato 2017).

It can be argued that the rise of Duterte occurred at the exact moment when the liberal reformist regime was most vulnerable. Its core narrative of good governance was eroded with the extraconstitutional ouster of populist Estrada in 2001, the contested presidential election of 2004, and the massive display of incompetence during the latter half of the second Aquino administration. Thus, by "challenging liberal reformism despite his predecessor Noynoy Aquino's personal popularity, Duterte was able to take advantage of the 'systemic disjunction' of this once dominant political order—due to the discrediting of the good governance narrative, the weakening influence of key 'strategic groups' backing it (particularly the Church and social democrats), and the vulnerability of key institutions" (Thompson 2016b, 59).

Duterte was able to tap into the "politics of anger" fueled by the general sense of frustration among the voters and the growing desire for a strong leader to restore law and order. Thus, "Duterte has taken advantage of the systematic vulnerability of liberal reformism to begin building a new elite coalition around his law and order narrative" (52).

The election of Duterte was a repudiation of the failures of the second Aquino administration. The Duterte phenomenon was not a revolt of the poor but was a protest of the new middle class who suffered from lack of public service, endured the horrendous land and air traffic, feared the breakdown of peace and order, and silently witnessed their tax money siphoned by corruption despite promises of improved governance.

The anger found form in a movement that gravitated around the antiestablishment and unorthodox mayor from the South who promised the coming of *tunay na pagbabago* (real change). Duterte proceeded in cobbling up an insurgent counter-elite coalition to neutralize the strategic interests that constitute the EDSA ruling elite. These include: the traditional politicians marginalized by the EDSA forces (i.e., the Marcos, Estrada, and Arroyo forces); the non-Manila business elites (i.e., former Marcos crony and banana magnate Antonio Floirendo, former Cory Aquino cabinet member Carlos Dominguez, Filipino-Chinese Lorenzo Te, Dennis Uy, and Samuel Uy); the new middle class (i.e., call center agents, Uber drivers, overseas Filipino workers); the communist national democrats; and the national police.

In Skowronekian terms, Duterte is a repudiator reconstructing the Philippine presidency. He ascended to power not simply by defeating the unpopular candidate of a popular reformist president but by riding the crest of voter anger and dissatisfaction with the EDSA regime narrative that has become hollow in the face of continuing poverty, corruption, and criminality. Through his controversial actions, he is changing the storyline—from the elite-led good governance crusade of EDSA to a counter-elite nationalist-populist law and order developmentalism. Already, he is setting the motion for constitutional change and the shift to a federal-parliamentary-semi-presidential system of government. If he succeeds, the Filipino nation will enter into a new era of the post-EDSA regime.

References

Abinales, Patricio N., and Donna J. Amoroso. 2005. *State and Society in the Philippines*. Manila: Anvil.

Anderson, Benedict. 1988. "Cacique Democracy and the Philippines: Origins and Dreams." *New Left Review* 169:3–33.

Arguelles, Cleve. 2016. "How the Philippines' Incomplete 'People Power' Revolution Paved the Way for Rodrigo Duterte." *The Conversation*, 10 December. https://theconversation.com/how-the-philippines-incomplete-people-power-revolution-paved-the-way-for-rodrigo-duterte-65972.

Bello, Walden. 1986. "Aquino's Elite Populism: Initial Reflections." *Third World Quarterly* 8:1020–30.

Burton, Sandra. 1989. *Impossible Dream: The Marcoses, the Aquinos, and the Unfinished Revolution*. New York, NY: Warner Books.

Casiple, Ramon C. 2016. "The Duterte Presidency as a Phenomenon." *Contemporary Southeast Asia* 38:179–184.

Castañeda Anastacio, Leia. 2016. *The Foundations of the Modern Philippine State: Imperial Rule and the American Constitutional*

Tradition in the Philippine Islands, 1898–1935. New York: Cambridge University Press.

Claudio, Lisandro E. 2013. *Taming People's Power: The EDSA Revolutions and Their Contradictions*. Quezon City: Ateneo de Manila University Press.

Coronel, Sheila. 1991. "Dateline Philippines: The Lost Revolution." *Foreign Policy*, 84:166.

Cullinane, Michael. 2003. *Ilustrado Politics: Filipino Elite Responses to American Rule, 1898–1908*. Quezon City: Ateneo de Manila University Press.

Curato, Nicole. 2017. "Flirting with Authoritarian Fantasies? Rodrigo Duterte and the New Terms of Philippine Populism." *Journal of Contemporary Asia* 47:142–53.

De Castro, Renato. 2007. "The 1997 Asian Financial Crisis and the Revival of Populism/Neo-populism in 21st Century Philippines." *Asian Survey* 47:930–51.

Doronilla, Amando. 1992. *The State, Economic Transformation, and Political Change in the Philippines, 1946–1972*. Singapore: Oxford University Press.

Ileto, Reynaldo C. 1993. "The 'Unfinished Revolution' in Philippine Political Discourse." *Southeast Asian Studies* 31:62–82.

Isaac, Francis, and Joy Aceron. 2016. "Making Sense of Digong Duterte." *Rappler*, 30 January. http://www.rappler.com/thought -leaders/120239-rodrigo-duterte-elections-2016.

Lieberman, Robert C. 2000. "Political Time and Policy Coalitions: Structure and Agency in Presidential Power." In *Presidential Power: Forging the Presidency for the Twenty-First Century*, ed. Robert Y. Shapiro, Martha Joynt Kumar, and Lawrence R. Jacobs, 274–310. New York: Columbia University Press.

Magcamit, Michael I., and Aries A. Arugay. 2017. "Rodrigo Duterte and the Making of a Populist Demigod: Part 1." *IAPS Dialogue*. https://iapsdialogue.org/2017/03/17/rodrigo-duterte-and-the-m aking-of-a-populist-demigod-part-1/.

Moffit, Benjamin. 2016. *The Global Rise of Populism*. Stanford: Stanford University Press.

Paredes, Ruby R., ed. 1989. *Philippine Colonial Democracy*. Quezon City: Ateneo de Manila University Press.

Putzel, James. 1992. *A Captive Land: The Politics of Agrarian Reform in the Philippines*. Quezon City: Ateneo de Manila University Press.

Quimpo, Nathan G. 2008. *Contested Democracy and the Left in the*

Philippines after Marcos. Quezon City: Ateneo de Manila University Press.

Regilme, Salvador Santino F. 2016. "Why Asia's Oldest Democracy is Bound to Fail." *Journal of Developing Societies* 32:220-45.

Rivera, Temario C. 1994. *Landlords & Capitalists: Class, Family, and State in Philippine Manufacturing.* Quezon City: Center for Integrative Development Studies/University of the Philippines.

———. 2002. "Transition Pathways and Democratic Consolidation in Post-Marcos Philippines." *Contemporary Southeast Asia* 24:466-83.

Rufo, Aries. 1998. "Alfredo Siojo Lim – Cory's Choice: Robocop for President." In *Showdown '98: The Search for the Centennial President*, ed. Malou Mangahas, 141-79. Metro Manila: The Manila Times and Ateneo Center for Social Policy and Public Affairs.

Skowronek, Stephen. 1997. *The Politics Presidents Make: Leadership from John Adams to Bill Clinton.* Cambridge, MA: Belknap Harvard.

———. 2011. *Presidential Leadership in Political Time: Reprise and Reappraisal.* 2nd ed. Lawrence, KS: The University of Kansas Press.

Tancangco, Luzviminda G., and Roger L Mendoza. 1988. "Elections and the Crisis of Legitimacy in the Philippines: A Comparative View of the Marcos and Aquino Regimes." *Philippine Journal of Public Administration* 32:268-98.

Teehankee, Julio C., and Mark R. Thompson. 2016. "Electing a Strongman." *Journal of Democracy* 27:125-34.

Teehankee, Julio C. 2016a. "Weak State, Strong Presidents: Situating the Duterte Presidency in Philippine Political Time." *Journal of Developing Societies* 32:1-29.

———. 2016b. "Duterte's Resurgent Nationalism in the Philippines: A Discursive Institutionalist Analysis." *Journal of Current Southeast Asian Affairs* 35:69-89.

Timberman, David G. 2016. "Elite Democracy Disrupted?" *Journal of Democracy* 27:135-44.

Thompson, Mark R. 1996. *The Anti-Marcos Struggle: Personalistic Rule and Democratic Transition in the Philippines.* Quezon City: New Day Publishers.

———. 2007. "Reform After Reformasi: Middle Class Movements for Good Governance After Democratic Revolutions in Southeast Asia." *Working Papers in Contemporary Asian Studies* 21. Sweden: Centre for East and South-East Asian Studies, Lund University.

———. 2010. "Populism and the Revival of Reform: Competing Political Narratives in the Philippines." *Contemporary Southeast Asia* 32:1-28.

———. 2013. "The Post-Marcos Presidency in 'Political Time.'" *SEARC Working Paper Series* 142. Hong Kong: Southeast Asia Research Centre University of Hong Kong.

———. 2014. "The Politics Philippine Presidents Make." *Critical Asian Studies* 46:430–66.

———. 2016a. "The Moral Economy of Electoralism and the Rise of Populism in the Philippines and Thailand." *Journal of Developing Societies* 32:246–69.

———. 2016b. "Bloodied Democracy: Duterte and the Death of Liberal Reformism in the Philippines." *Journal of Current Southeast Asian Affairs* 35:39–68.

Velasco, Renato S. 1997. "Philippine Democracy: Promise and Performance." In *Democratization in East and Southeast Asia*, ed. Anek Laothamatas, 77–112. Singapore: Institute of Southeast Asian Studies.

Wurfel, David. 1988. "Filipino Politics: Development and Decay." Quezon City: Ateneo de Manila University Press.

Wurfel, David. 1983-1984. "Trends in National Political Elite Composition-Cause and Consequences: The Philippines Since the 1960s." *Anuaryo/Annales: Journal of History and Political Science* 12, no. 1–2:39-66.

WHO SUPPORTS RODRIGO DUTERTE?

Ronald D. Holmes

Rodrigo Duterte is a record breaker many times over. He is the first local official immediately elected to the highest position of the land. He is the first president hailing from Mindanao. He is the first head of state in the Philippines to announce the nation's "separation" from the United States, to show the middle finger to the European Union for meddling in the country's human rights situation, to call the United Nations Secretary General "the devil," and the Pope a son of a whore.

To make things more interesting, Duterte also registers the highest trust and performance ratings relative to previous presidents, as captured by Pulse Asia Research, Inc. (Pulse Asia) and the Social Weather Stations (SWS)—two of the county's major survey organizations.

These records are partly remarkable. I say partly inasmuch as Duterte shares a similar record of prior presidents after 1986—except for Gloria Macapagal-Arroyo—who have garnered significant majority approval/satisfaction ratings that they retained for a period of at least a year. I say remarkable, however, because Duterte's approval and trust ratings remained unchanged despite the contentious issues his regime faces. Most controversial of these issues is the president's bloody war against drugs, leaving over thousands dead within his first nine months in power.

This chapter examines the level and sources of support for Duterte in the first months of his administration. In doing so, this chapter argues that Duterte's performance and trust ratings are not bound to significantly change, save for two conditions: an unexpected or unpredictable critical incident that would put into serious doubt Duterte's commitment to change or his trustworthiness and integrity as an individual; and a catastrophic downturn in economic conditions. For all the warts, missteps, and arrogation of power that Duterte and his cohorts have exhibited, he and his administration have been able to effectively sustain the connection with the public, which explains the positive performance and trust ratings.

From a Mediocre Student to a Well-rated President

By his own admission, Duterte was an unexceptional student. In a televised debate during the presidential campaign, Duterte was asked what his programs would be should he win as president. Duterte said that he would just copy the good plans of the other contenders. After all, he had mastered copying the answers of his classmates as a grade school student. In several press conferences and speeches after he assumed the presidency, Duterte boasted that the people he appointed to the cabinet got far better grades than he did when they were students. Duterte has caricatured himself as a "late bloomer" and blossomed he did as he won the presidency and set significant majority performance and trust ratings.

Tables 1 and 2 show Duterte's performance and trust ratings in the surveys conducted by Pulse Asia and the SWS within the first six months of the current administration.

Table 1. President Duterte's Performance Rating (figures in percent)[*]

	September 2016			December 2016		
	Approval	Indecision	Disapproval	Approval	Indecision	Disapproval
Pulse Asia	86	11	3	83	13	5
	Satisfaction	Indecision	Dissatisfaction	Satisfaction	Indecision	Dissatisfaction
SWS	76	13	11	77	10	13

Table 2. President Duterte's Trust Rating

	June (SWS)/ July (Pulse) 2016			September 2016			December 2016		
	Trust	Indecision	Distrust	Trust	Indecision	Distrust	Trust	Indecision	Distrust
Pulse Asia	91	8	0.2	86	11	3	83	13	4
SWS	84	11	5	83	9	8	81	10	9

[*] Figures in this and the subsequent tables may not add up to 100%, given rounding-off and the exclusion of "don't know/refused to answer" responses.

The variance in performance and trust ratings between Pulse and SWS surveys may be attributed to differences in question phrasing and sampling. Notwithstanding this divergence, Duterte obtained consistently majority approval/satisfaction and trust ratings in both Pulse and SWS September surveys. From survey to survey, there are only marginal changes in Duterte's performance and trust ratings.

Breaking Down the Performance and Trust Ratings

What is driving these numbers? Table 3 shows the breakdown of Duterte's performance ratings by geographic area, locale, socioeconomic class, and sex.

Table 3. Duterte's Disaggregated Performance Ratings (figures in percent)

	Pulse Asia						SWS					
	Approval		Undecided		Disapproval		Satisfied		Undecided		Dissatisfied	
	Sept	Dec	Sept	Dec	Sept	Dec	Sept	Dec	Sept	Dec	Sept	Dec
Area												
PH	86	83	11	13	3	5	76	77	13	10	11	13
NCR[1]	80	79	14	15	6	6	74	75	10	9	16	16
BL[2]	84	78	13	15	3	7	70	74	17	12	13	14
Vis[3]	88	84	9	13	3	3	75	76	11	8	14	15

Min⁴	93	91	6	7	1	2	88	82	8	9	4	8
Locale												
Urban	86	81	11	13	3	6	74	79	14	9	12	13
Rural	86	84	11	12	3	4	78	75	11	11	11	14
Socio-economic class												
ABC	82	69	12	26	6	4	69	73	18	6	13	21
D	86	84	12	11	3	5	76	77	12	10	11	13
E	88	85	8	11	4	5	76	74	12	13	11	13
Sex												
Male	84	84	12	11	4	5	79	79	13	9	8	13
Female	88	81	10	14	2	5	72	74	13	12	15	14

¹National Capital Region; ²Balance Luzon; ³Visayas; ⁴Mindanao

In terms of geographic area, Mindanao registers significantly higher appreciation for Duterte's performance, coupled with consistent single digit dissatisfaction. The higher appreciation from Mindanaoans is expected as Duterte hails from the island and has continued to root himself in his hometown, Davao City, periodically holding office in the Malacañang of the South, in Panacan. Moreover, in many of his speeches, during the campaign and in his presidency, Duterte underscores the historical injustices suffered by Mindanaoans. Further, he anchors his proposal to shift to a federal structure chiefly to liberate Mindanao from conflict.

Performance ratings are invariant regardless of locale, socio-economic class, and sex, given each survey's margin of error. Nonetheless, one should note the marginal decline in approval from Class ABC in Pulse Asia's surveys, and the marginal increase in dissatisfaction from the same socio-economic class in the Social Weather Stations' September–December 2016 surveys.

A similar story emerges in Duterte's trust ratings. The president's significant majority trust rating has been buoyed by the almost universal trust conferred by Mindanaoans. From the September–December surveys of both Pulse and SWS, there are only marginal reductions in the trust rating of the president in the National Capital Region (NCR); the Balance of Luzon (BL, for the Pulse September–December 2016 survey); in Visayas (for the SWS September–December 2016 surveys); in both urban and rural locales and for both sexes; and for socio-economic class ABC and D (for Class E, there is a marginal decline in trust for the president in the Pulse December 2016 survey). In general, trust for the president is invariant across the areas and socio-demographic groups. This is indicated in Table 4.

Table 4. Duterte's Trust Ratings (figures in percent)

	Pulse Asia						SWS					
	Trust		Undecided		Distrust		Trust		Undecided		Distrust	
	Sept	Dec	Sept	Dec	Sept	Dec	Sept	Dec	Sept	Dec	Sept	Dec
Area												
PH	86	83	11	13	3	4	83	81	9	10	8	9
NCR[1]	81	79	13	16	6	5	83	76	11	12	7	11

BL[2]	82	77	13	17	4	6	78	79	12	11	10	10
Vis[3]	86	87	12	11	2	2	82	78	8	13	8	13
Min[4]	96	92	3	5	1	2	94	90	4	5	2	5

Locale

Urban	86	82	10	13	4	5	82	82	11	9	7	8
Rural	86	83	11	13	3	3	85	80	7	10	8	9

Socio-economic class

ABC	85	72	8	25	7	3	82	75	7	7	10	16
D	85	83	12	12	3	5	84	81	10	10	6	9
E	88	85	7	12	4	3	80	80	7	11	13	8

Sex

Male	85	84	11	11	4	5	84	83	9	10	7	8
Female	87	81	11	15	2	4	82	79	10	10	8	10

What explains these high approval and trust ratings? Part of this could be rooted in the public's general regard that he has fulfilled his campaign promise of fighting criminality in general or combatting illegal drugs in particular. There are survey data that support this interpretation, illustrating a significant majority approval or satisfaction of the administration's performance in fighting criminality. In the September and December 2016 Pulse Asia surveys, the administration obtained an 89 percent and 84 percent approval in addressing the issue, the highest level of approval across all issues that the administration was performance-rated. In the SWS December 2016 survey, the Duterte administration generated a significant majority satisfaction rating (67 percent) in fighting crimes. Though this level of satisfaction was not the highest recorded across issues that the survey elicited performance ratings of the administration, the highest satisfaction registered on helping the poor (78 percent), the Duterte administration's performance rating on fighting crimes remains the highest across all administrations, as shown in Figure 1.

Figure 1.   Net Satisfaction with the National Administration on Fighting Crimes, Social Weather Stations Surveys, November 1990–December 2016

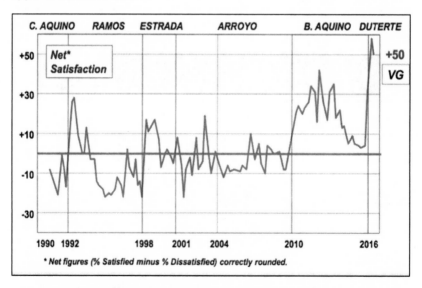

On the specific campaign against illegal drugs, the December 2016 SWS survey found that 85 percent of the public were satisfied (53 percent very satisfied and 32 percent somewhat satisfied) with the administration's performance. In addition, 88 percent of the public agreed that the drug problem declined after Duterte assumed the presidency.

Aside from receiving a satisfactory rating on fighting crimes and illegal drugs, the majority of the public was also satisfied with the administration's performance in promoting human rights (70 percent satisfied, 16 percent undecided, 14 percent dissatisfied) and solving the problem of extra-judicial killings (59 percent satisfied, 20 percent undecided, 19 percent dissatisfied) according to the SWS December 2016 survey. For those appalled by the increasing number of casualties in the campaign against illegal drugs, these data may be perplexing. However, other results from the SWS December 2016 survey indicate that the public remains concerned about extra-judicial killings. The December 2016 SWS survey found that a significant number of Filipinos are somewhat worried/very worried that someone from one's family will be a victim of extra-judicial killing, 33 percent and 45 percent, respectively. Moreover, 69 percent of the public considered extra-judicial killings a somewhat or very serious problem. Notwithstanding these concerns, 70 percent of the public believed that the Duterte administration was serious (38 percent very serious and 32 percent somewhat serious) about solving the problem of extra-judicial killings.

Comparing Duterte with Prior Presidents

Duterte's highly positive performance ratings are not distinct from public appreciation for former presidents at the beginning of their terms. Table 5 captures the performance ratings of previous presidents in the first six months of their respective terms. As this table reveals, Duterte scores the second highest gross satisfaction rating, 77 percent (in the December 2016 survey), slightly lower than the highest satisfaction ratings posted by Corazon Aquino (78 percent in the October 1986 SWS survey) and former President Joseph Estrada (78 percent in the June 1999 SWS survey). Pulse surveys, on the other hand, register the highest approval rating for Duterte. As discussed earlier, this is primarily due to his near-universal approval in Mindanao.

Table 5.   Performance ratings of post-1986 presidents in the first six months of their term (figures in percent, month/year)

President	SWS (date of survey) Gross Satisfaction		Pulse (date of survey) Gross Approval	
Corazon Aquino	60 (5/1986)	78 (10/1986)	Not applicable (Pulse established in 1999)	
Fidel Ramos	70 (9/1992)	68 (12/1992)		
Joseph Estrada	69 (9/1998)	73 (11/1998)		
Gloria Maca-pagal Arroyo (2001)	42 (3/2001)	46 (7/2001)	63 (3/2001)	57 (6/2001)
Gloria Maca-pagal Arroyo (2004)	57 (6/2004)	38 (12/2004)	55 (6/2004)	41 (10/2004)
Benigno S. Aquino III	71 (9/2010)	71 (12/2010)	79 (9/2010)	74 (3/2011)[1]
Rodrigo Duterte	76 (9/2016)	77 (12/2016)	86 (9/2016)	83 (12/2016)

*There was no quarterly survey conducted by Pulse in December 2010.

How long can the incumbent president sustain the high approval/satisfaction ratings? Figure 2 shows the public assessment of the performance of previous presidents based on SWS surveys. The figure reveals that all except one president after 1986, Gloria Macapagal Arroyo, sustained majority satisfaction ratings for a relatively lengthy period: Corazon "Cory" Aquino for a period of thirty-nine months (May 1986–August 1989); Fidel Ramos for thirty-three months (September 1992–June 1995); Joseph Estrada for thirteen months (September 1998–October 1999); and Benigno "Noynoy" Aquino III for fifty-one months (September 2010–December 2014). Despite fluctuations in their performance ratings, two previous presidents ended with majority satisfaction ratings in SWS surveys: Fidel Ramos and Benigno Aquino III.

A review of the developments that transpired during the terms of former presidents indicates that certain critical incidents led to an erosion of satisfaction for each of the presidents.

In the case of President Cory Aquino, the first decline in her performance rating came soon after the August 1987 coup attempt. The 28 August 1987 coup was preceded by work stoppages and labor protests after the government announced an increase in oil prices, with a national strike held on 26 August 1987. The October 1987 SWS survey posted a 21 percentage point drop in her satisfaction rating, from 76 percent in March 1987 to 55 percent; and her first double-digit disapproval, at 20 percent (from 7 percent in March 1987). While there were other survey observations where Cory Aquino's satisfaction rating declined, it was in the November 1990 SWS survey where her satisfaction rating was less than a majority, at 38 percent (down from 54 percent in May 1990). The drop in the satisfaction rating (with a 14 percentage point increase in dissatisfaction, from 17 percent to 31 percent), may have been triggered by the power crisis that started to be felt in many parts of the country by the second quarter of 1990 and a series of natural disasters (e.g., July 1990 earthquake, March 1991 Pinatubo eruptions) that the government failed to effectively respond to. After the November 1990 survey, Cory Aquino failed to regain a majority satisfaction rating with her end-of-term performance rating standing at 38 percent satisfied, 30 percent undecided, and 31 percent dissatisfied.

With respect to President Fidel Ramos, the first significant decline in his performance rating was recorded in the August 1994 SWS survey, a drop from 75 percent satisfaction in April 1994 to 66 percent in August 1994. However, the major drop occurred in March 1995 when Ramos obtained a 49 percent satisfaction rating, down

Figure 2. Social Weather Stations Gross Satisfaction Ratings of Presidents, May 1986–December 2016

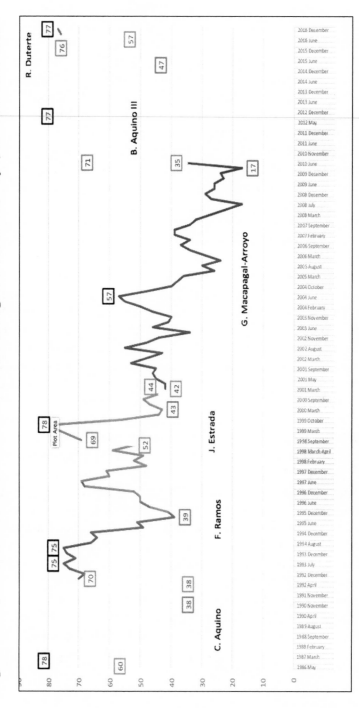

from 66 percent satisfaction recoded in December 1994. The critical incident that occurred prior to the survey was the execution of the Singapore-based Overseas Filipino Worker Flor Contemplacion. While Ramos recovered a majority satisfaction rating (51 percent) in the subsequent survey (June 1995), his performance rating dipped again in October 1995, at 39 percent satisfaction (with 23 percent undecided and 38 percent dissatisfied) after the implementation of the Value Added Tax (VAT). Ramos's satisfaction-rating final slump was registered in January 1998 just before the election campaign for the presidential elections of 1998 started.

After holding on to a significant majority satisfaction rating for four surveys, President Joseph Estrada's satisfaction rating fell from 78 percent in June 1999 to 56 percent in October 1999. In the December 1999 SWS survey, Estrada's satisfaction further declined to 44 percent and remained less than a majority in the SWS surveys until the end of his term. The same erosion was registered in Pulse's *Ulat ng Bayan* surveys where his approval declined continuously from 74 percent in May 1999, 61 percent in September 1999, and 53 percent in December 1999. The primary cause of Estrada's declining performance rating was a worsening economy that started even before he assumed the presidency in mid-1998. In 1998, the Philippine economy recorded its first negative growth in the post-Marcos period, with real GDP declining by 0.5 percent (Rodlauer & Loungani 1999). Aside from a contraction of the economy, a series of oil price increases triggered a wave of renewed protests (Cororaton 2000).

With respect to President Gloria Macapagal Arroyo, with her satisfaction ratings already middling, the significant changes that can be observed are in the increases in her dissatisfaction or disapproval ratings, specifically when these ratings hit majority dissatisfaction/disapproval in the middle of 2005, alongside the so-called "Hello Garci" scandal. The scandal broke out when a recording of a conversation between Arroyo and a Commission on Election official, Virgilio "Garci" Garcillano, was leaked with the allegation that Arroyo instructed the latter to pad her votes in the 2004 presidential elections. In the July 2005 Pulse survey, her disapproval stood at 58 percent. In both SWS and Pulse surveys from 2005, Arroyo was unable to recover public appreciation as public dissatisfaction/disapproval of her performance remained higher than levels of satisfaction/disapproval.

Finally, while President Benigno S. Aquino III can claim the record of having maintained a favorable assessment of his performance from the public for the longest time, his satisfaction/approval rating considerably declined given the Mamasapano incident in January 2015. The incident caused the death of forty-four policemen and several combatants of the Moro Islamic Liberation Front and civilians. This drew so much flak for Aquino given that he approved the operation to capture a wanted terrorist implicated in the Bali bombing. Given the incident, Aquino registered his first lower than a majority satisfaction/approval rating, at 47 percent (in the SWS survey of March 2015) and 38 percent (in the March 2015 Pulse survey).

The record of presidents' performance ratings points to common factors that result in decline in public support. The first are critical events that expose the lack of competence or compassion of an administration. The second would be economic difficulties caused by public policies adopted by an administration or internal/external vulnerabilities. For Duterte to sustain his majority public approval/satisfaction, therefore, he would need to continually exhibit the capacity to address important issues, avoid a major blunder, and hope that the forecast of economists that the Philippine economy would continue to grow in the foreseeable future is correct.

Describing Duterte

In three successive surveys, Pulse Asia asked respondents to describe President Duterte in a single word or phrase. Nearly all (a negligible 0.1/0.2 percent) replied to the question with the verbatim responses categorized in Table 6. What is clear from such results is that President Duterte remains to be seen as a resolute leader. A third describes him as courageous. About a fifth says that he is a person of his word, one with conviction, and a competent leader who effectively enforces the law. From the September 2016 survey, however, Duterte's campaign against drugs has definitely gained more traction as more Filipinos described him as one who resolutely fights illegal drugs.

Table 6. Word/Phrase that best describes President Duterte, Pulse Asia Research Inc. Ulat ng Bayan Surveys, July 2016; September 2016; December 2016 (in percent, rounded off figures, bold figures as top five in each survey)

Response category	Jul-16	Sep-16	Dec-16
Matapang/astig/brusko/palaban (courageous/firm/brusque/fighter)	35	36	30
May isang salita/may palabra de honor (man of his word/with word of honor)	11	9	16
May paninindigan/may matibay na desisyon/determinado/may prinsipyo (person of conviction/with a firm decision/determined/ principled)	9	7	5
Mabait/mabuting tao/matulungin/may malasakit (good person; helpful; with compassion)	6	2	2
Magaling mamuno/Mabuting mamuno/ magaling magpatupad ng batas/tumutupad sa tungkulin (competent leader/ effective enforcer of the law/fulfills his responsibilities)	5	4	3
Laban sa droga/corruption (fights drugs/corruption)	3.1	15	15
Palamura/masama ang pananalita/ bastos (curses/foul mouth/impolite)	1.7	6	6

Q: *Para sa inyo, ano ang isang salita o ilang salita na pinakanaglalarawan kay Presidente Rodrigo "Rody/Digong" Duterte?* (What one word or phrase that best describes President Rodrigo "Rody/ Digong" Duterte)

In the December 2016 Pulse Asia survey, only a small proportion of the respondents provided negative characterizations. Only 2
percent of the respondents described Duterte as one who disregarded/
violated human rights. Almost the same proportion (1.9 percent)
asserted that Duterte flip-flops (*pabago-bago ng desisyon*) in his decisions and less than 1 percent described him as light-headed (*wala sa
sarili*, 0.6 percent); arrogant (0.5 percent); dictatorial (0.3 percent);
hard to understand (0.3 percent); feared (0.3 percent); focused only on
the drug problem (0.2 percent); not fulfilling his promise (0.2 percent);
impulsive (0.1 percent); moody (0.1 percent); quick-tempered (.1
percent); a liar (.1 percent); and does not listen (0.05 percent). Only one
respondent refused to give a description of Duterte out of fear that
what he/she might say may be taken against him or her. For the most
part, Filipinos have a positive view of Duterte.

The Populism of Fear:
Will the Fear of Populism be Forthcoming?

Duterte's fight against illegal drugs has definitely gone into full
swing. His campaign promise has been translated into his administration's flagship program called Operation Double Barrel
(Philippine National Police 2016). The unyielding implementation of
this program may have produced the significant majority approval/
satisfaction and trust conferred on the president. This is not to say,
however, that the public has not been mindful of the repercussions
of such a plan, especially the increasing death toll that has, as of
the end of 2016, gone past 6,000 (Regencia 2016). It is undeniable,
though, that Duterte has succeeded in imprinting on the minds of
the public the fear of crime to continually enlist popular support,
what a scholar referred to as the "populism of fear" (Chevigny 2003).
Eventually, though, the fear of crime might be upended by the fear
of those who were designated to combat crime, the law enforcers.
There are already signs of the latter fear evolving, captured by the
public's concern about extra-judicial killings and most recently
buoyed by the acts of crooked policemen who have used the cover
of the anti-illegal drug operation to engage in kidnap for ransom
activities.

Duterte himself has admitted that the police force is "corrupt to the core" (France-Presse 2017). Accordingly, Duterte vowed to cleanse the agency as he promised to wage the war against drugs until the last day of his term, a departure from his campaign promise of weeding out illegal drugs within the first six months of his term.

Duterte's extension of the drug war can be taken as an admission that there really are other more serious problems that his administration has yet to attend to: pervasive corruption, unending poverty, and continuing inequality, to name a few. These are prolonged woes that breed with each other and produce other social concerns, including the proliferation of illegal drug use. If Duterte continues with his myopic war against drugs and fails to take cognizance of and act with even more resolute fashion to address these more serious ills that Philippine society confronts, such narrow-mindedness may bring about a greater fear of his brand of populism and a steady erosion of his approval and trust ratings.

Epilogue

In the March 2017 Pulse Asia *Ulat ng Bayan* survey, Duterte's approval rating appears to hold, marginally down from 83 percent to 78 percent. Duterte's trust rating, however, shows a significant decline, from 83 percent in December 2016 to 76 percent in March 2017. The decline can be attributed to the shift toward ambivalence of the most populous socio-economic class D, a seven-percentage point decline (also from 83 percent in December 2016 to 76 percent in March 2017).

The significant majority's appreciation and trust for Duterte may indicate that the president remains impervious to certain political and economic developments that occurred prior to the survey. These developments include the testimony of a witness in a Senate investigation pointing to Duterte as the initiator of the alleged Davao Death Squad (DDS). The testimony spurred the first impeachment complaint against Duterte filed by an opposition legislator. Within the first quarter of 2017, Duterte has also been decried by a couple of international human rights organizations, the United States, the European Parliament, and several international media outfits for the "death toll of the war on illegal drugs," with some asserting that Duterte should be held criminally liable for the killings. On the economic front, inflation hit a more-than-two-year high in February 2017, the Philippine peso depreciated against the dollar, and power rates and public transportation fares went up in Metro Manila.

Perhaps the sustained significant majority approval and trust ratings result from an image of resoluteness that the president projects. Despite all the criticisms, Duterte vowed to continue the war on drugs even if it means his death or incarceration as he claims he is engaged in the campaign to prevent the country from becoming a failed state. He and his cohorts have also shown zeal in hitting and demolishing critics by accusing them of being protectors of drug lords or destabilizers. An arch-critic, Senator Leila de Lima, is now incarcerated after three cases were filed against her for her alleged involvement in the illegal drug trade. Vice President Leni Robredo is faced with her own impeachment complaint. Finally, Duterte boasts of his unwavering stance against corruption when he swiftly terminated from an appointive office even his former official spokesperson in the presidential campaign, Peter Laviña, who was accused of an anomalous transaction. In firing Laviña, Duterte remarked: "even a whiff of corruption, *talagang tatanggalin kita* [I will sack you]."

In the coming years, Duterte is certain to face additional challenges, possibly even more difficult than those confronted within the first few months of his term. The greatest challenge will be to show concrete measures of performance that positively impact on the lives of people, which means extending beyond the war on drugs.

References

Chevigny, Paul. 2003. "The Populism of Fear." *Punishment and Society* 5(1):77–96.

Cororaton, Caesar. 2000. "Oil Price Increase." *Policy Notes* 10. Philippine Institute for Development Studies. http://dirp4.pids.gov.ph/ris/pdf/pidspn0010.PDF.

"Duterte Extends Deadly Drug War." 2017. *Philippine Daily Inquirer.* http://newsinfo.inquirer.net/866493/duterte-extends-deadl y-drug-war.

France-Presse, Agence. 2017. "Duterte extends deadly drug war." *Inquirer.net*, 30 January. http://newsinfo.inquirer.net/866493/ duterte-extends-deadly-drug-war.

Philippine National Police. 2016. "Memorandum Circular 20 Project Double Barrel." Philippine National Police. http://didm.pnp.gov. ph/Command Memorandum Circulars/CMC 2016-16 PNP ANTI-ILLEGAL DRUGS CAMPAIGN PLAN %E2%80%93 PROJECT DOUBLE BARREL.pdf.

Regencia, Ted. 2016. "Duterte's Drug War: Death Toll Goes Past 6,000." *Al Jazeera.* http://www.aljazeera.com/blogs/asia/2016/12/duterte-drug-war-death-toll-6000-161213132427022.html.

Rodlauer, Markus, and Prakash Loungani. 1999. "Philippines: Selected Issues." Washington: International Monetary Fund. https://www. imf.org/external/pubs/ft/scr/1999/cr9992.pdf.

Rodrigo Duterte: A Fascist Original

Walden Bello

Fascism comes in different forms to different societies. When people expect fascism to develop in the "classic way," they fail to recognize it even when it is already upon them.

In 2016, fascism came to the Philippines in the form of Rodrigo Duterte. This event continues to elude a large part of the citizenry, some owing to fierce loyalty to the president, some out of fear of what the political and ethical consequences would be of admitting that naked force is now the ruling principle in Philippine politics.

Why Duterte Fits the "F" Word

At a panel that I was part of one month after Duterte ascended to the presidency, there was considerable hesitation in using what panelists euphemistically called the "F" word to characterize the new Executive. There is an understandable reluctance to use the term fascist, undoubtedly because the word has been applied very loosely to all kinds of movements and leaders that depart, in some fashion, from liberal democratic practices, such as their propensity to resort to the use of force to achieve their political objectives.

However, there would probably be considerably less objection to the use of the word to describe Duterte if we see as central to the definition of a fascist leader (a) a charismatic individual with strong inclinations toward authoritarian rule who (b) derives his or her strength from a heated multiclass mass base, (c) is engaged in or supports the systematic and massive violation of basic human, civil, and political rights, and (d) proposes a political project that contradicts the fundamental values and aims of liberal democracy or social democracy.

If one were to accept these elements provisionally as the key characteristics of a fascist leader, then Duterte would easily fit the bill.

A Fascist Original

Having said that, one must nevertheless acknowledge that Duterte is a fascist personality that is an original.

His charisma is not the demiurgic sort like Hitler's, nor does it derive so much from an emotional personal identification with the people and nation as in the case with some populists. Duterte's charisma would probably be best described as "cariño brutal," a volatile mix of will to power, a commanding personality, and gangster charm that fulfills his followers' deep-seated yearning for a father figure who will finally end what they see as the "national chaos."

Duterte is not a reactionary seeking to restore a mythical past. He is not a conservative dedicated to defending the status quo. His project is oriented toward an authoritarian future. He is best described, using Arno Mayer's term, as a counterrevolutionary.[1] Unlike some of his predecessors, like Hitler and Mussolini, however, he is not waging a counterrevolution against the left or socialism. In Duterte's case, the target—one can infer from his discourse and his actions—is liberal democracy, the dominant ideology and political system of our time. In this sense, he is both a local expression as well as a pioneer of an ongoing global phenomenon: the rebellion against the values and discourse of liberal democracy that Francis Fukuyama had declared as the "end of history" in the early 1990s.[2]

Counterrevolutionaries are not always clear about what their next moves are, but they often have an instinctive sense of what would bring them closer to power. Ideological purity is not high on their agenda, with them putting the premium on the emotional power of their message rather on its ideological coherence. The low priority accorded to ideological coherence is also extended to political alliances. Duterte's mobilization of a multiclass base and his ruling with the support of virtually all of the elite is unexceptional. However, one of the things that makes him a fascist original is that he has brought the dominant section of the left into his ruling coalition, something that would have been unthinkable with most previous fascist leaders.

But perhaps Duterte's distinctive contribution to fascism as a political phenomenon is in the area of political methodology. The stylized paradigm of fascism coming to power has the fascist leader or party begin with violations of civil rights, followed by the power grab, then indiscriminate repression. Duterte turns around this "Marcosian model" of "creeping fascism." He begins with impunity on a massive scale, that is, the extra-judicial killing of thousands of alleged drug users and pushers, and leaves the violations of civil liberties and the grab for absolute power as mopping up operations in a political landscape devoid of significant organized opposition.

A Product of EDSA

Duterte's ascendancy cannot be understood without taking into consideration the debacle of the EDSA liberal democratic republic that was born in the uprising of 1986. In fact, EDSA's failure was a condition for Duterte's success.

What destroyed the EDSA project and paved the way for Duterte was the deadly combination of elite monopoly of the electoral system, the continuing concentration of wealth, and neoliberal economic policies and the priority placed on foreign debt repayment imposed by Washington. By 2016, there was a yawning gap between the EDSA Republic's promise of popular empowerment and wealth redistribution and the reality of massive poverty, scandalous inequality, and pervasive corruption.[3]

And the EDSA Republic's discourse of democracy, human rights, and rule of law had become a suffocating straitjacket for the majority of Filipinos who simply could not relate to it owing to the overpowering reality of their powerlessness. Duterte's discourse—a mixture of outright death threats, *basagulero* language, and frenzied railing coupled with disdainful humor directed at the elite, whom he called "coños" or cunts—was a potent formula that proved exhilarating to his audience who felt themselves liberated from the stifling hypocrisy of the EDSA discourse.

Fascism in Power

Probably no fascist personality since Hitler came to power in Germany, in 1933, has used the mandate of a plurality at the polls to reshape the political arena more swiftly and decisively than Duterte in 2016. Even before he formally assumed office, the extra-judicial killings began; the elite opposition disintegrated, with some 95 percent of the so-called "Yellow Party," the Liberals, joining the Duterte Coalition; and Duterte achieved total control of both houses of Congress.

The Supreme Court, shying away from a confrontation, chose not to challenge the president's decision to have the former dictator, Ferdinand Marcos, buried in the Libingan ng mga Bayani, or the National Heroes' Cemetery. A traditional bulwark of defense of human rights, the Catholic Church exercised self-censorship, afraid that in a confrontation with a popular president who threatened to expose bishops and priests with mistresses and clerical child abusers; it was going to be a sure loser.[4]

A novice in foreign policy, Duterte was able to combine personal resentment with acute political instinct to significantly reshape the Philippines' relationship with big powers, notably the United States. What surprised many, though, was that there was very little protest in the Philippines at Duterte's geopolitical reorientation given the stereotype of Filipinos being "little brown brothers." What protest there was came mainly from traditional anti-American quarters, which evinced skepticism about the president's avowed intentions.

Here, Duterte again showed himself to be a masterful instinctive politician. As many have observed, coexisting with admiration for the United States and US institutions exhibited by ordinary Filipinos is a strong undercurrent of resentment at the colonial subjugation of the country by the United States, the unequal treaties that Washington has foisted on the country, and the overwhelming impact of the "American way of life" on local culture. One need not delve into the complex psychology of Hegel's master-servant dialectic to understand that the undercurrent of the US-Philippine relationship has been the "struggle for recognition" of the dominated party (Hegel n.d.). Duterte has been able to tap into this emotional underside of Filipinos in a way that the Left has never been able to with its anti-imperialist program.

The anti-American comments from Duterte supporters that filled cyberspace were just as fierce as their attacks on critics of his war on drugs. Like many of his authoritarian predecessors elsewhere, Duterte has been able to splice nationalism and authoritarianism in a very effective fashion, though many progressives have seen this as mainly motivated by opportunism.

What Surprises Are in Store For Us?

So what other surprises should we expect from this fascist original?

Perhaps the best way to approach the question of what is likely to come is to ask the following: What are the chinks in Duterte's armor? How would they affect the pursuit of Duterte's program? What are the prospects for the opposition?

There are chinks in the Duterte armor, and one of them is the health and age of the president. Duterte has been candid about his medical problems and his dependence on the drug fentanyl, reportedly a strongly addictive substance that is 50–100 times stronger than morphine and has the same effects as heroin. The age factor is not unimportant, considering that the president is turning 72. Hitler became chancellor at forty-four and Mussolini became prime minister at thirty-nine. For the successful pursuit of an ambitious political project, one's energy level is not unimportant.

More problematic is the issue of institutionalizing the movement. The force driving Duterte's electoral insurgency has not yet been converted into a mass movement. Duterte's key advisers have recognized this, their analysis being that Joseph Estrada was ousted in 2001 because he was not able to fall back on an organized mass movement to protect him. Jun Evasco, the secretary of the Cabinet and a long-time Duterte aide, is the key person the president is relying on to fill the breach by forming the Kilusang Pagbabago (Movement for Reform) that was launched in August 2016.

Evasco's vision is apparently a mass organization along the lines of those of the National Democratic Front, where he cut his political teeth. This won't be easy since, as some analysts have pointed out, he would have to contend with competing projects from Duterte's political allies, like the Pimentels, the Marcoses, and the Arroyos, who would prefer an old-style political formation that brings together elite personalities.[5] Needless to say, a political formation along the lines of the latter would be the kiss of death for Duterte's electoral insurgency.

A bigger hurdle would be failure to deliver on political and social reforms. Practically all of the key political and economic elites have declared allegiance to Duterte, so that one finds it difficult to see how he can deliver on his political and economic reform agenda without alienating key supporters.

The Marcoses, who still have their ill-gotten wealth stashed abroad, the Arroyos, who have been implicated in so many shady deals, and so many other elites, many of whom have cases pending before the Ombudsman, are not likely to be disciplined for corruption, especially given their very close links to Duterte. Nor will the Visayan Bloc, which has come in full force behind Duterte, agree to a law that will extend the very incomplete agrarian reform program. Nor will the big monopolists like Manuel Pangilinan and Ramon Ang, who have pledged fealty to him, submit without resistance to being divested of their corporate holdings.

This is not to say that Duterte is a puppet of the elites. Having a power base of his own that he can easily turn on friend or foe, he is beholden to no one. Indeed, one can argue that most of the elite have joined him mainly for their own protection, like small merchants paying protection money to the mafia. The issue, rather, is how serious he is about social reform and how willing he is to alienate his supporters among the elite.

The same goes for economic reform. Ending contractualization (or ENDO, for "End of Contract"), one of the president's most prominent promises, is currently bogged down in efforts to arrive at a "win-win" solution for management and labor, and all the major labor federations are fast losing hope the administration will deliver on this.

As for macroeconomic policy, any departure from neoliberal principles on the part of orthodox technocrats like Budget Secretary Benjamin Diokno and National Economic and Development Authority Director General Ernesto Pernia is far-fetched. Again, the question lies in how convinced Duterte is that neoliberalism is a dead end and how willing he is to incur the technocratic and bureaucratic displeasure and loss of confidence on the part of foreign investors that would be elicited by adopting a different economic paradigm.

Social and economic reform is Duterte's Achilles's heel, and the president himself is aware that popularity is a commodity that can disappear quickly in the absence of meaningful reforms. Dissatisfaction is fertile ground for the build-up of opposition. This spells danger for the country in the medium term.

Even if he is able to quickly create a mass-based party, Duterte, to stay securely in power, would find that he would need to resort to the repressive apparatuses of the state to quell discontent and opposition. This may not be too difficult a course to follow. As noted earlier, having led a bloody campaign that has already claimed over 7,000 lives, the suspension of civil liberties and the imposition of permanent emergency rule would be in the nature of "mopping up" operations for Duterte. Indeed, the strategic aim of the EJK campaign is not to win the war on drugs. It is to promote a broader authoritarian agenda by establishing a climate of intimidation and fear that will make the destruction of democratic political institutions and political rights and their remaking in an authoritarian direction a "walk in the park." That is why the president can be so cavalier about how many more people will have to be killed—about 20,000 to 30,000 more—and about the timeline of the campaign—from six months to six years.

The Opposition

Does the opposition matter? The elite opposition is extremely weak at this point, with most of the Liberal Party having joined the Duterte bandwagon out of opportunism or fear.[6] An opposition led by Vice President Leni Robredo, who resigned from Duterte's Cabinet after being told not to attend meetings, is not likely to be viable.

While undoubtedly possessing integrity, Robredo has shown poor judgment, receptiveness to bad advice, and little demonstrated capacity for national leadership, and is, in the view even of some of her supporters, largely a political creation of Liberal Party operatives who wanted to convert the name of her deceased husband, former Department of the Interior and Local Government head Jesse Robredo, into political capital.

Moreover, her continuing strong ties to the double-faced Liberal Party and the former administration lend her to becoming easily discredited among both Duterte supporters and opponents.

The Left in Crisis

This brings up the Left.

Duterte's coming to power created a crisis for the Left. For one sector of the Left, Akbayan, the social democratic Left that had allied itself uncritically with the Aquino administration, Duterte's ascendancy meant their marginalization from power along with the Liberal Party, for which they had, with their leadership's eyes wide open, become the grassroots organizing arm.

For the traditional left, or what some called the "extreme left," Duterte posed a problem of another kind. While the National Democratic Front and Communist Party had not supported Duterte's candidacy, they accepted Duterte's offer of three cabinet or cabinet-level positions, as secretaries of the Department of Agrarian Reform and the Department of Social Welfare and Development and chair of the National Anti-Poverty Commission. They also accepted the president's offer to initiate negotiations to arrive at a final peace agreement.

For Duterte, the entry of personalities associated with the Communist Party into his Cabinet provided a left gloss to his regime, a proof that he was progressive, "a socialist, but only up to my armpits," as he put it colorfully during his victory speech in Davao City on 4 June 2016.[7]

It soon became clear that Duterte had the better part of the bargain. As the regime's central policy of killing drug users and pushers without due process escalated, the Left's role in the Cabinet became increasingly difficult to justify. This dilemma was compounded by the fact that no new land reform law was passed that would allow agrarian reform to continue, there was little move-ment in the administration's promise to end contractualization, and macroeconomic policy continued along neo-liberal lines.

The Left, however, found it hard to shelve the peace nego-tiations, from which they had already made some gains, and to part from heading up government agencies that gave them unparalleled governmental resources to expand their mass base.

Duterte had again displayed his acute political instincts. Knowing that the traditional Left was at an ebb in its fortunes, he gambled that they would accept his offer of Cabinet positions. And having accepted these and agreeing to open up peace negotiations from which it could get many more concessions than it would have gotten under previous administrations, the Left, he knew, would find it extremely difficult to part from the positions of power it had gained.

The price, the leaders of the Left realized, would be high, and this was their association with a bloodthirsty regime. The Communist Party and its mass organizations tried to alleviate the contradiction by issuing statements condemning Duterte's bloody policies.[8] But this only made their dilemma keener, since people would ask, why then do you continue to provide legitimacy to this administration by staying on in the Cabinet? Unlike Hitler and Mussolini, Duterte brought the Left into his regime, but in doing so, he has been able to sandbag it and subordinate it as a political force. Recent developments confirmed Duterte's having the upper hand. After he broke off the peace talks, calling the New People's Army terrorists, the Left pleaded with him to resume negotiations and their representatives remained in the Cabinet.

Whether he is fully conscious of it or not, Duterte's ascendancy has severely shaken all significant political institutions and political players in the country, from right to left.[9]

The Military

Interestingly, the one institution that could effectively undermine Duterte is the military. The president knows this, and to keep the Armed Forces of the Philippines (AFP) on his good side, Duterte has appointed several former generals to key positions in his cabinet and takes every opportunity to visit military camps. The military is central to his agenda of imposing martial law, which he has threatened several times. Yet, it may also prove to be the biggest obstacle.

Contrary to the perception of many, the military does not relish martial law, which Duterte has threatened to do if, in his view, conditions warrant it. This is not because it loves civilian rule, but because it is severely overextended. This is the reason the AFP command was one of the strongest backers of the Bangsa Moro Basic Law, which promised a political conclusion to the nearly 50-year-old Muslim insurgency whose containment has been the military's main preoccupation. The project collapsed when a US-supported raid into insurgent territory by Philippine police forces authorized by former President Aquino in January 2015 went awry and derailed the negotiations, much to the chagrin of many in the AFP high command.

With only 220,000 frontline troops, the AFP is one of the smallest standing armies in Southeast Asia and one of the most underequipped, having relied for so many years on hand-me-down weaponry from the United States. It has had its hands full battling several major insurgencies. Given its current strength, plus the fact that insurgencies demand principally political, not military solutions, the best it has been able to do is battle these insurgent movements to a stalemate, not eliminate them.

The surest way to demoralize the military is to overextend it by pushing it to assume political and police functions for which it is ill equipped. This could be the unintended byproduct of politicizing the military, which martial law would inevitably do. A politicized military that exercises police powers is a plague on the people, but it also stirs discontent and rebellion in its ranks, as happened during the Marcos dictatorship. Like Marcos, he may think he is riding the tiger, and like him, he might well end up inside it.[10]

Civil Society Mobilizes

Opposition to Duterte has developed over the last six months from the civil society. A leading force is iDefend, a broad grouping of over fifty people's organizations and non-governmental organizations that has waged an unremitting struggle against the extra-judicial killings (Castillo 2016). Another is the coalition against the Marcos burial at the Libingan ng mga Bayani.

While Malacañang has painted these formations as "dilawan," or yellow, the reality is that most of their partisans are progressives that are as opposed to a "yellow restoration" as they are to Duterte's policies, as well as newer and younger forces drawn from the post-EDSA and millennial generations that have become alarmed at Duterte's fascist turn.

This growing opposition does not seek a reprise of 1986, perhaps heeding Marx's warning that "history first unfolds as tragedy, then repeats itself as farce." It is increasingly realizing that the fight for human rights and due process must be joined to a revolutionary program of participatory politics and economic democracy—to socialism, in the view of many—if it is to turn the fascist tide. There is no going back to EDSA.

What the opposition still has to internalize, though, is that opposing fascism in power will not be, to borrow a saying from Mao, "a dinner party," that it will indeed be exceedingly difficult and demand great sacrifices. Moreover, there is no guarantee of success in the short or medium term. Fascism in power can be extraordinarily long-lived. The Franco regime in Spain lasted thirty-nine years, while Salazar's Estado Novo in neighboring Portugal went on for forty-two years.

Like the anti-Marcos resistance four decades back, the only certainty members of the anti-fascist front can count on is that they're doing the right thing. And that, for some, is a certainty worth dying for.

Endnotes

[1] Here, I find Arno Mayer's distinction among "reactionaries," "conservatives," and "counterrevolutionaries" still very useful. Fascism, in Mayer's typology, falls into the counterrevolutionary category. See Mayer 1971. Mayer's work, despite its brevity, has become one of the classic inter-disciplinary references for 20th-century right-wing movements.

[2] See Fukuyama 1992. This is not to say that liberal democracy was not also a subject of derision on the part of Hitler and Mussolini. However, the principal target of both leaders was the socialist project and the workers' movement and they played on the threat of a working class revolution to unite the right on their way to power.

[3] The income of the top 10 percent relative to the bottom 40 percent increased from 3.09 in 2003 to 3.27 in 2009, while the gini coefficient, the best summary measure of inequality, increased from 0.438 in 1991 to 0.506 in 2009. See Martinez, Western, Tomazewski 2014, 96–115. According to the National Statistical Coordination Board, people from the high-income class, which account for between 15.1 and 15.9 percent of the country's population, enjoyed a 10.4-percent annual growth in income in 2011. In contrast, incomes of people in the middle-income segment grew by only 4.3 percent, and incomes of those in the low-income group by 8.2 percent. Overall inequality thus increased as the incomes of the top bracket increased faster than other brackets (Remo 2013).

[4] After months of low-key responses to Duterte's extra-judicial execution of drug users and pushers, the Catholic Bishops Conference finally came out with a careful condemnation of the campaign, without naming Duterte. See Emasquel 2017.

[5] For some interesting reports on the status of Kilusang Pagbabago, see Burgos 2016; and "Exposing Duterte's Kilusang Pagbabago" 2016.

6   A "loyal opposition" was created in the House with the assistance of the majority, to prevent a real oppositionist, Rep. Teddy Baguilat of the Liberal Party, from becoming head of the minority. See Cepeda 2016.

7   Full speech Pres. Rodrigo Duterte Victory Party at Maa, Davao City, 4 June 2016, https://www.youtube.com/watch?v=R54TiPbaF00.

8   See, for instance, Communist Party of the Philippines 2016.

9   But—and this is an important caveat—Duterte has not been completely free of institutional restraints. This is true especially with respect to the military. The collapse of the peace talks was the price Duterte had to pay to keep the loyalty of the military. The 50-year-old AFP-NPA conflict has spilled so much blood on both sides that it has achieved the epic proportions of a blood feud—a "rido," to borrow a term from Mindanao—that is no longer mainly determined by political rationality. The two sides are extremely sensitive to the other getting even the slightest advantage, so that the dynamics of negotiations becomes that of preventing the other side from gaining tactical advantage rather than accumulating momentum toward an agreement. To succeed, the peace process requires a minimum degree of trust and a willingness to make concessions that may not be immediately reciprocated but advance the talks strategically. The release of 400 NDF captives could have been such a concession. The release would have had no impact on the military equation and could have led to a political breakthrough but the military leadership could not countenance something that could be perceived by its officer corps and rank and file as an institutional defeat. Duterte wants a deal with the CPP-NPA but the success of his ambitious authoritarian agenda entails keeping the military happy, and that means giving the military leadership veto power in what it jealously guards as its turf: its blood feud with the CPP-NPA. In this area, the civilian leadership, even one as powerful as Duterte, takes a back seat.

10   At the time of writing, the scenario painted above may have come closer to being realized. The military's failure to retake Marawi City from what some say are scarcely more than a hundred Muslim irregular fighters has drawn attention to its woeful fighting capabilities, with incidents like friendly fire from Philippine Air Force planes killing Philippine Army troops drawing universal dismay. Even as the army is being outfought by Maute irregulars in Marawi,

its commander in chief has added a massive new task with his declaration of martial law for Mindanao, which is to perform police functions in a whole region, in preparation for exercising police functions nationwide in his design to establish a nation-wide dictatorial regime. Duterte, say some analysts, has provided a gift to the Communist New People's Army and the different insurgent Muslim groups by releasing AFP units now containing them to assume police functions regionally.

References

Burgos, Raymond. 2016 "Out of Order: Kilusang Pagbabago." *Abante*, 8 November. http://www.abante.com.ph/order-kilusang-pagbabago. htm.

Castillo, Galileo. 2016. "iDEFEND Marks Philippine President Duterte's First 100 Days in Office with March, Candle Lighting, and Ringing of Bells." *Focus on the Global South*, 9 October https://focusweb.org/ content/idefend-marks-philippine-president-dutertes-first-100-days-office-march-candle-lighting-and.

Cepeda, Mara. 2016. "Baguilat's Allies to Protest Suarez' Minority Leadership before SC." *Rappler*, 27 July. http://www.rappler.com/ nation/141072-baguilat-allies-protest-suarez-house-minority-leadership-sc.

Communist Party of the Philippines. 2016. "Worsening Violations of Human Rights." *PRWC*. https://www.philippinerevolution.info/ statements/20161207-worsening-violations-of-human-rights.

Esmaquel, Paterno II. 2017. "CBCP Denounces 'Reign of Terror' in Duterte Drug War." *Rappler*, 5 February. http://www.rappler.com/ nation/160503-cbcp-statement-killings-duterte-drug-war.

"Exposing Duterte's Kilusang Pagbabago." 2016. *Superficial Gazette of the Republic of the Philippines* (blog). https://superficialgazette. wordpress.com/2016/12/15/exposing-kp/.

Fukuyama, Francis. 1992. *The End of History and the Last Man*. New York: Free Press.

Hegel, Georg Wilhelm. "Hegel by Hypertext." https://www.marxists.org/ reference/archive/hegel/.

Martinez, Arturo Jr., Mark Western, Michele Haynes, and Wojtek Tomazewski. 2014. "Is There Income Mobility in the Philippines?" *Asian-Pacific Economic Literature* 28 (1):96–115.

Mayer, Arno J. 1971. *Dynamics of Counterrevolution in Europe, 1870–1956: An Analytic Framework.* New York, NY: Harper and Row.

Remo, Michelle V. 2013. "Rich-Poor Divide in Philippines Widening." *Philippine Daily Inquirer.* http://newsinfo.inquirer.net/441817/rich -poor-divide-in-ph-widening.

Dutertismo, Maoismo, Nasyonalismo

Lisandro E. Claudio
Patricio N. Abinales

Rodrigo Duterte is the first Philippine president to not render even the minimum obeisance to liberal democratic politics. He openly promises to use the coercive powers of the state to destroy a drug scourge that he claims to be upending the foundations of society. None of his predecessors were as candid as he has been: even the late dictator Ferdinand Marcos embellished his autocratic pronouncements with some rhetorical deference to constitutional politics. Pundits, political scientists, and the literati once trusted Marcos when he promised that constitutional authoritarianism was only transitory, and that it would eventually blossom into a much superior form of democratic politics indigent to Filipinos. "If President Marcos is a dictator," explained diplomat and public intellectual Salvador P. Lopez in 1974, "he is not ruthless enough to be an effective one." Lopez believed Marcos to be a "crypto-democrat" who would not easily outgrow his "democratic upbringing" (1974, 16).

Duterte has shown no inclination to parrot the post-authoritarian "keep-democracy-alive policies affirmations" of post-Marcos presents. The republic's 16th president's diatribes revolve around vague terms like "the people" and phrases like "saving the nation." The words "justice," "freedom," or "democracy" are not part of his political lexicon. In Duterte's world, individual rights (from the freedom of expression to the presumption of innocence in judicial proceedings) are inconsequential when compared to a national interest that he equates with his own political victories. During the election, Maria Ressa predicted the broad contours of Duterte's *punto de vista*.

> Duterte is brazen in what he plans to do if he wins: establish a dictatorship that would discipline Filipinos, establish law and order, eradicate corruption, and bring growth and development. . . . In short, he would bring the existing political system upside down, capturing the zeitgeist to build transparent systems and institutions that reward doing the right thing. (Ressa 2016)

L'etat c'est moi.

Ressa has been proven mostly correct, although to what extent the Philippines is now in a "dictatorship" is open to debate. What is clear are Duterte's dictatorial intentions. In less than a year as president, he has allowed for the killing of thousands of drug suspects (the exact number is immaterial considering the moral depravity), and is willing to run roughshod over those who criticize his drug war.

That this is an authoritarian thoroughbred is no question. Whether the regime is European garden-variety fascism or a variation of the Asian values dogmatism out of Singapore and Malaysia is, however, debatable. Mark Thompson's (2016, 10) description of Duterte as "a kind of Filipino Sukarno or Mahathir" has merit in allowing us to compare him to other Southeast Asian strongmen. And, indeed, his conception of broad national unity under a strong, anti-Western leader has resonances with these figures. Yet conceptual provision must also be made for the president's uniqueness. In certain ways, he is exceptionally Filipino, reflecting the unique circumstances not just of the political moment but also the era of his political socialization.

In this paper, we argue that Duterte's politics is the fusion

of two seemingly opposing streams of the unfinished nationalist project. On the one hand, he is the heir to elite attempts to
centralize a system of a multi-polar oligarchic democracy, the best-
known example of which is Ferdinand Marcos's vision for a "New
Society." On the other hand, his populism is rooted in a form of
socialist nationalism that flourished in the 1960s through the leadership of the Maoist Communist Party of the Philippines (CPP).

These streams may be on the opposite sides of the barricades,
but they share something in common—a penchant for top-down
leadership and a disdain for liberal democracy. For both Ferdinand
Marcos and the CPP, the people's voice is inconsequential. It is only
tapped to legitimize policy or political action under a controlled
environment, perennially balanced by a "strong" executive in the
case of Marcosians and a vanguard Party in the case of the Maoists.

The other element that unites these two streams is their prov-
enance. Both emerged out of a frustration with the liberal democratic system that flourished from the immediate postwar period
until the mid-1960s. During martial law, these two forces became
ensconced in the center of political debates, with Marcos's New
Society on the right and Maoist "National Democracy" on the Left.
Where do we trace these philosophies? And how do they intersect in
the figure of Rodrigo Duterte?

The Philippine Age of Extremes

The historian Eric Hobsbawm (1996, 563) famously labeled the
twentieth century an "age of extremes"—a time when the political impulses of the nineteenth century turned "militant and
bloodthirsty." Radical fascism on the right—represented by the
Axis powers—collided and competed with a militant Leninist
Communism on the left. Both extremes sought to eradicate constitutional government and centralize power in single parties with
strong leaders. For François Furet (2000, 11), these two doctrines'
"great secret" was a "common enemy" that existed despite their
mutual opposition: "quite simply, democracy"—a democracy that
he defined in liberal terms. The Philippines was not exempted from
these 20th-century pressures.

Vicente Rafael (2013, 483) calls the Marcos period "the long 1970s"—a time when counter-cultural youths "were at once critical of, but also anxious about, collaborating with those in power or those who aspired to be in power, whether this was Marcos or the Communist Party." The period was a time of contradictions: both the Party and Marcos opposed each other, yet both aspired for a strong national unity.

What unified these various, contradictory impulses of the time was a mutual impatience and disdain for the elite, bureaucratic liberalism of the immediate postwar period. The life of the Philippine Second Republic was one anchored on the broad precepts of *ilustrado* and American liberalism, modified to suit the needs of a burgeoning intellectual/bureaucratic class. For a certain generation of liberal bureaucrat-scholars, the newly independent state was a fulfillment of optimistic dreams about liberal self-governance (Claudio 2017). Yet the promise would not correspond to reality.

By 1965, this system's weaknesses had already been exposed. The 1950s and 1960s were decades of brutal economic austerity (45–80), a period of laggard growth and stagnant improvements in employment (Paderanga 2014), which compromised the long-term integrity of the Philippine export industry (Power and Sicat 1971, 41; Sicat 1986, 12; Valdepeñas and Bautista 1977, 183). The paucity in economic innovation, despite the veneer of an import-substitution policy, left much room for experiments in developmentalism during the Marcos period (Hau 2017, 165–223).

Politically, the two-party system, wherein the Nacionalista and Liberal Parties merely competed in dispensing patronage with little regard for large-scale political reform (Thompson 1995: 15–32), reinforced the power of Filipino local oligarchs leading to what Anderson (1988, 15) has referred to as the "Heyday of Cacique Democracy." In many ways, the period of 1945–1965 was like the period of 1986–2016: 30 years of slow, seemingly feckless reform within an elite democracy that was not delivering the economic goods despite claims regarding liberal democratic progress.

Both Marcosianism and Maoist peasant Communism were directly targeting this system of liberal democracy. Marcos's "New Society" sought to target oligarchs on the right and Communists on the left. It was a laudable goal on paper, but his "democratic revolution from the center" became a justification for an *autogolpe*, which allowed him to destroy the nominally democratic system that had sired him. In true Leninist fashion, on the other hand, the CPP aimed to overthrow state power through revolution led by a centralized vanguard party. Had they won, they would certainly have acted like all other Leninist parties that have taken power: they would have centralized state control through systematic terror. As a leading ex-cadre notes, "Thank goodness, we didn't win in 1986. If we had, the Philippines would have ended up with a regime worse than Marcos's—a totalitarian dictatorship" (cited in Francisco 2012).

Duterte's political consciousness evolved during these years, and, as we shall see, he partook of both of the period's extremes. Now, as president, he carries with him the various tensions of the era that made him.

Maoist Nationalism?

Perhaps nothing marks Duterte more as being rooted in the Marcos era than his anti-Americanism. As Nathan Quimpo (2011, 29–33) argues, political analysis during this period was centered on America's influence in the Philippines. It was a time when activists and leftwing political pundits decried unfair economic treaties between the United States and the Philippines, the American bases that were used to fight a war in Vietnam, and the superpower's support for the tyrant in the palace. Amid a growing anger for the country's former colonizer also emerged new forms of history writing that emphasized the perennial subjugation of "the Filipino people" against foreign rule (Ileto 2011). The anti-imperialist sentiments of the period were most strongly articulated by CPP and its aboveground "national democratic" organizations, which defined the grammar of activism for an entire generation. It became commonplace to view the Philippines as a dependent neo-colony of the United States that required national liberation.

Analysts suggest that Duterte's personal encounters with American hubris inform his hatred for the United States, but this hatred has older roots. The president refers to his politics as "socialist" (unexplained) and he was once a member of the Communist Party of the Philippines' (CPP) youth front, the Kabataang Makabayan. During his time as Davao mayor, he often claimed continued affinity with the **Communists and their aboveground organizations (Tuazon 2016). Duterte has also expressed his gratitude to the CPP's eternal chairman, Jose Ma. Sison, for his political education. "Sison,"** according to Duterte on the campaign trail, **"contaminated us early on and we became the first KM members." He added that, "If I make it, God-willing, to the presidency, I will be the first left President of this country"** (quoted in Garcia 2016).

As president, he has been consistently anti-American. He has, among other things, dredged up the massacres of Muslims by American troops in the 1900s and, in a speech during his visit to the People's Republic of China, declared his/his country's (the two are confused) "separation" from the United States. **No other Filipino president or Filipino politician has been brave enough to speak out on the United States' historical transgressions as a colonial master since the birth of the republic in 1946.**

Communists have been jubilant over their political windfall of having elected an anti-imperialist, supposedly left-wing president. Since his election, **the CPP has praised Duterte for his anti-American stance, saying in a recent statement that "the situation now exists for the forging of a patriotic alliance between his anti-US regime and the revolutionary and patriotic forces" (Communist Party of the Philippines 2016).**[1] When Duterte offered them a part of the spoils of the presidency, the CPP gladly accepted and sent some of its top cadres to occupy senior positions in the Cabinet. The Party's representatives in the lower house joined the president's allies in the majority, and its front organizations scaled down their already elfin anti-state urban protests. On the military front, the Armed Forces of the Philippines and the Communist New People's Army (NPA) declared a mutual ceasefire, then renewed peace talks after Duterte released the Party's jailed senior (and aging) leaders. Although these talks have been derailed by recalcitrant Communist commanders who continue with small-scale anti-government attacks and military officers who are wary of their commander in chief's closeness to their sworn enemy, there has never been so much goodwill between the Republic of the Philippines and the CPP's National Democratic Front.

True enough it did not take long for the fighting to renew. At the start of 2017, each side was already accusing the other of violating the temporary cessation of hostilities in the countryside. The communists were the first to break the ceasefire on 1 February, accusing the AFP of launching attacks on NPA units. Three days later, Duterte ordered the military to renew its counter-insurgency operations (**"Duterte Ends Unilateral Ceasefire with NPA"** 2017). The peace talks were suspended but both sides agreed to resume the peace talks a month later, agreeing to issue joint statements as part of their mutual "confidence-building" measures (Manlupig 2017). This time, however, there was no ceasefire (Romero 2017).

This nationalist solidarity based on a shared derision of the United States gains additional traction from a common belief that Duterte and the Communists are heirs to a long line of nationalists (and radicals) fighting for "genuine" national independence against American imperialism. Both the president and the politburo see themselves as vanguards of a movement that will bring about the birth of the nation, beginning with distancing the country from the United States.[2]

Yet Duterte's nationalism is not simply derivative of his past dalliances with the Filipino Ayatollah. It needs further explanation in the light of the CPP's inability to slay liberal bourgeois nationalism. In fact, the Communists are cognizant that Duterte's anti-Americanism is vintage bourgeois nationalist in origin. The mantra the president and his advisers invoke—for a neutral foreign policy to break away from the "shackling dependency" that has made the Philippines America's "little brown brothers"—can be traced back to the arguments made by Senators Claro M. Recto, Jose W. Diokno, and Lorenzo Tañada (Abinales 2001, 192–228). The Communists know that anti-American nationalism is never a guarantee of a proletarian, socialist outlook.

In a statement reminiscent of his criticisms of Recto, Sison praised Duterte for being "the first Left President of the Philippines who is determined to uphold national independence, expand democracy for the people, carry out national industrialization and genuine land reform, and realize an independent foreign policy." He then warned Duterte that while Communists believe his authenticity, "there are elements in his own government . . . who wish to prolong the already discredited bankrupt US-dictated neoliberal economic policy and perpetuate foreign and feudal domination" (Sison 2016). Duterte may thus proclaim himself anti-imperialist and leftwing, but like Recto, Diokno, and Tañada, he is also compromised by the presence of rightwing supporters in their midst. Hence the CPP will work with him *but also* keep him at a safe distance as it once did with Tañada and Diokno during the Marcos era. It also makes it easy to split from any alliance with these "bourgeois reformists" when it came time to draw a line in the sand. The classic example of the first was the Left-Center coalition to boycott the 1980 demonstration elections staged by Marcos, and of the second was the disastrous 1980 Bagong Alyansang Makabayan founding congress that the CPP undercut after realizing it granted too many concessions to the other side (Manansala 1986).

The potentials of a similar break under Duterte are already festering. Assorted small-scale attacks by individual NPA commanders have compromised peace talks, proving that not all members of the CPP are enamored with Duterte. In its March 2017 statement announcing the conclusion of its only second congress since its founding in 1967, the CPP attacked the government "for bowing to the demands of the U.S. [and] called for 'people's war toward complete victory'" ("Filipino Communists Reaffirm" 2017). On the legal front, aboveground organizations are already chafing at having to support a president whom they view as waging a war on drugs that disproportionately targets the poor. Moreover, the tensions between the Communist Cabinet members and their bourgeois colleagues is becoming more acute. Apart from the usual suspicions from the defense establishment, the Maoists in government are making enemies of some of Duterte's closest advisors. Most recently, the Department of Social Welfare and Development and its Communist secretary Judy Taguiwalo criticized the influential finance department (under the powerful Davao businessman, Carlos Dominguez) on the department's website (see Social Marketing 2017)—an unusual public breach of comity within the Cabinet.

Finally, Communist suspicion will likely grow exponentially as it becomes clearer and clearer that Duterte's anti-Americanism does not mean major policy shifts aimed at disengaging the country from American global hegemony. Early on, the president's economic team had promised that the country would be a cosigner in a "World Trade Organization (WTO) agreement aimed at facilitating the flow of goods among signatories to improve customs administration" and make easier the free flow of traded commodities (Pillas 2016). Duterte had expressed a strong preference to develop stronger trade ties with other members of the Association of Southeast Asian Nations (ASEAN). Yet the Philippines' recent agricultural agreement with Thailand followed norms laid out by the WTO (Vibar 2017).

The most serious strain to the Duterte-CPP alliance is, of course, military. Despite Duterte's belligerence, both the United States and the Philippines remain close allies and the AFP and Defense Department leaderships have repeatedly stood by their American partners. US-Philippine joint operations against Islamic terrorists remain while Duterte's Defense Secretary Delfin Lorenzana announced on 26 January 2017 that the Enhanced Defense Cooperation Agreement (EDCA) signed by the two countries during the term of President Benigno Aquino III "is still on." This means that the US Defense Department will continue the establishment of "EDCA-chosen [American-controlled] camps" in four Philippine Air Force bases. There is likewise no sign that the Duterte administration was moving to eliminate the annual Balikatan (Shoulder-to-Shoulder) joint military exercises (Parameswaran 2017). Moreover, a seeming meeting of *macho* minds between Duterte and American President Donald J. Trump has reduced the rancor that festered during the time of President Barack Obama. There is evident cooling in Duterte's anti-Americanism and he has redirected his bile at the European Union of late. But can the Communists spin a new imperialist target and call it "EU imperialism" instead of "US imperialism"? Doubtful.

The fraught alliance between *Dutertismo* and *Maoismo* leaves no room for long-term compromises. Either the Communists wholly abandon proletarian nationalism for its ideological vacuity, or Duterte take the next step as a "socialist" and embrace the Party's national democratic revolution. However, it is unlikely that Duterte will become a full-blown socialist because, as the above economic and military policies indicate, he will remain within the United States' security umbrella. More importantly, Duterte's obeisance to elite politics remains, and nothing is better proof of this than his allegiance to the family of Ferdinand E. Marcos, the original sworn enemy of the CPP.

Supreme Cacique Redux

Duterte "doesn't consider himself part of the Philippine ruling class or the feudal system cemented in place by paternalism, private armies and decades of largesse" (McBeth 2016). This is, however, not an entirely accurate picture: Duterte does disdain the old elite, but he was congenial to the new elites that emerged after World War II, the most prominent of which is the Marcos family. Since the fall of Marcos, anti-authoritarian fears have always revolved around the threat of a new Marcos. In the late 1990s, when then President Fidel Ramos attempted to revise the constitution ostensibly to extend his term, anti-Marcos forces led by former President Corazon Aquino blocked him, declaring they would "never again" allow the Constitution to be manipulated ("6,000 Attend Rizal Park Rally" 1997). In the early 2000s, when President Joseph Estrada was surrounding himself with a coterie of cronies, commentators once again warned about the "ghost of Marcos" ("Philippines—the Ghost of Marcos" 1999) And, finally, President Gloria Macapagal Arroyo, who placed the Philippines under a "state of rebellion" to dampen protests against her and who aimed to build a centralized "strong republic," was similarly tainted with a Marcosian brush. Yet nobody has lived up to the Marcosian legacy more than Rodrigo Duterte.

Since the election, ties between Duterte and the Marcos family have only become more pronounced. Under the president, not only has Marcos been buried in the Heroes' Cemetery, his son, Ferdinand Jr. ("Bongbong"), has also risen to prominence as a close adviser of the president. Despite his failed vice-presidential bid, Bongbong's influence over national politics has never been more pronounced, with him having the president's ear and a throng of pro-dictatorship "trolls" at his disposal to spread history-revisionist material about the "golden era" of martial law. And because of the increasingly acrimonious relationship between Duterte and Marcos Jr.'s chief rival, Vice President Leni Robredo, the Marcos-Duterte alliance has found a despised common foe.

The relationship between the Dutertes and Marcoses has always been portrayed as a patronage relationship dating back to when then President Marcos rewarded Duterte's father's loyalty with a senior government position (Placido 2016). Even in the twilight of Marcos's presidency, the dictator believed he could call on Rodrigo to quell anti-government sentiment in Davao City, even if these protests were being led by the former's own mother (Andes 2017).

But the relationship is more than one of dependency and mutual benefit. It is now clear that Duterte has a deep admiration for the Marcosian legacy. No post-authoritarian president has publicly mused about the declaration of martial law as much as Duterte. In his speeches since October 2016, he has alluded to martial law at least once a month, usually discussing it as a potential prong of his anti-drug war (Ranada 2017). What we see in Duterte is a genuine belief in Marcos's strong arm tactics and the late dictator's capacity to justify his actions on legal-constitutional grounds. If there was one political leader that Duterte appeared to have modeled himself during his years as mayor, it was Marcos. Like the latter, he used deadly force to achieve results (hence, the Davao Death Squad) but he also repeatedly reminded his constituents that he did so as a prosecutor, i.e., someone familiar with the law. He was strongman and disciplinarian yet also a constitutionalist—the 21st-century version of his pin-up Ferdinand Marcos. Like Marcos, moreover, Duterte's hatred for the "oligarchy" and the elite stems less from a genuine desire at social leveling. As with Marcos, Duterte demonizes the oligarchs so that he may reign over them.

The desire to centralize power amid an unwieldy, localist, and oligarchic system has a long tradition that goes back to the beginning of the republic. It can be traced to Commonwealth President Manuel Quezon (McCoy 1989), the country's first strongman president, who, like Duterte, tended to equate the state with himself.

Quezon's efforts at centralization, however, were disrupted by World War II, and it would take Marcos to renew the project.

Anderson (1988, 17–20) notes that Marcos nationalized the logic of local oligarchic rule. Instead of multiple caciques with private armies, martial law created one "supreme cacique" in the presidential palace, whose private army was not a group of local thugs, but the Armed Forces of the Philippines. Duterte is attempting a similar centralization, acting, in the words of his advisors, as "the mayor of the Philippines." And if, as a local cacique in Davao, he used the Davao Death Squad as a private armed group to kill drug users, as president he now has a national-level DDS. It is called the police. With a pliant House of Representatives, an emasculated minority in the Senate, and a Supreme Court that will prove more pliant as the president appoints more justices, there are few checks against government impunity. Duterte is not yet as powerful as Marcos was—his greater murder rate notwithstanding—but he is obviously trying to match his idol.

How much power will Duterte be able to arrogate unto the presidency? How far will he be able to use the national DDS to further his goals? Will Duterte use the national DDS to silence dissent? And will Duterte be able to fortify his praetorian guard with members of the military (a necessary measure for a budding dictator given how inferior the police are to the military)? Duterte's Marcosian project seems to be a work-in-progress, and it has not been articulated in as rigorous a way as Marcos's New Society. Yet, this early, we see attempts at statist centralization and strengthening unparalleled in the post-EDSA presidency. Congress approved the increased allocation to the Office of the President from PhP 2.87 billion ($61.44 million) in 2016 to PhP 20.03 billion ($430.3 million) for 2017, an increase of more than PhP 17 billion, or about $370 million (Cepeda 2016). Thus, while Duterte may deploy Sisonite rhetoric, his actions are pure Marcosian.

Conclusion

In the years to follow, this volume is likely to be succeeded by a plethora of essays and studies about a singular figure in Philippine political history. Scholars will continue to ask: What kind of politician is Rodrigo Roa Duterte? As early as now, the president has been classified in multiple ways: populist (Curato 2016; David 2017), authoritarian (Santos 2016), and even fascist (Bello 2017). More ascriptions are soon to follow. These labels will point to something accurate about the president, but they will miss out on certain things. If Duterte's own political biography proves anything, it is his unorthodoxy and his various contradictions. He will continue to confound scholarship.

But if we can neither completely define Duterte nor ascertain what he is for, it is easier to see what he is against. As Walden Bello (2017) categorically notes, for Duterte, "the target is liberal democracy—the dominant ideology and political system of our time." It is in this respect that Duterte becomes comparable to various other contemporary strongmen like America's Trump, Turkey's Erdogan, Russia's Putin (Duterte's self-proclaimed idol), and even the various advocates of authoritarian Asian values. We hope to have shown, however, that Duterte's hatred for liberal democracy, along with his various contradictory relationships with other anti-liberals, can be traced to the peculiarity of mid-twentieth century Philippine politics when the two extremes of authoritarian and communist nationalism rushed to the foreground of Philippine politics. Duterte is a product of this period and therefore reflects a political mindset shared by many individuals who gained political maturity over the same years. His perspective, in other words, is one that carries the latent anti-democratic tendencies of the Philippine baby boomers. He represents a dangerous, extremist past—a past naïve liberals had once assumed banished—folding into the Philippine present. This peculiar past, represented by a peculiar leader, operating in a peculiar present, will continue to confound.

The irony is that those who share in Duterte's illiberalism and nostalgia for the authoritarian era have forgotten that the freedom of expression that they are passionately defending now were "enabled by a liberal order," and will be the first to be disposed of if that authoritarian order comes to being.[3]

Endnotes

[1] Communist glee was best represented by this gnathonic compli-
     ment over Duterte's having begun "the task of evoking/invoking
     the accursed past." The Communist writer E. San Juan (2016) called
     Duterte the "oral tribune, with prophetic expletives . . . coming
     down [from the mountains] with the task of reclaiming the collec-
     tive dignity of the heathens – eulogized by Rudyard Kipling, at the
     start of the war in February 1899 as 'the white men's burden.'"
[2] Writes the *Wall Street Journal*: "Mr. Duterte's nationalism echoes
     sentiments common among left-leaning Filipinos that America
     never atoned for invading the archipelago in 1898 and violently
     subduing the former Spanish colony" (Moss 2016).
[3] We are grateful to Carol Hau for this insight.

References

"600,000 Attend Rizal Park Rally: It Was Cory Magic All Over." 1997.
     Philippine Daily Inquirer, 27 September.

Abinales, Patricio N. 2001. *Fellow Traveler: Essays on Filipino Communism*.
     Quezon City: University of the Philippines Press.

Anderson, Benedict. 1988. "Cacique Democracy in the Philippines:
     Origins and Dreams." *New Left Review* 169 (3):3–31.

Andes, She. 2017. "People Power Sa Davao." *I-Witness*. GMA 7, 25
     February.

Bello, Walden. 2017. "Philippine President Rodrigo Duterte Is a
     Wildly Popular Fascist." *The Nation*, 10 January 10. https://
     www.thenation.com/article/philippine-president-rodrigo-du
     terte-is-a-wildly-popular-fascist/.

Cepeda, Mara. 2016. "Office of the President Gets P17-B Increase
     in 2017 Budget." *Rappler*, 15 August. http://www.rappler.com/
     nation/143136-office-president-budget-2017.

Claudio, Lisandro E. 2013. *Taming People's Power: The EDSA Revolutions
     and Their Contradictions*. Quezon City: Ateneo de Manila University
     Press.

———. 2017. *Liberalism and the Postcolony: Thinking the State in
     20th-Century Philippines*. Quezon City: Ateneo de Manila University
     Press.

Communist Party of the Philippines. 2016. "Tasks After 100 Days Under
     Duterte." *Ang Bayan*, 7 October. https://www.philippinerevolution.

info/ang_bayan/20161007-tasks-after-100-days-under-duterte/.

Curato, Nicole. 2017. "Flirting with Authoritarian Fantasies? Rodrigo Duterte and the New Terms of Philippine Populism." *Journal of Contemporary Asia* 47 (1):142–53.

David, Randy. 2017. "Duterte, Trump, and Populism." *Philippine Daily Inquirer*, 5 March. http://opinion.inquirer.net/102168/duterte-trump-populism.

Dizon, Nikko. 2016. "Benevolent Dictator? There's No Such Thing." *Philippine Daily Inquirer*, 8 May. http://newsinfo.inquirer.net/783937/benevolent-dictator-theres-no-such-thing.

"Duterte Ends Unilateral Ceasefire with NPA." 2017. *Mindanews*, 3 February.   http://www.mindanews.com/peace-process/2017/02/duterte-ends-unilateral-ceasefire-with-npa/.

"Filipino Communists Reaffirm 'People's War' on US Imperialism." 2017. *Telesur*, 29 March. http://www.telesurtv.net/english/news/Filipino-Communists-Reaffirm-Peoples-War-on-US-Imperialism-20170329-0044.html.

Francisco, Mariel N. 2012. "A Book Against Forgetting." *Philippine Daily Inquirer*, 23 September, Lifestyle Section. http://lifestyle.inquirer.net/67866/a-book-against-forgetting/.

Furet, Francois. 2000. *The Passing of an Illusion: The Idea of Communism in the Twentieth Century*. Translated by Deborah Furet. Chicago and London: University of Chicago Press.

Garcia, Arturo. 2016. "Why Duterte Hates American Imperialism." *Justice for Filipino-American Veterans*, 9 September.

Hau, Caroline S. 2017. *Elites and Ilustrados in Philippine Culture*. Quezon City: Ateneo de Manila University Press.

Hobsbawm, Eric J. 1996. *The Age of Extremes: A History of the World, 1914–1991*. 1st Vintage Books. New York: Vintage Books.

Ileto, Reynaldo C. 2011. "Reflections on Agoncillo's *The Revolt of the Masses* and the Politics of History." *Southeast Asian Studies* 49 (3):496–520.

Lopez, Salvador P. 1974. *The Dillingham Lecture Series: The Philippines Under Martial Law*. Quezon City: University of the Philippines Press.

Manlupig, Karlos. 2017. "Gov't-NDF Peace Talks to Resume Joint Statement." *Philippine Daily Inquirer Net*, 21 March. http://newsinfo.inquirer.net/879884/govt-ndf-peace-talks-to-resume-joint-statement.

McBeth, John. 2016. "Why Rodrigo Duterte Hates America." *The National Interest*, 25 October. http://thediplomat.com/2016/11/why-the-philippines-rodrigo-duterte-hates-america/.

McCoy, Alfred W. 1989. "Quezon's Commonwealth: The Emergence of Philippine Authoritarianism." In *Philippine Colonial Democracy*, ed. Ruby R. Paredes, 114–60. Quezon City: Ateneo de Manila University Press.

Manansala, Aida. 1986. "Polarization in Philippine Politics: Interviews with Leandro Alejandro, BAYAN Secretary-General, Emanuel Soriano, Bandila Executive Vice-President and Karina David, UP KAAKBAY Chapter Head." *Diliman Review* (January–February): 36–37.

Moss, Trefor. 2016. "Behind Duterte's break with the U.S. is a lifetime of resentment." *The Wall Street Journal*, 21 October. https://www.wsj.com/articles/behind-philippine-leaders-break-with-the-u-s-a-lifetime-of-resentment-1477061118.

Paddock, Richard C. 2016. "Mysterious Blast in Philippines Fuels Rodrigo Duterte's 'Hatred' of U.S." *The New York Times*, 13 May. https://www.nytimes.com/2016/05/14/world/asia/philippines-president-rodrigo-duterte.html.

Paderanga, Cayetano. 2014. "The Macroeconomic Dimensions of Philippine Development." Keynote Speech for the Philippine Studies Conference in Japan. Center for Southeast Asian Studies, Kyoto University, 28 February.

Parameswaran, Prasanth. 2017. "Where is the New US-Philippine Military Pact under Duterte." *The Diplomat*, 28 January. http://thediplomat.com/2017/01/where-is-the-new-us-philippines-military-pact-under-duterte/.

"Philippines—The Ghost of Marcos." 1999. *Foreign Correspondent*. Australian Broadcasting Corporation, 12 November.

Pillas, Catherine. 2016. "Duterte Set To Sign PHL's Ratification of WTO-TFA." *Business Mirror*, 4 October 4. http://www.businessmirror.com.ph/duterte-set-to-sign-phls-ratification-of-wto-tfa/.

Placido, Dharel. 2016. "Duterte: My Father Stood by Marcos." 4 October. http://news.abs-cbn.com/news/10/04/16/duterte-my-father-stood-by-marcos.

Power, John H., and Gerardo P. Sicat. 1971. *The Philippines: Industrialization and Trade Policies*. London, New York, and Kuala Lumpur: Oxford University Press.

Quimpo, Nathan Gilbert. 2008. *Contested Democracy and the Left in the Philippines after Marcos*. Quezon City: Ateneo de Manila University Press.

Rafael, Vicente L. 2013. "Contracting Colonialism and the Long 1970s." *Philippine Studies: Historical and Ethnographic Viewpoints* 61 (4):477–94.

Ranada, Pia. 2017. "Understanding Duterte's Martial Law Remarks." *Rappler*, 20 January. http://www.rappler.com/newsbreak/in-depth /158810-understanding-duterte-martial-law-remarks.

Ressa, Maria. 2015. "Duterte's end game for leadership," *Rappler*, 28 October. http://www.rappler.com/nation/110952-duterte-end-gam e-leadership.

Romero, Alexis. 2017. "Gov't-NDF Peace Talks Resume." *PhilStar Global*, 3 April. http://www.philstar.com/headlines/2017/04/03/1687235/ govt-ndf-peace-talks-resume.

San Juan Jr., E. 2016. "Anti-Americanism in the Philippines. President Duterte's Subaltern Counter-Hegemony: Guerilla Incursions from the Boondocks." *Global Research*, 14 November. http://www. globalresearch.ca/anti-americanism-in-the-philippines-presi-dent-dutertes-subaltern-counter-hegemony/5556831.

Santos, Vergel O. 2016. "Duterte's Descent into Authoritarianism." *The New York Times*, 15 November. https://www.nytimes.com/2016/11/16/ opinion/dutertes-descent-into-authoritarianism.html.

Sison, Jose Maria. 2016. "Filipino Communist Rebels Support Duterte's Rift with US Policy." *Telesur*, 25 October. http://www.telesurtv.net/ english/opinion/Filipino-Communist-Rebels-Support-Dutertes-Rift-with-US-Policy-20161025-0014.html.

Social Marketing. 2017. "Http://www.dswd.gov.ph/dswd-Stand-on-Finance-Depts-Tax-Reform-Package-We-Have-Deep-Reser-vations-Because-of-Its-Impact-on-the-Poor/." Department of Social Welfare and Development, 14 March. http://www.dswd.gov. ph/dswd-stand-on-finance-depts-tax-reform-package-we-have-deep-reservations-because-of-its-impact-on-the-poor/.

Thompson, Mark R. 2016. "The Early Duterte Presidency in the Philippines." *Journal of Current Southeast Asian Affairs* 35 (3):3–14.

———. 1995. *The Anti-Marcos Struggle: Personalistic Rule and Democratic Transition in the Philippines*. New Haven and London: Yale University Press.

Sicat, Gerardo P. 1986. "A Historical and Current Perspective of Philippine Economic Problems." Philippine Institute for Development Studies. http://opendocs.ids.ac.uk/opendocs/handle/123456789/3476.

Tuazon, Bobby M. 2016. "Duterte's Socialist Experiment." *Philippine Daily Inquirer*, 21 May, sec. Opinion. http://opinion.inquirer. net/94843/dutertes-socialist-experiment.

Valdepeñas Jr., Vicente B., and Germelino M. Bautista. 1977. *The Emergence of the Philippine Economy*. Manila: Papyrus Press.

Vibar, Ivy Jean. 2017. "Philippines Forges Agri Deals with Thailand in Duterte Visit." *ABS-CBN News*, 21 May 21. http://news. abs-cbn.com/news/03/21/17/philippines-forges-agri-deals-with -thailand-in-duterte-visit.

The Mindanaoan President

Jesse Angelo L. Altez

Kloyde A. Caday

The euphoria of the 2016 presidential race was staggering. It marked the first time someone from Mindanao actually had a chance of becoming the president of the republic. With such possibility, the inhabitants of Mindanao delivered, unsurprisingly throwing their support behind Rodrigo Roa Duterte of Davao City. Duterte won all six administrative regions of Mindanao, and cemented a "solid south" vote. This is a rarity in a region marred by ethnolinguistic, religious, economic, and socio-political divide. Six months into his administration, Pulse Asia reports that Duterte enjoys a 96 percent trust rating in Mindanao (see Holmes in Chapter 3). This is the highest trust rating a sitting president has ever had in the region.

This chapter situates Duterte among the Mindanao constituency and traces the profound connection he brokered with them. Contrary to the essentialist assertion of plain regionalism, it will be argued that the solid south vote emanates from a legitimate longing for inclusion among the diverse people of Mindanao, perceived to be *misunderstood* and left out by the central government run by the

northerners, underscored by the region's problems of underdevelopment and innumerable socio-political and security concerns as
manifested by the persistent armed conflict. The chapter also presents a brief historical narration of the formation of the three political segments of the contemporary Mindanaoan[1]—the Islamized
indigenous peoples (Moro), the non-Islamized indigenous peoples
(lumad[2]), and the migrant-settlers from Luzon and Visayas. From
here onwards, the term "Mindanaoan" shall be employed to refer to
the tri-people.[3] The chapter then characterizes the struggles of each
of these groups, and explains how Duterte captured their imaginations by understanding their anxieties, aspirations, and needs.[4]

Much Ado About Land Conflict

Perhaps no work of literature has rightly captured a person's
connection to the land but Pearl S. Buck's *The Good Earth*: "Out of
the land we came and into it we must go."

Land conflicts in Mindanao and its systematic tolerance
transformed the landscape of the island—millions were displaced,
natural resources were exploited by corporations, and land claims
have infringed along with other claims. A typical interpretation of
this problem has mainly focused on the economic aspects, but what
has been overlooked is the fact that land laws that are supposed
to defend people are the laws that permit the destruction of the
social stability and cultural heritage of the indigenous inhabitants
of Mindanao. Land dispossession has penetrated on a personal
level, especially to the lumad and Moros who claim to be not just the
rightful owners of the lands, but more so, of their community. In a
Transitional Justice and Reconciliation Commission (TJRC) consul-
tation, one Meranao[5] left a rhetorical question: "Now that we have
no lands, who are we?" (TJRC 2017b, 146).

The TJRC (2016) traced the roots of conflict and waves of land
dispossession. The first wave dates from 1898 to the Commonwealth
period, with the Regalian doctrine as the guiding principle of
land titling, stating that all private lands belonged to the Spanish
crown. It was promulgated as early as Spanish occupation, but
this has become the foundation of several laws, severing most

ethnolinguistic groups in Mindanao from their ancestral domains.

When the Americans took control of the Philippines from the Spaniards, the succeeding land laws and policies under the American rule—such as the Bates Agreement, National Land Settlement Act, among others—legitimized marginalization as they exploited the vast resources of Mindanao. These were the agents that lacked oversight for they failed to monitor the entry of corporate lands into the territories of indigenous inhabitants. The state-sanctioned migration promised to resolve the problems of overpopulation and to attain national development while the whole scenario is marred by anomalous motives to benefit the elites. Even worse, the implementation of these settlements was not well supervised and regulated, resulting in corruption and exorbitant financial loss (Abinales 2016).

In the 1970s–1980s, the heavy militarization during Ferdinand Marcos's dictatorial regime heightened the disenfranchisement of the lands and properties in the island as the government used it as a battlefield to wage war against the troops of the Moro National Liberation Front and the armed-wing of the Communist Party of the Philippines, the New People Army's (TJRC 2016). Dictatorship may have been overthrown, but the current situation complicated the land conflicts in the areas through land-related policies (e.g., Comprehensive Agrarian Reform Law in 1988, Mining Act of 1995, and Indigenous Peoples' Rights Act of 1997), which negate each other and confuse land claims. This was also the time of the regional autonomy of Autonomous Region in Muslim Mindanao (ARMM), a "breeding ground" of local Moro elites who did not address this conflict, but instead abused their control to acquire more lands and be complicit in horizontal conflicts that displaced inhabitants of ARMM from the land they owned (TJRC 2016).

In a 2017 report, the World Bank and the International Organization for Migration challenges the notion that all migrant-settlers in Mindanao are purely responsible for the land dispossession. That the Moro leaders welcomed the settlers in 1950s and had acquired large land titles in their names prove they have also engaged in marginalizing the Mindanaoans' territory and identity (WB-IOM 2017). This protracted conflict reflects "weakness of state apparatus" (WB-IOM 2017, 43–44); land laws were imposed

nationally—even in the Cordilleras and Mindoro—but little attention was given to govern Mindanao to provide its people the same
protection.

The Prelude to a Solid South

Never has there been a Philippine president who is able to locate
himself on the ground of Mindanao until Rodrigo Duterte. What
propelled his triumph is the unison of voices of the Mindanaoans
to associate themselves with him, with the progress of Davao City
as the microcosm of the Mindanao dream where the tri-people live
side by side despite their differences.

Peace Talks and Why They Take Too Long

One of the nuances that drove the tri-people of Mindanao to rally
behind Rodrigo Duterte, a fellow Mindanaoan, was the obstinate
armed conflict that kept the region lagging behind its northern
counterparts in terms of human development. In the Family Income
and Expenditure Survey (FIES) conducted by the Philippine Statistics
Authority (PSA) in 2016, eleven out of the twenty poorest provinces
in the Philippines are from Mindanao. Since the '70s, the central
government has attempted to put a closure to the Moro insurgency
by engaging them in several attempts for a peaceful settlement, but
to no avail.

At the heart of every peace pact is the hope for greater political
participation and eradication of poverty and violence in Mindanao.
Nevertheless, its journey suggests it is bound to undergo a cycle
of "Sisyphean ordeal,"[6] that one improvement encounters another
setback. The state may have granted ARMM as a product of Moro
thought leaders' resistance against the central government, yet
statistics show that three out of four individuals in ARMM experienced deprivations in 2009. Apart from sustained insecurity in
ARMM, what has been maintained in the region since 1989 is the
poor socioeconomic conditions of its people (Monsod 2016).

The peace-building initiatives between 1989 and 2009 were
carried out against a backdrop of 5,642 violent conflicts (Monsod

2016), showing how the peace process was unable to stop bullets. The dialogues consisted of several traps that should have been evaded by its actors, resulting in failures to recognize significant stakeholders, to institutionalize and develop the implementation of the autonomy, and to advance trust over deep-seated bias against the Mindanaoan.

The Tripoli Agreement that established ARMM is very Moro-specific and has failed to understand that Mindanao is a tri-people land. It has sidelined the participation and cause of the settler population, most significantly of the non-Muslim indigenous peoples. The lumad have always been told what to do; a Teduray[7] development worker alleged the accords to be a mere "political accommodation," thereby keeping disempowerment among the lumad (Dictaan-Bang-oa 2004, 166). The ill-fated 2008 Memorandum of Agreement on Ancestral Domain (MOA-AD) did not learn from this lesson when it attempted to expand ARMM and included areas with migrant-settler and lumad majority, deeming it unconstitutional and leading to skirmishes within migrant-settler communities (International Crisis Group 2016).

The realities evident in Muslim Mindanao reveal that regional autonomy was not offered at all. The one-size-fits-all formula of the Ramos regime lacked both the capacity-building measures for the Moro leaders and the safeguards that could monitor regional transactions and expenditures, which led to corruption. As a result, it cultivated patronage politics and feudal powers, resulting in prolonged poor governance, violence, and poverty. The Misuari activism waned, and he was charged with corruption and jailed for rebellion (ICG 2016).

The Comprehensive Agreement on the Bangsamoro (CAB) in 2014 seemed to have learned from these traps, and promised to place the peace process as a national agenda by including several sectors of women, lumad groups, and the like. It highlighted mechanisms in asymmetrical governance for transitioning the Bangsamoro polity, with the ideals on confidence-building measures and livelihood programs in the envisioned area, yet it did not have a place in Congress before the end of the Aquino administration. This situation validated that prejudice against the Moro lies deep in public consciousness, which was worsened by the Mamasapano incident and the orchestration of anti-Moro propaganda springing from it.[8]

The Mamasapano fiasco in January 2015 quickly stirred biases against the Moro, leading legislators to withdraw their support for the BBL because they treated the incident as the onset of Moro separatism without looking into the intricacies of the matter (ICG 2016). As a result, peace talks were deferred and BBL was down and out by the time the 16th Congress was adjourned, perpetuating the cycle of Sisyphus.

Still recuperating from this loss, the Moros suffered yet again another perceived injustice from the northerners. At this time, Rodrigo Duterte showed inclinations of joining the presidential derby, launching a 30-day listening tour across the country in January 2015, discussing his plans to replicate nationwide the mechanisms he instituted in Davao City (Herrera 2015). On the day the Mamasapano debacle unfolded, Mr. Duterte was in Zamboanga City, preaching the miracles of Davao and ranting about the failures of the central government to understand the cultural and social realities in Mindanao.

One of Us

In his campaign sortie in the municipality of Buluan, in Maguindanao, a month before the elections, Mr. Duterte exhorted a Muslim audience. The gist of his speech was about his understanding of the Mindanao problem: "If I become president, if Allah gives his blessing, before I die since I am old, I will leave to you all a Mindanao that is governed in peace" (Ranada 2016). In an area torn by armed conflict for decades, Mr. Duterte's words are perceived as a commitment forged in blood—a kin's word vouched to be fulfilled.

The conflict dynamics and politico-economic inequity in Mindanao quickly overturned the Moro into the minority, with a decline of the Moro population from 70 percent in the 1990s to 20 percent (Coronel-Ferrer 2016). This dramatic decrease is ascribed to a perceived disregard of the indigenous inhabitants of Mindanao's cultural ties with land, several policies that escalated conflicts, heavy militarization, and the encroachment of corporate bodies.

The magnitude of the conflict escalated when Moros started

to assert their birthright during the Marcos administration. The Marcos years envisioned national progress and linkages in Mindanao by investing in development projects. It also challenged the old Moro elites by reconfiguring the state's political network in Muslim Mindanao, and increasing military surveillance in the area in neutralizing religious battles in the island (Abinales 2016).

However, one incident that triggered resistance was the Jabidah Massacre on 18 March 1968. Twenty eight out of 200 Moro military trainees (most of them belonging to Tausug and Sama groups from Sulu and Tawi-Tawi) allegedly were summarily executed in Corregidor after refusing to fight against Malaysians for the claim of Sabah (Buendia 2008). Despite the grave brutality in the massacre, nobody was held responsible after several investigations in the Senate and Congress. This injustice insinuated neglect of the central government toward the political rights and welfare of the Moro.

The MNLF was born of frustration with the exclusivist government and suspicious collusion between their own leaders and Manila politico-economic elites. It was through the MNLF that the different ethnolinguistic groups practicing Islam (e.g., Meranao, Maguindanaon, Tausug, and Iranon) were united against the repressive state, through one political identification that connotes pride and consciousness: Moro (Buendia 2005).

Mr. Duterte's link with the Moro goes beyond being a Mindanaoan. His maternal grandmother was a full-blooded Meranao, so he is seen by the Moro people as "one of us." Despite growing up in a Christian family, such blood connection made him a strong bearer of the legitimate grievances that the Moros harbored for decades. In a culture that values blood next to God, Mr. Duterte is seen as an opportunity bound by familial commonality: a space for negotiation where the Mindanao orthodoxy of Christian-Muslim divide can meet through a rightful compromise (Mawallil 2016).

True to his commitment to the Moro cause, his public speeches bring to the national consciousness the historical injustices that the Moro people had experienced at the hands of the colonizers and then of the Philippine government. During the third presidential debate, he argued that the problems in Mindanao can only be fixed if the government recognizes the historical injustices inadvertently committed against the indigenous peoples of Mindanao, especially the Moro, citing that Mindanao was already Muslim prior to the arrival of the colonizers ("Complete Transcript of the Final Presidential Debate" 2016). Early on in his presidency, Mr. Duterte, in one of his speeches, mentioned the incident in Bud Dajo and Bud Bagsak in Sulu where Moro women and men made their last stand and fought to the death as they resisted the American rule (Llanes 2016).

The failure of the peace agreements in the past is perceived by the Moro people as a continued exercise of wanton prejudice and disenfranchisement by the Christian-dominated Philippine society against Muslim Mindanao. Mr. Duterte's bonds with the Moro is seen as an opportunity for them to be represented in the central government.

With the aging population of the leaders of the MILF comes a crucial time to strike an enduring peace deal with the Moro people. The entry of cross-border extremists willing to exploit the frustration of the Muslim population of Mindanao is now mobilizing the homegrown lawless elements, brandishing the flag of the Islamic State. On 4 January 2016, a video released by an affiliate of the Islamic State claimed the unification of the four pro-ISIS groups in the Philippines—namely, the Maute Group, based in Lanao del Sur; Bangsamoro Islamic Freedom Fighters, based in Maguindanao; Abu Sayyaf, based in Basilan and Sulu; and the Ansarul Khilafah, based in Sarangani Province. In the same video, Isnilon Hapilon of the ASG-Basilan was anointed Amir of the Islamic State in the whole Southeast Asia, connecting him with the vast resources of the extremist groups based in Indonesia and Malaysia (Institute for Policy Analysis of Conflict 2016).

The siege of Marawi in Lanao del Sur, where alleged ISIS-supported extremists attempted to take over the city, is a testament to the gravity of the situation in Muslim Mindanao. It reinforces the importance of the peace talks not just for the Moro people but also for the entire population of Mindanao.

The Sympathetic Advocate

Duterte's connection with the lumad goes a long way. Genuine or not, the image that Mr. Duterte fashioned for himself in the eyes of the indigenous peoples of Mindanao was that of a sympathetic advocate capable of understanding their plight and hardships and keen to offer them social protection from the hegemonic forces that render the lumad feeble and helpless.

With Mr. Duterte at the rudders of the local government of Davao City, the city was transformed into what is *perceived* today as the most progressive city in Mindanao in terms of human development and security. The indigenous peoples benefited from this when, in many instances, Mr. Duterte opened the doors of *his* city to accommodate them, instituted deputy mayors representing the cultural minorities to advance their inclusion in the city's decision-making (Gonzales 2005), made explicit pronouncements supporting their cause, and pushed for the passage of policies aimed at protecting their rights under his jurisdictions.

During the opening ceremony of the Kadayawan Festival[9] in Davao City in August 2007, Mr. Duterte lamented how the commercialization of the festival led to the marginalization and bastardization of cultural ritual and traditions of the indigenous peoples. In his speech laden with sound bites, the mayor reiterated that the annual festival was instituted to pay tribute to the lumad who "beat the hardest stone" and "the first to cultivate and took care" of Davao City (Fiel and Velez 2007).

Every Christmas season, it has been the tradition of the local government of Davao City to take good care of the visiting lumad from the neighboring regions. Without discriminating, the mayor's instruction was clear: to make sure that the visiting indigenous peoples, insensitively seen by many as mendicants, are sheltered in time for their holiday stay (Alviola 2014).

On the policy side, reports about discrimination against minority groups, including the indigenous peoples in the city, prompted Mr. Duterte to urge the Sangguniang Panlungsod of Davao City to pass the Anti-Discrimination Ordinance (the first in the Philippines) to minimize prejudice (Mellejor 2012).

On September 2015, Mr. Duterte made headlines when he opened Davao City to the displaced indigenous peoples of Davao del Norte and Bukidnon (Manlupig 2015). In what was dubbed as the "Stop Lumad Killings" campaign, Mr. Duterte joined the throngs of advocates calling for the protection of the lumad and urged the military to leave their ancestral lands so that the indigenous peoples could return home peacefully.

These, among many others, are some of the ways in which Mr. Duterte forged himself with the lumad. He appeared to be understanding and passionate about their struggles, putting at the forefront the incontrovertible truth that many seem to have forgotten: the indigenous peoples are the remnants of Mindanao's precolonial past and they are vulnerable victims of marginalization.

Such compassion, amplified by unswerving media coverage, created the image of Mr. Duterte as a protector of the lumad. Beyond the Davao region, the indigenous peoples of Mindanao are facing a lot of challenges, most of which have to do with their ancestral lands: the issue of ownership, encroachment, and contesting claims.

It cannot be overstated that the identity of the indigenous peoples go hand in hand with their ancestral lands. The two notions are so intertwined that one cannot characterize the former without the latter. Despite the Indigenous Peoples Rights Act of 1997, it is common knowledge that the Philippine IPs continually suffer disenfranchisement from their ancestral lands. The lumad are no different. And what makes some lumad groups' claim even more contentious is the overlapping claims they have with other minority groups, particularly that of the Moros in what the latter call their Bangsamoro homelands (Erasga 2008).

Son of Migrants

The migrant-settlers of Mindanao came in droves through migration policies implemented by the American colonial government and continued by the independent Philippine government.[10] The goals of these resettlement policies were to decongest the central and northern islands of the Philippines, maximize agricultural output of Mindanao, and assimilate the indigenous population of Mindanao to the way of life of the migrant-settlers to hasten the process of socio-cultural integration (TJRC 2017a). The series of resettlement laws and pro-migrant policies led to the gradual land dispossession and minoritization of the indigenous inhabitants of Mindanao. Such diaspora provided a rife avenue for disputes where the perceived marginalization of both the Moros and the lumad by the migrant-settlers led to the intensification of the conflict among the three political segments (Cagoco-Guiam 2005).

Mr. Duterte himself was the son of a migrant-settler. His lineage can be traced back to the Duranos of Cebu, and he was raised in a devout Catholic family. Such credential proved to be pivotal to the 70 percent migrant-settler population of Mindanao. With the challenges of underdevelopment that marked the region, plus the consistent failure of the Luzon-based government to come to terms with the Moro grievances that usually result in a full-blown armed conflict, Mr. Duterte was able to rally behind him a dissatisfied constituent, sick of and worn out by the alien policies of the Manila-based government perceived to be naïve about what's happening in Mindanao.

One of the contentious issues that knit together the tri-people is land. While land dispossession victimized the lumad and the Moro, the migrant-settlers were the ones who benefited from the series of resettlement policies, as up to 24 hectares of land were awarded to each migrant household at the onset of the implementation of these policies (Abaya-Ulindang 2015).

It is noteworthy to reiterate that among those who opposed the 2008 MOA-AD between the Philippine government and the Moro Islamic Liberation Front were the migrant-rich areas of Mindanao that were supposed to be annexed to the proposed Bangsamoro Juridical Entity. More than the question of constitutionality, the ordinary migrant landowner feared that if they were annexed to the Bangsamoro lands, they would lose their land. The same irrational fear was displayed in some segment of the migrant populations throughout the deliberations of the Bangsamoro Basic Law during Mr. Aquino's presidency.

Mr. Duterte's perceived closeness with the Moro, his Visayan heritage, and his grounding in Mindanao are his main selling points. The problem in Mindanao can only be fixed by a Mindanaoan who understands the intricacies of the segments of the population, including the migrant-settlers, who practically developed the lands that were granted to them by the government.

Concluding Comments

Mr. Duterte has not only won the elections; he has successfully allied himself with the lumad, Moros, and the migrant-settler populations. Sensing that the president's groundbreaking victory is also theirs, these people feel empowered, more eager to participate in nation-building, and more hopeful for a transformed Mindanao.

For the majority of the Mindanaoans who have witnessed and encountered underdevelopment, armed conflict, corruption, and elitism from the imperial North, electing a leader who understands their grievances and who shares their frustrations is worth the shot. Never mind that Rodrigo Duterte is tough-talking, never mind that his remarks against big fishes are uncalled for, and never mind his unconventional ways and policies. After several attempts, the northern elites failed to solve the persistent problems in Mindanao. What the people of Mindanao look forward to are tangible results through political will, inclusive development, equal opportunity, and, most of all, whether real or imagined, a community safe from impunity—aspirations of a chronically marginalized population that Rodrigo Duterte has embodied.

Acknowledgments

Special thanks to Prof. Rufa Cagoco-Guiam, Jade Mark Capiñanes, and Dr. Noel Pingoy.

Endnotes

[1]   There's an on-going debate among Mindanao scholars on how to refer to the diverse peoples of Mindanao. For the purposes of this piece, "Mindanaoan" shall refer solely to the island's constituency

regardless of ethnological inclinations and upbringings.

2   Lumad is a Bisayan term meaning "native." This commonly accepted identification persists, but is otherwise confronted with issues of representation (See Lim 2015).

3   The term "tri-people" has been devised and cultivated by Mindanao-based development workers and NGOs to acknowledge the tripartite nature of the contemporary Mindanaoans. It is an initiative to rally the Mindanao constituents, irrespective of their backgrounds, to acknowledge one another as legitimate stakeholders to the destiny of Mindanao (Paredes 2015).

4   While this chapter paints the story of the Mindanaoans, the focus will be on Duterte in relation to them. Hence, some historical accounts may not be mentioned considering editorial limitations and the ultimate objective of the piece.

5   One of the thirteen Islamized ethnolinguistic groups in Mindanao whose ancestral lands form part of the present Central Mindanao.

6   See Wadi 2012.

7   The Teduray people is one of the lumad groups found mainly in the province of Maguindanao.

8   For more on the conflict dynamics of the Mamasapano incident, see de Jesus and de Jesus 2016.

9   Celebrated annually on the third week of August, the festival was instituted to pay tribute to the bounties of nature, commemorating the pre-colonial history and tradition of the people of Davao City and its neighboring regions.

10   For a list of resettlement policies implemented in Mindanao, see TJRC 2016, 48.

References

Abaya-Ulindang, Faina C. 2015. "Land Resettlement Policies in Colonial and Postcolonial Philippines: Key to Current Insurgencies and Climate Disasters in Its Southern Mindanao Island." Paper presented at the Academic Conference on Land Grabbing, Conflict, and Agrarian-Environmental Transformations: Perspectives from Southeast Asia, Chiang Mai University. https://www.iss.nl/file-admin/ASSETS/iss/Research_and_projects/Research_networks/LDPI/CMCP_54-Abaya-Ulindang.pdf.

Abinales, Patricio. 2016. "War and Peace in Muslim Mindanao: An Orthodoxy." In *Mindanao: The Long Journey to Peace and Prosperity*, ed. Paul Hutchcroft, 39–61. Mandaluyong: Anvil.

ABS-CBN News Staff. 2016. "What are the 20 Poorest Provinces in the Philippines?" *ABS-CBN News.* http://news.abs-cbn.com/focus/v2/03/24/16/what-are-the-20-poorest-provinces-in-the-philippines.

Alviola, Derek. 2014. "48,000 Lumads go to Davao City for Christmas." *Rappler.* http://www.rappler.com/nation/78547nativeslumadsdavaochristmas.

Buendia, Rizal. 2008. "Looking Into the Future of Moro Self-Determination in the Philippines." *Philippine Political Science Journal* 29, no. 52. doi:10.1080/01154451.2008.9723506.

———. 2005. "The State-Moro Armed Conflict in the Philippines: Unresolved National Question or Question of Governance?" *Asian Journal of Political Science* 13(1):112–13. doi:10.1080/02185370508434252.

Cagoco-Guiam, Rufa. 2005. "Mindanao: Conflicting Agendas, Stumbling Blocks, and Prospects Toward Sustainable Peace." In *Searching for Peace in the Asia Pacific: An Overview of Conflict Prevention and Peacebuilding Activities*, ed. A Heijmans, N. Simmonds, and H. van de Veen, 483–504. Boulder, CO: Lynne Rienner.

"Complete Transcript of the Final Presidential Debate." 2016. *Philippine Daily Inquirer.* http://newsinfo.inquirer.net/781485/read-complete-transcript-of-final-presidential-debate.

Coronel-Ferrer, Miriam. 2016. "Forging a Peace Settlement for the Bangsamoro: Compromises and Challenges." In *Mindanao: The Long Journey to Peace and Prosperity,* ed. Paul Hutchcroft, 99–131. Mandaluyong: Anvil.

De Jesus, Edilberto, and Melinda de Jesus. 2016. "The Mamasapano Detour." In *Mindanao: The Long Journey to Peace and Prosperity*, ed. Paul Hutchcroft, 159–95. Mandaluyong: Anvil.

Dictaan-Bang-oa, Eleanor P. "The Question of Peace in Mindanao." In *Beyond the Silencing of the Guns*, edited by Chandra K. Roy, Victoria Tauli-Corpuz, and Amanda Romero-Medina, 166. Baguio: Tebtebba Foundation, 2004.

Erasga, Dennis S. 2008. "Ancestral Domain Claim: The Case of the Indigenous People in Muslim Mindanao (ARMM)." *Asia-Pacific Social Science Review* 8 (1):33–44. https://www.researchgate.net/publication/250278425_Ancestral_Domain_Claim_The_Case_of_the_Indigenous_People_in_Muslim_Mindanao_ARMM.

Fiel, Tyrone, and Cheryll Velez. 2007. "'New' Kadayawan Goes Back to Its Tribal Roots." *Bulatlat.* http://bulatlat.com/main/2007/08/18/'new'-kadayawan-goes-back-to-its-tribal-roots/.

Gonzales, Daisy. 2005. "The Rise and Rise of Rodrigo Duterte." *Bulatlat*. http://www.bulatlat.com/news/5-40/5-40-duterte.htm.

Herrera, Christine. 2015. "Duterte Sets Presidential Bid, 30-day Visayan Sortie." *Manila Standard*. http://manilastandard.net/news/top-stories/169075/duterte-sets-presidential-bid-30-day-visayan-sortie.html.

International Crisis Group. 2016. *The Philippines: Renewing Prospects for Peace in Mindanao*. Belgium: ICG. https://www.crisisgroup.org/asia/south-east-asia/philippines/philippines-renewing-prospects-peace-mindanao.

Institute for Policy Analysis of Conflict. 2016. "Pro-ISIS Groups in Mindanao and their Links to Indonesia and Malaysia." *Institute for Policy Analysis of Conflict*. http://file.understandingconflict.org/file/2016/10/IPAC_Report_33.pdf.

Lim, Frinston. 2015. "1,000 Mindanao Tribal Chiefs Want 'Lumad' Term Dropped." *Philippine Daily Inquirer*. http://www.newsinfo.inquirer.net/742061/1000-mindanao-tribal-chiefs-want-lumad-term-dropped.

Llanes, Ferdinand C. 2016. "Remembering Bud Dajo and Bud Bagsak." *Philippine Daily Inquirer*. http://opinion.inquirer.net/97415/rememberingbuddajoandbudbagsak.

Manlupig, Karlos. 2015. "Duterte: 'Stop Lumad Killings.'" *Rappler*. http://www.rappler.com/nation/106132dutertestoplumadkillings.

Mawallil, Amir. 2016. "Duterte and the Bangsamoro Connection." *ABS-CBN News Online*. http://news.abscbn.com/blogs/opinions/10/17/16/opinionduterteandthebangsamoroconnection.

Mellejor, Ayan. 2012. "Davao Council Bans Discrimination vs Gays, Minority, Differently Abled." *Philippine Daily Inquirer*. http://newsinfo.inquirer.net/324189/davao-council-bans-discrimination-vs-gays-minority-differently-abled.

Monsod, Toby. 2016. "Human Development in the Autonomous Region in Muslim Mindanao: Trends, Traps, and Immediate Challenges." In *Mindanao: The Long Journey to Peace and Prosperity*, ed. Paul Hutchcroft, 199–241. Mandaluyong: Anvil.

Paredes, Oona. 2015. "Indigenous vs. Native: Negotiating the Place of Lumads in the Bangsamoro Homeland." *Asian Ethnicity* 16 (2):166–85.

Ranada, Pia. 2016. "Duterte in ARMM: I Am the Moro People's President." *Rappler*. http://www.rappler.com/nation/politics/elections/2016/129082dutertearmmmoropeoplepresident.

The World Bank and International Organization for Migration. 2017. *Land: Territory Domain, and Identity*. http://documents.worldbank.org/curated/en/968161490797321335/Land-te rritory-domain-and-identity.

Transitional Justice and Reconcilation Commission. 2016. *Report of the Transitional Justice and Reconciliation Commission*. Makati: TJRC. http://www.tjrc.ph/skin/vii_tjrc/pdfs/report.pdf.

———. 2017a. *Dealing with the Past and Land Dispossession in the Bangsamoro: Land Report*. Makati City: TJRC. http://www.tjrc.ph/ skin/vii_tjrc/pdfs/TJRC%20Land%20Report.pdf.

———. 2017b. *Listening Process Report 2017*. Makati: TJRC. http://www. tjrc.ph/skin/vii_tjrc/pdfs/TJRC%20Listening%20Process%20 Report%20PPT.pdf.

Wadi, Julkipli. 2012. "The Philippines and Bangsamoro Polity: Breaking the 'Sisyphean Ordeal.'" *Asian Studies* 48 (1&2):35–46. Edited by Eduardo Tadem.

HIDE THE LOOKING GLASS
DUTERTE AND THE LEGACY OF AMERICAN IMPERIALISM

Adele Webb

"Who is he to question me about human rights and
extrajudicial killings?"[1]

Even for the man who has earned international notoriety for his
brash talk and bad manners, the episode of September 2016
when President Duterte "cursed" the then United States leader
Barack Obama seemed to reach a new low. As news of the incident
made headlines across the globe, the international community stood
aghast—especially given that the target of this crude tirade was a
stately and diplomatically spoken figure like Obama. The contrast
couldn't have been more pronounced.

Yet to a large audience at home, the incident itself, and the
international backlash that followed, only served to cement the
president's support. It drew attention to a puzzle that has shad-
owed much of the international analysis of the extraordinary rise
to national prominence of the former local mayor. It is a puzzle-
ment that has only deepened with the unfolding of the president's
controversial policy on drugs. Why does a political leader who
attracts criticism on the international stage for being a threat to
human rights and democratic governance command what appears
to be both a large and stable supporter base at home? And why does

condemnation from international media and human rights groups only seem to bolster the determination of supporters to defend the president and his administration?

The incident brings to the forefront a discussion of the historical legacies of the United States in the Philippines; it also prompts a revisiting of the question of why the dignity of "the people" remains an incendiary political narrative. This chapter tries to understand the resonance of a political figure like Duterte by taking a historical view of political narratives and political discourses in the Philippines over the long twentieth century. After first discussing Duterte's populist discourse, and opening the puzzle of why it seems to fall on fertile ground, the chapter explores the way America's policies of "benevolent imperialism" and "democratic tutelage" beginning in 1898, in seeking to legitimize US authority over the Islands, discursively constructed the "Filipino" as behaviorally and innately subordinate and incapable of self-rule. Next, it argues that the American colonial discourse left a legacy in the post-independence political consciousness, in the form of a collective anxiety around questions of freedom and sovereignty, before going on to show how this anxiety has created opportunities for its deployment by populist leaders and movements since 1946. Finally, the chapter suggests that while Duterte is not the first political leader to use the hypocrisy of American intervention in the Philippines to appeal for popular support, his successful mobilization of a state-led nationalist discourse demonstrates that the legacy of American imperialism, and the desire to overcome the humiliation and infantilization of its central premise, continue to haunt contemporary Philippine politics.

Duterte and "The People"

In the period leading up to the May 2016 national election, Mayor Duterte made many promises. He promised an end to the hollow talk and "motherhood statements" of traditional politicians: "What you say in public, you must do . . . Shut up and just do it."[2] He promised an end to favoritism in the application of laws: "I would insist that everybody follows the law, whether you're rich or you're poor,

whether you are my son or my daughter."[3] And he promised decisive leadership: "It's going to be a dictatorship. The police and the
military will be the backbone. If the leading policemen and military
agree with you, then after six years there will be a new set up; maybe
a federal type, less corruption, and fresh air for the next generation."[4] Alongside the promises, Duterte stressed that it wasn't for
money that he would choose to run for the highest office, claiming
not to need any more money than he already had.[5] Neither was it
out of ambition that he would run: "I am already happy with what I
have achieved," he said in the same one-on-one recorded interview.
What was his motivation for becoming president? "I am Rodrigo
Duterte. I am a Filipino. I love the Philippines because it is the home
of my people."[6]

Language is always central to politics, but the centrality of the
notion of "the people" is a striking feature of populist discourse.
A history of populism across the globe would suggest that populist
leaders find fertile ground in becoming themselves a signifier that
promises meaning to the notion of a unified and "whole" people,
especially in the context of great societal divides. Another key feature
of populist political discourse is the imbuing of the non-elite with
dignity and legitimacy, the power of which lies in the stark contrast
to the signifiers of subordination in everyday life (Panizza 2005, 25).

During the press conference at Davao International Airport in
September 2016, at which the president (in)famously rejected the
right of the United States to interfere in the Philippines' business,
he stated:

> I am a president of a sovereign state. And we have long ceased to
> be a colony. I do not have any master but the Filipino people.[7]

It came as part of a lengthy and irritated monologue during which
the president not only granted himself the status of both spokesman
and defender of "the people" but also claimed that given the historical record of the United States in the Philippines, President Obama
had no credibility in holding him to account, and that past actions of
American governments toward the Filipino people belie any feigned
concern about human rights now. Asked about the prospect of being
confronted with human rights concerns by Obama, he said:

> You must be kidding. Who is he to confront me? America has
> one too many to answer for the misdeeds in this country . . . As a
> matter of fact, we inherited this problem from the United States.
> Why? Because they invaded this country and made us their subju-
> gated people.

It reflects another of the president's favored discursive strategies. Rather than acknowledge the substance of the criticism, he
recriminates by attacking the questioner's hypocrisy. He used a
similar tactical deflection in more recent criticism coming from
Catholic Church leaders over his administration's "war on drugs."
In a January speech he said: "I challenge you now, I challenge the
Catholic church, you are full of shit *at mabaho rin kayong lahat* [and
you all stink too], corruption and all," before asking how the bishops
could justify receiving monetary benefits from the political elite
while other Filipinos go hungry.[8] Russian President Vladimir Putin
along with US President Donald Trump are both well known for the
same tactic.

Yet recognizing this language as a populist discursive strategy
is only one side of the story. Such discursive strategies only work
when they resonate with the intended audience, especially when
they tap into historical narratives and questions of identity around
which linger uncomfortable emotions such as anxiety, fear, or
shame. The resonance of Duterte's words suggests that this incendiary notion of "the people" has deep historical roots.

America's "Empire of Liberty" in the Philippines

Much of the American scholarly and popular literature presents
America's involvement in the Philippines during the first half of
the twentieth century as, at best, benevolent, and, at worst, benign.
In fact, although the encounter of the United States with the
Philippines from 1898 was a significant turning point in American
history, the question of what America's colony in the Philippines
means for US history and culture has, at least until quite recently,
been understudied (Bascara 2014). This is likely explained, in part,
by the fact that until the last two decades it was a widely held belief
in the United States that, as William Appleman Williams wrote in

1955, "one of the central themes of American historiography is that there is no American empire" (1955, 379).

Only since the US military interventions in Iraq and Afghanistan have debates about "American empire" resurged. But rather than remaining a radical discourse of international relations, the language of "empire" and "imperialism" in relation to US foreign policy has become normalized, and generally used in positive terms (Mabee 2004, 1359–62). Even liberal thought has been revised to accommodate popular use of the term "empire" by insisting that the American version of empire takes unique form, since "[w]hile European empires suppressed liberty, rights and democracy, America's empire has been aimed at spreading them" (Go 2007, 75–76).

This "liberal exceptionalism" thesis resonates strongly in contemporary popular American discourse, and America's role in the Philippines is presented as the "model par excellence" (Go 2007). For example, Stanley Karnow's 1989 book, *In Our Image: America's Empire in the Philippines*, which won the prestigious Pulitzer Prize, doesn't spare many of the unpleasant details of the encounter, but concludes that America's intentions in the Philippines were "relatively benign" (1989, 434) and certainly more liberal than the past colonial powers of Europe. In 2003, Wall Street Journalist Max Boot wrote an account of the Philippine-American encounter as an analogy for the ongoing occupation of Iraq. The military campaign of conquest in the Philippines, according to Boot, represented one of the "small wars" in American history; "savage wars of peace" that accomplished the divine mandate of the country's military machine to rescue and defend the "downtrodden" natives. Whatever the cost in lives, it was needed to maintain and expand "the empire of liberty" (Boot 2003).

Arguably, American empire in the Philippines was only "exceptional" in the sense that it unleashed a new paradox that the world had not previously seen—"the business of hoisting the flag of democracy at gunpoint" (Keane 2009, 374). The American government and its people wished to teach the Filipinos about political freedom and self-government; but this "democratic tutelage" came in the form of the forceful imposition of a direct rule.

It was this founding contradiction that preoccupied many

Americans at the time, including the famous author Mark Twain, who wrote about the paradox at the heart of this "democratizing" mission. Penned in 1901, Twain's most widely circulated essay on the topic reads:

> The Person Sitting in Darkness is almost sure to say: "There is something curious about this—curious and unaccountable. There must be two Americas: one that sets the captive free, and one that takes a captive's new freedom away from him, and picks a quarrel with him with nothing to found it on; then kills him to get his land." (Twain 1901, 170)

And yet this and other anti-imperialist writings of Mark Twain about the Philippine-American War of 1899–1902 remain little-known even to students of American literary history.[9] The silencing even of one of America's most famous humorists signals the weight and dominance of US Colonial Rhetoric in constructing a historiography of Philippine-American relations that persists even until today.

The de-politicization of terms like "empire" and "imperialism" in US narratives of its own history has prompted more critical scholars to revisit the details of American colonialism in the Philippines (for example, see Doty 1996; Harris 2011; Wesling 2011). The United States' self-identification as an "exceptional" nation, to whom the values of liberty and freedom are innate, prohibits the invasion and conquest of democratic and sovereign foreign peoples. This raises the question of how the American government and colonial authorities at the turn of the last century could build domestic support for their first annexation of a foreign territory outside the Americas, while leaving intact the United States' own national identity.

Roxanne Lynn Doty (1996) analyzed the way in which the United States, through the discourse of politicians and early colonial officials, produced "knowledge" about itself, and about the Filipino "'native,' that was disseminated and put to use to justify US conquest, violence, and subsequent control" (Doty 1996, 37). In order to indefinitely defer the promised independence to the Philippines, and to sustain a policy of colonial administration and control for another four decades, this contradiction was perpetuated through rhetorical constructions of, on the one hand, an American subject who was a benevolent and kind teacher to the Philippines and signifier of this highest ideal, and on the other, a Filipino subject who was without reasoning processes and intellectual capacity, belonging to "liberty's infant class" of those who had "not yet mastered the alphabet of freedom" (Harris 2011, 79). Colonial representations rendering Filipinos "in need of guidance, tutoring, and uplifting" legitimized the denial of Filipino agency. At the same time, this very denial of agency presupposed America's mandate to act. It made it possible, even necessary, to ignore, silence, or forcefully repress Filipino attempts to exercise agency, and framed all such policy decisions and practices as acts of "deliverance and salvation rather than conquests and exploitations" (Doty 1996, 39–44).

Post-Independence Continuities

By the time the American General Douglas MacArthur walked ashore in Leyte, in October 1944, and uttered the famous words, "People of the Philippines: I have returned," the Second World War was almost over, and the American government had its sights set on more pressing geopolitical challenges.

For most Filipinos, the years of Japanese rule had been brutal, and laden with suffering, which made MacArthur's return an exhilarating national experience; the "liberation era," as it became known, was an extraordinary period of what historian E. P. Patanne called "stateside guzzling," when the ingesting of American-labeled commodities was "a form of ritual" designed to reassure the Filipinos of the "good old days" (1960, 111).

It was during this same period that post-independence relations between the United States and the Philippines were being negotiated, especially relating to America's trade and military access to the newly sovereign islands. While it might have been the case that the former American colony was free to enjoy the idea of political independence from 4 July 1946, the Islands' economy remained subject to the preferential relationship of the colonial era. The

United States retained the economic advantages of a colonial power but without responsibility for Philippine welfare (Jenkins 1954, 69). Economic power remained concentrated and under monopolistic control, with profits of the money-crop system going to landlords and compradors, while most of the population struggled to pay for imported commodities including rice, which though it could have been produced locally, was not. As journalist Teodoro Locsin wrote in 1950: "While benevolent America was building schools and roads (largely with local taxes), introducing modern sanitation, and cutting down disease, imperial America was perpetuating a medieval economic system incompatible with the development of a healthy internal economy."

Particularly striking about this early independence period was not only America's ability to continue intervention in the Philippines without needing to claim the status of sovereign power, but how the asymmetrical relationship between the two countries, which had been constructed and legitimated by a colonial regime of "democratic tutelage," continued to constrain the space for Filipino democratic agency. Within colonial discourse, but even more so in the Cold War era, the United States constructed itself as the fixed signifier and a "global emblem" of democracy. Those who affirmed the positivist narrative of American benevolence in the Philippines were deemed to be on the side of "democracy." Those who contested the history, including the violence and economic self-interest with which American soldiers had established the Pacific colony, were deemed ungrateful and dangerous, and even excluded from formal contests for power because they were advocating a politics that fell outside the democratic pale.[10]

For example, when the terms of the Philippine Trade Bill were being negotiated in late 1946, including the controversial "parity clause" that would see United States citizens granted equal economic rights to Philippine natural resources as Filipino citizens, not only did the United States make access to postwar rehabilitation funds contingent on the acceptance of this clause (even though when passed by US Congress the clause was in breach of the Philippine Constitution), many middle class Filipinos saw their approval of continued American rights to Philippine resources as something akin to an act of loyalty and gratitude. As one person wrote in a letter to the *Philippines Free Press* newspaper at the time, approving the granting of parity rights to American citizens was an opportunity to "show [his] undying gratitude for 42 years of benevolent tutelage, for the redemption of the promise of liberation after three and one half dark years of Japanese oppression, and for their honouring of our long-cherished dream of independence."[11] Or as another wrote in his letter to the paper's mailbag, "to reject parity to our benefactor and liberator (America) would be tantamount to violating the essence and principles of character training."[12]

Post-independent Philippines remained haunted by its colonial past. It wasn't only the way the American government continued to interfere in domestic political and economic affairs even long after formal independence, it was also the visceral sense of being watched, and of having to perform "democracy" correctly in order to earn legitimacy in the eyes of the former ward. As one reader implored his fellow countrymen in 1947, "Let us not give Mother America and the world the painful and shameful impression that we are a corrupt, degenerate people, who toy with our liberties and do not have respect for the time-honoured democratic processes."[13]

It was a collective experience of humiliation and infantilization that was not easily forgotten. Four decades under foreign gaze left an anxiety within many in the Philippines about the capacity to correctly inhabit this democratic freedom. Hau describes this collective Filipino subject of history as an "object of anxiety"—a doubled subject who is, on the one hand, "free in its capacity to strive for perfection and respond to the ethical imperative of transforming the determinants of its existing conditions," and yet at the same time "irreducibly constrained by these determinants and her history" (Hau 2000, 27).

The contradictions of Philippine democracy's founding legitimacy left an ambivalence, too, about democracy itself. The dominant historiography celebrated the American colonial period as a kind of sacred path along which the Philippine nation needed to travel to reach the ultimate goal of freedom, for which national heroes and martyrs of the past had long struggled. And yet to memorialize history as such was to legitimize and perpetuate the narrative of a

Filipino subject as being of dubious capacity for self-government, prone to misbehavior and vice. It left the question unresolved: could the constraints of this hierarchical ordering—the American "teacher" and the Filipino "pupil"—ever be overcome?

In Search of a "Revolutionary Break" With the Past

It is little surprise that from the early 1950s onwards, the writing of Philippine history became a site of contest, as nationalist historians tried to claw back a Filipino dignity and political agency that was all but lost in colonial accounts, especially in relation to the late nine-teenth-century events of a populist revolution against the former colonial power of Spain, and the national resistance movement against American forces that immediately followed. But it wasn't only on the pages of history books where such battles were fought.

Nationalist discourses of a resurrected "people" began to be mobilized by political elite as they competed with the discourses of the political "left," to capture a national imaginary seeking a redemptive path in order for the Philippine nation to transcend the humiliation and indignities of the colonial past.

It is precisely because the national imaginary had been compromised by the experiences of the colonial and neocolo-nial past, Hau argues, that the imperative of radical transforma-tion has been kept alive—the task of the "unfinished revolution," and the need to "exorcise the ghost of colonialism" (2000, 280–81). The fragile interpellation of "the Filipino," along with the histor-ically compromised notions of "freedom" and "sovereignty," have provided fertile political terrain for populist discourse claiming to resolve the ambiguities of the past. The post-independence political landscape has long been marked by populist appeals that claim to fully enact a reconciled and restored "Filipino people," and offer "a promise of emancipation after a journey of sacrifice" (Panizza 2005, 23). Key to these appeals have been an imbuing of "the people" with dignity and value, and the turning of everyday markers of subordi-nation on their head.

President Diosdado Macapagal (1961–1965) was the first to bring the language of revolution within state discourse, declaring the

1896 Revolution "unfinished," before announcing that his administration's Land Reform Program was, in fact, a "revolution in itself," and "part of a peaceful, ambitious, unfinished revolution which we are now waging to win for our people an adequate measure of prosperity and well-being."[14] The Filipino "people," he said on the one-hundredth birth anniversary of the "great plebeian" leader Andres Bonifacio, suffer from the errors of the past colonial regimes and from "the thwarted hopes of our historical struggles." It is time for "our people" to have the dignity they deserve.[15]

Macapagal was defeated in the 1965 election for president. But his successor, Ferdinand Marcos, became the master of a discourse of populist nationalism.[16] Beginning with his very first inauguration speech, Marcos evoked the vision of a Philippines that had lost its way, overtaken by greed and corruption by those in power; the Filipino subject, a brave hero of history, had been left without dignity and facing despair. Words had become cheap in the Philippines, he told his audience: "Justice and security are as myths rendered into elaborate fictions to dramatize our so-called well-being and our happy march to progress."[17] But his mandate from "the people" was one of action. The sovereignty of "the people" was being derided by the extravagant lifestyles and conspicuous consumption of the political class, and mocked by lawless elements and "syndicated crime." People had lost "faith" in the government. It was time for the long-suffering citizens of the Philippines to stop being the ones to bear the burden. He was calling on the people to "join hands" with him so that he could bring change that was "bold" and "meaningful," and restore the Philippines to the democratic republic the nation's "forefathers" intended:

> This is a vision of our people rising above the routine to face formidable challenges and overcome them. . . .
>
> It is our people bravely determining our own future.[18]

Like the current president, Marcos built his system of concentrated power from a large base of middle class "loyalists," who rationalized that the only hope for transformation rested on the acquisition of power by an alternative force to the landlords and oligarchs, given that the latter's grip on Congress seemed impenetrable through a "business as usual" approach (Bello 1988, 216).

Almost two decades later, in 1983, another populist discourse was sinking roots and gaining resonance within a popular middle-class consciousness, facilitated paradoxically by the oppressiveness of President Marcos's authoritarian regime. When Benigno Aquino Jr. was assassinated on the tarmac of Manila's international airport upon the opposition leader's much anticipated return from exile, groups from across the political spectrum—National Democrats, Social Democrats, Christian Democrats, and Liberal Democrats—issued a Manifesto in which they declared:

> THE TIME has come to speak with one voice and act with one will . . . "THE FILIPINO PEOPLE will no longer tolerate the loss of their liberties, the exploitation of their labor, the plunder of their natural resources, the shameless looting of public funds, the arbitrary arrests, brutal torture and ruthless murders of their children and their leaders, the arrogant presence of alien military bases on their land, the mockery of elections, and the denigration of their sovereignty—all perpetuated by a government that has forcibly imposed itself upon them with the support of the US government . . . "WE SHALL NOT CEASE our struggle until our people are truly free and sovereign, and our country is truly democratic and independent.[19]

The signature appearing at the top of the page was that of the recently widowed, soon-to-be-new president, Cory Aquino.

People rose to the challenge. A revolutionary spirit swept through many parts of the country, capturing the imagination of many, and stirring them to stand and fight. As writer Melba Maggay wrote in her "Diary from the Barricades" during those extraordinary four days of February 1986:

> Casual grit. That was what it was the afternoon the tanks came charging. The engines began to roar, but the people refused to move, a defenseless but determined wall of restraint against the tidal lust for bloodshed. It was a war of nerves, but perhaps, more deeply, a trial of faith: faith in the rightness of standing there,

quaking yet fortified by an instinctive sense that the doing of that which is right will pay off somehow.[20]

Learning the Lessons of History:
Is Duterte the Hope for Democracy or Its Peril?

Thirty years after EDSA I, frustration with the failure of the nation to reconcile and overcome the determinants of history has again made fertile the political ground: Duterte is a "revolutionary" political figure who calls on "the people" to lay the burden of sacrifice at his feet, and to trust him as a redemptive leader who can deliver his "people" out of the wilderness. His rhetoric bears a striking resemblance to that of Marcos, and his resonance is not simply about the desire for effective government; it demonstrates that redemption is about overcoming anxiety and restoring dignity. To an audience in October 2016 he said:

> I can lose the presidency anytime. If Congress would oust me, fine. That is part of the destiny of my presidency because I won without money and machinery. If I lose my life, that's part of the territory of being president. But I would never allow our dignity and honor to be just like a doormat before the international public . . . If there is one thing I would like to prove to America and to everybody is that there is such a thing as the dignity of the Filipino people.[21]

In telling Obama to mind his own business, the president behaved badly, but in this very subversiveness lies his appeal. The more his erratic and undisciplined behavior draws the disapproval of an international crowd, the more compelling to many is his leadership. Why? Because he embodies the scrutinized Filipino "native" subject of history, subordinated and looked down upon by the "foreign" outsider; in standing up for "the people," he signifies a refusal to continue the indignity of the past.

While the lessons from history are plentiful, two seem particularly pertinent to understanding the politics of these contemporary times. First, America's conquest of the Philippines in the name of "democratic tutelage" is a cautionary tale. Beginning with the annexation of Manila Bay in 1899, American foreign policy over the long twentieth century has used a discourse of "democracy" to legitimize international hegemonic power. We can no longer ignore the fact that to a large extent, the "global spread of democracy" has enabled the continuation of a form of imperialism by creating an asymmetry between those who "democratize" and those who are "democratized" (Slater 2006, 1382–83), and that this imbalance of power, and the indignity it involves, has compromised the very ideal of democracy itself. In the Philippines, the result is an unresolved anxiety amongst citizens about their democratic agency, a longing for political legitimacy and worth, and an ambivalence about democracy which plays into the hands of populist politicians like Duterte (Webb forthcoming).

Second, "there is no new thing under the sun," as the saying from the Book of Ecclesiastes reminds us. And as this chapter has sought to demonstrate, neither is the current president and his populist appeal an entirely new feature on the Philippine political landscape. The search for a "revolutionary break" with the past, and the appeal of redemptive leadership, has been a feature of Philippine democracy throughout the post-independence period. While the longing to overcome the experience of indignity and humiliation can be recognized as a legacy of a colonial past, the dark history of the Marcos era, along with the experience of populist leaders globally, begs the heeding of a warning: that what may be advocated as democratic renewal and the awakening of democratic consciousness may in fact become its peril. Populist leaders such as Duterte, in claiming a radical mandate, might be able to dislocate from power those who would normally occupy it—whether that be traditional politicians, oligarchs, or leaders of organized crime and drug cartels. Yet such leaders, time and again, instead of opening the space of contest that democracy requires, appropriate that central place of power for themselves.

Many of the chapters in this book attest to the fact that violence and the use of arbitrary power, rather than defeating the evils of concentrated power, simply lead to its manifestation in other forms. Indeed, under the cover of speaking for a "rectified" and "whole"

Filipino people, the current president is exercising a level of discretionary power that belies the democratic agency and the freedom of the very people he purports to protect. If Duterte wishes to hold up a long-hidden looking-glass to America, to expose the hypocrisy of its treatment of Philippine human rights in the past, he had best be prepared to do the same himself.

Endnotes

1   Transcript, "Duterte on Obama." See Duterte 2016.
2   Mayor Rodrigo Duterte, interview by Maria A. Ressa of Rappler, 26 October 2015. See Ressa 2015.
3   Ibid.
4   Ibid.
5   Ibid.
6   Ibid.
7   Transcript, "Duterte on Obama," 6 September 2016.
8   Quoted in Salaverria 2017 and Ranada 2017.
9   Shelly Fisher Fishkin, Director of American Studies at Stanford University, recently posed the question in a recent article on Twain's anti-imperialist writing: "Why was it not featured more prominently in American literary history—and American social and political history? And why was the Philippine-American War itself so off the radar screen not only when it came to criticism on America's most famous author, but in American history textbooks as well?" (see Fishkin 2010, 22–28).
10 The six candidates from the newly formed Democratic Alliance political party who had, in a landmark election result, won congressional seats in the November 1946 national ballot—all of whom were known for advocating against the acceptance of the terms of the United States-Philippine trade deal, and who signaled the potential for electoral threat from a coalition of peasants, workers and progressive middle class elements—were denied the right to take up their seats in the House of Representations under President Manual Roxas. This exclusion from formal politics, based on an "anti-Americanism" that was not so much against America as it was for the political and economic sovereignty of the Philippines, became the basis for the largest peasant uprising the country had ever seen, the Hukbalahap rebellion, which was eventually defeated by the Philippine government with the help of the United States'

anti-communist counterinsurgency in the early 1950s. See Jenkins 1954 and Kerkvliet 1977.

[11]   "Free Press' Readers and Parity," *Philippine Free Press*, 1 March 1947, 38–39.

[12]   Ibid.

[13]   See Pamor 1947, 45–46.

[14]   Address of President Macapagal at the signing of the Agricultural Land Reform Code, 8 August, 1963: http://www.officialgazette.gov.ph/1963/08/08/address-of-president-macapagal-at-the-signing-of-the-agricultural-land-reform-code/.

[15]   Speech of President Macapagal at the Bonifacio Centenary Ceremonies, 30 November 1963: http://www.officialgazette.gov.ph/1963/11/30/speech-of-president-macapagal-at-the-bonifacioc entenary-ceremonies/.

[16]   Bello even called Marcos "a figure of Machiavellian brilliance" (Bello 1988, 216).

[17]   Inauguration Address, President Marcos, 30 December 1965: http://www.officialgazette.gov.ph/1965/12/30/inaugural-address-of-presi dent-marcos-december-30-1965/.

[18]   Ibid.

[19]   "21 September, 'Manifesto of Freedom, Democracy, and Sovereignty'" (Filipiniana Collection, Rizal Library, Ateneo de Manila University).

[20]   Melba Padilla Maggay, "Diary from the Barricades," first published in 1985–1986 Philippines Yearbook of the Fookien Times. http://mpmaggay.blogspot.com.au/2011/02/diary-from-barricades.html.

[21]   Speech of President Duterte during the Philippine Economic Forum, Convention Hall, Prince Park Tower Hotel, Tokyo, Japan, 26 October 2016. http://pcoo.gov.ph/oct-26-2016-speech-of-president-rodri go-roa-duterte-during-the-philippine-economic-forum/.

References

Appleman Williams, William. 1955. "The Frontier Thesis and American Foreign Policy." *Pacific Historical Review* 24 (November):379–95.

Bascara, Victor. 2014. "God's Arbiters: Americans and the Philippines, 1898–1902/Empire's Proxy: American Literature and US Imperialism in the Philippines." *American literature: A Journal of Literary History, Criticism and Bibliography* 86 (1):189–91.

Bello, Walden. 1988. "From Dictatorship to Elite Populism: The United States and the Philippine Crisis." In *Crisis and Confrontation: Ronald*

Reagan's Foreign Policy, ed. M. H. Morley. Totowa, NJ: Rowman & Littlefield.

Boot, Max. 2003. *The Savage Wars of Peace: Small Wars and the Rise of American Power*, Vol. 1st pbk. New York: Basic Books.

Doty, Roxanne Lynn. 1996. *Imperial Encounters: The Politics of Representation in North-South Relations*. Minneapolis: University of Minnesota Press.

Duterte, Rodrigo. 2016 "Duterte on Obama." Speech, ASEAN Summit, Laos, 6 September. *Rappler*. http://www.rappler.com/nation/145337 -transcript-duterte-obama-human-rights.

Fishkin, Shelley Fisher. 2010. "Reflections." *The Mark Twain Annual* 8 (1): 22–28.

Go, Julian. 2007. "The Provinciality of American Empire: 'Liberal Exceptionalism' and U.S. Colonial Rule, 1898-1912." *Comparative Studies in Society and History* 49 (1):74-108. doi: 10.1017/S0010417507000412.

Harris, Susan K. 2011. *God's Arbiters: Americans and the Philippines, 1898–1902*. Oxford; New York: Oxford University Press.

Hau, Caroline S. 2000. *Necessary Fictions: Philippine Literature and the Nation, 1946–1980*: Quezon City: Ateneo de Manila University Press.

Jenkins, Shirley. 1954. *American Economic Policy toward the Philippines*. Stanford: Stanford University Press.

Karnow, Stanley. 1989. *In Our Image: America's Empire in the Philippines*. New York: Random House.

Keane, John. 2009. *The Life and Death of Democracy*. New York; London: Simon & Schuster.

Kerkvliet, Benedict J. 1977. *The Huk Rebellion: A Study of Peasant Revolt in the Philippines*. Berkeley: University of California Press.

Locsin, Teodoro M. "Fil-American: The Story of a Relationship." *Philippines Free Press*, 24 June 1950.

Mabee, Bryan. 2004. "Discourses of Empire: The US 'Empire', Globalisation and International Relations." *Third World Quarterly* 25 (8): 1359–78. doi: 10.1080/0143659042000308410.

Pamor, Florentino. 1947. "Annul the Elections!" *Philippines Free Press*, 20 December.

Panizza, Francisco. 2005. "Introduction: Populism and the Mirror of Democracy." In *Populism and the Mirror of Democracy*, ed. F. Panizza, 1–31. London; New York: Verso.

Patanne, E. P. 1960. "The Liberation Era Lingers on." *Progress* 1960 (110–14):111.

Ranada, Pia. 2017. "Duterte to Catholic Church: You're Full of Shit." *Rappler*, 24 January. http://www.rappler.com/nation/159370-du terte-catholic-church-full-shit

Ressa, Maria A. 2015. "Duterte, His 6 Contradictions and Planned Dictatorship." *Rappler*, 26 October. http://www.rappler.com/nation/ politics/elections/2016/110679-duterte-contradictions-dictatorship

Salaverria, Leila B. 2017. "Duterte: Catholic Church 'Full of Shit.'" *Inquirer.net*, 24 January. http://newsinfo.inquirer.net/865123/ duterte-catholic-church-full-of-shit

Slater, David. 2006. "Imperial Powers and Democratic Imaginations." *Third World Quarterly* 27: 1369–86. doi: 10.1080/01436590601027230.

Twain, Mark. 1901. "To the Person Sitting in Darkness." *North American Review* CLXXIL:161–76.

Webb, Adele. Forthcoming. "'Why Are the Middle-Class Misbehaving?' Exploring Democratic Ambivalence and Authoritarian Nostalgia." *Philippine Sociological Review* 65 (S1).

Wesling, Meg. 2011. *Empire's Proxy: American Literature and US Imperialism in the Philippines*. New York: NYU Press.

Duterte's "War on Drugs"

The Securitization of Illegal Drugs and the Return of National Boss Rule

Nathan Gilbert Quimpo

Of all the undertakings pursued by the irrepressible and mercurial President Rodrigo Duterte, none have proven as controversial as his deadly "war on drugs." After only eight months of the Duterte presidency, the "war"[1] has already claimed the lives of over 8,000 people, with many drug suspects killed extra-judicially by police and anonymous vigilantes. Tens of thousands more of drug suspects have been arrested, many of them packed into the country's already densely overpopulated prisons. Fearing summary execution, over a million drug users and pushers have surrendered to law enforcement forces.

In justifying his "war on drugs," Duterte has depicted the drug trade as a grave threat to Philippine society and to national security, asserting that it "has infected every nook and corner of this country, involving generals, mayors, governors, and so many ninjas [police who protect drug syndicates]" (Ranada 2016). Duterte has often been quoted by media as saying that drugs are the country's biggest problem. During the 2016 election campaign, Duterte even warned that because of the growing drug menace, the Philippines was on the brink of becoming a "narco-state."

Domestic and international human rights groups, Catholic Church officials, opposition politicians as well as some Western governments, however, have decried the wave of drug-related killings. The Catholic Bishops' Conference has expressed deep concern over the many killings and the "reign of terror" in urban poor communities. Amnesty International and Human Rights Watch have denounced the widespread, deliberate, and organized executions of drug suspects as a flagrant violation of international human rights law and as possibly amounting to "crimes against humanity."

Despite all the criticisms against the extra-judicial killings, the Duterte administration has continued to enjoy an "excellent" net satisfaction rating of +77 (85 percent satisfied, 8 percent dissatisfied) among Filipinos in its campaign against drugs, as a December 2016 survey of the Social Weather Stations (SWS) has shown.[2] Moreover, satisfaction, approval, and trust ratings in the Duterte government itself have remained very high in SWS and Pulse Asia surveys. The remarkable ratings of the Duterte administration have held in all classes and in all the main geographical divisions of the country (Metro Manila, Luzon, Visayas, and Mindanao).

Given such a controversial and complicated issue as the "war on drugs," certain basic questions need to be asked. Why has Duterte embarked on the "war on drugs"? Are illegal drugs as much of a threat to Philippine society and to national security as they are being touted to be? How successful has Duterte been in achieving his objectives in the fight against drugs? What are the prospects of this "war" in the coming years?

As a framework of analysis, I use the theory of securitization as developed by the Copenhagen School and by other security studies scholars. Securitization theory examines how security threats are constructed and how extreme measures in addressing such threats are justified. In addition, I return to the concept of "bossism," which John Sidel and Peter Kreuzer have extensively investigated in their studies on local strongman rule in the Philippines.

I argue that the populist Duterte has shrewdly picked on an issue of broad popular concern—drug trafficking—and securitized it. He has hyperbolized the drug menace to justify the deadly "war on drugs." For Duterte, much more than just burnishing his "tough on crime" and "man of action" persona and broadening his popular appeal, the "war on drugs" constitutes a key instrument for turning the national police machinery into his power base and into a quasi-private army with some Davao Death Squad features, for bringing back national boss rule and for pursuing a national development strategy anchored on a perverse view of law and order. While Duterte currently still basks in broad popular support, the prospects of the "war on drugs" and of boss rule are most uncertain.

The Securitization of Illegal Drugs

As conceptualized by the Copenhagen School, securitization involves the transformation of an issue that is managed within the normal political domain into a security matter. A securitizing actor or agent, such as a political leader, government, the military, or a pressure group, portrays a certain issue or problem as constituting a threat to the very survival of a referent object, such as the state, society, or the economy, and demands that extraordinary measures be undertaken to deal with the threat. The securitizing move is deemed successful if it convinces the targeted audience, such as the public, or at least gains its acceptance, about the existential threat and the need for the exceptional measures to counter it (Buzan et al. 1998; Emmers 2016).

Before Duterte assumed the presidency, he already set the stage for the securitization of drugs on a national scale. Before and during the 2016 election campaign, Duterte repeatedly harped on the message about illegal drugs being the country's biggest problem and being a grave threat to society and national security. He intensified his warnings in the weeks prior to his inauguration as president.

The drug menace is a social problem that is broadly perceived to have not been satisfactorily addressed by past administrations, but Duterte has blown it way out of proportion. On what basis has he determined that it is the country's topmost problem or security threat—over and above such other problems as poverty, social disparities, corruption, insurgency, environmental degradation, human rights violations, and organized crime apart from drug trafficking?

Duterte's claims on the gravity of the drug problem are belied by the government's own figures. In his first state-of-the-nation address in July 2016, Duterte estimated that the country had 3.7 million drug addicts. Two months later, the Dangerous Drugs Board (DDB), the government's policy-making and strategy-formulating body on drug prevention and control, declared that the Philippines had 1.8 million current drug users. The DDB did not specify how many of them were actually addicts. The United Nations Office on Drugs and Crime (UNODC) estimates that the Philippines has an estimated prevalence of drug use rate of only 1.69 percent, way below the overall global rate of 5.2 percent (Diola 2016). The Philippine Drug Enforcement Agency (PDEA) reports that in 2015, a whopping 92 percent of Metro Manila's barangays were plagued by the drug menace. But illegal drugs are mainly a problem of major cities. Contrary to Duterte's "every nook and corner of this country" assertion, only about 26 percent of the country's barangays were drug-affected, the PDEA report also indicates.

The claim of the Philippines' being on the brink of becoming a narco-state needs to be examined more closely. "A narco-state exists," writes Paul Reston Kan (2016, 51), "where the institutions of government direct drug trafficking activities or actively collude with drug traffickers, creating conditions where the illicit narcotics trade eclipses portions of the country's legitimate economy and where segments of society begin to accrue benefits from drug trafficking. A narco-state thrives due to its ability to exploit qualities of the state's links to the legitimate global economy." David Jordan (1999) defines narco-states more simply as "states where the criminalization of the political system has reached the point that the highest officials of the government protect and depend on narcotics trafficking organizations." Drug traffickers need considerable resources and machinery to be able to bribe and coerce politicians and law enforcement officials, manipulate elections, and dictate policy at the *national level*. Thus, narco-states have only emerged in major producing or transit countries in the global illegal drug trade, which is estimated to have an annual turnover of hundreds of billions of dollars.

In Latin America, the term *narco-state* has been applied,

sometimes loosely, to a number of countries—Colombia, Mexico, El Salvador, Honduras, Suriname, etc.—involved in the production (including processing), smuggling, and distribution of illegal drugs, particularly cocaine. The main destination of the drugs within the Americas is the United States, the world's largest consumer of illegal drugs. Apart from fighting bloody wars against law enforcement forces, drug cartels engage in deadly competition among themselves. Mainly because of these drug cartels, majority of the world's fifty most violent cities are in Latin America, topped by San Salvador, El Salvador (181 murders per 100,000 people in 2015), and followed by San Pedro Sula, Honduras; Acapulco, Mexico; and Guatemala City, Guatemala ("Revisiting the World's Most Violent Cities" 2016).

Guinea-Bissau, one of the world's poorest countries, has been described by the United Nations as Africa's first narco-state. Colombian and Mexican drug cartels have turned it into a major transshipment hub, mainly for the lucrative European cocaine market (Loewenstein 2016; O'Regan 2012).

Afghanistan, the world's top producer of opiates (opium, heroin, morphine, etc.), has long been widely tagged as a narco-state. Over the past decade, however, neighboring Tajikistan, which has become a key transit country for opiates to countries of the former Soviet Union and which has grown very dependent on the illegal drug industry, is said to have joined the ranks of narco-states, too (Paoli et al. 2007).

In the Philippines, the trade in illegal drugs--amphetamines, marijuana, cocaine, inhalants, solvents, ecstasy, etc.—is a PhP 55.5-billion industry, according to the DDB. The country's main drug problem is crystal methamphetamine, a synthetic chemical locally known as *shabu*. Most of the methamphetamine is smuggled in from China, but some of it is locally produced. China is also the Philippines'—and Asia's—biggest source of methamphetamine precursors. Marijuana has long been produced in certain remote rural areas of the Philippines. Although this is mainly for local consumption, some of it is smuggled to other countries. The Philippines has also been used in the past by Mexican and West African traffickers as a transshipment point for cocaine.

The Philippines is a long way from narcostatization. International drug monitoring agencies such as the UNODC, as well as the US government, have not tagged the Philippines as a major drug producer or hub.[3] Drug lords are known to have made some inroads in a number of local governments but there has been no evidence showing that their power and influence have become virulent or widespread at the regional or national level. There are hardly any signs that drug traffickers are anywhere close to mustering the wherewithal for capturing state power.[4]

Way before assuming the presidency, Duterte made it starkly clear to everyone that he would resort to extraordinary—even extreme—measures in cracking down on the illegal drug trade. During the 2016 election campaign, he warned: "You drug pushers, hold-up men and do-nothings, you better go out. Because I'd kill you." He promised to slaughter 100,000 criminals in his first six months as president and dump their bodies in Manila Bay to fatten all the fish there. As president-elect, he called on police and ordinary citizens to kill drug pushers and addicts fighting back or resisting arrest.

So very quickly upon inauguration, Duterte did come up with the ultimate extreme means: the "war on drugs." He picked the new chief of the Philippine National Police, Ronald "Bato" Dela Rosa, a former police chief of Davao City with vast experience in anti-drug campaigns, as the chief enforcer of the "war."[5] As Duterte has promised, the "war on drugs" has been a relentless, sustained, and bloody campaign. Drug suspects have been killed during police operations (such as "buy-bust" operations), killed by unidentified assailants (often riding on motorcycles), or killed in an unknown place, their bodies dumped away from the crime scene (ABS-CBN 2017). The "war" has resulted in the deaths of thousands of Filipinos—a "bloodbath," in the words of James Ross (2016) of Human Rights Watch. The vast majority of those killed have been poor urban slum dwellers.

A major feature of this war has been Oplan Tokhang,[6] consisting of community-level operations in which police knock on people's houses without prior notice, ostensibly to persuade drug pushers and addicts to give themselves up and mend their ways. "In affluent neighborhoods of gated communities and estates," reports the *New York Times* (Berehulak 2016), "there is, indeed, sometimes a polite knock on the door, an officer handing a pamphlet detailing the repercussions of drug use to the housekeeper who answers. In poorer districts, the police grab teenage boys and men off the street, run background checks, make arrests and sometimes shoot to kill."

On the basis of the high satisfaction ratings of the "war on drugs" and of his administration, it can well be said that Duterte's endeavor to securitize the illegal drug trade has been a great success. As pointed out by Taub (2016), the wide acceptance of the "war on drugs" indicates public loss of confidence in state institutions, particularly the judicial system. "Frustration with the government's inability to provide basic security," she writes, "led to rising public demand for new leaders who would take more decisive action to provide security."

The "war on drugs" has withstood criticism from the media regarding Duterte's exaggerated claims on the drug problem, as well as denunciations of human rights groups, particularly of extra-judicial killings. Senator Vicente Sotto, who supports the "war on drugs," justifies Duterte's inflated drug statistics, saying they could induce drug users to quit: "If they make people alarmed, then why not? It doesn't hurt anyone," he said. "People don't care how it's done as long as it's done" (Baldwin and Marshall 2016).

Duterte and the Davao Death Squad

The securitization model, as conceptualized by the Copenhagen School, has had its fair share of criticisms. I draw attention here to one particular shortcoming of the model pointed out by two scholars, Mely Caballero-Anthony and Ralf Emmers (2006, 5), who have come up with their own insights on securitization:

> [W]hile the Copenhagen School tells us who securitizes and how securitization takes place, it does not address the question of *why* securitization occurs. In response, we identify motivations that encourage securitizing actors to articulate a matter in security terms. Importance is thus given to answering a simple question: why securitize an issue? Every securitizing act involves a political

decision. A series of motives and intentions can explain an act of securitization. Securitizing injects urgency into an issue and leads to a mobilization of political support and a deployment of resources. (Emphasis in original)

Why has Duterte securitized illegal drugs? The answer has something in part to do with Duterte's populism.

As defined by Cas Mudde (2004, 543), populism is "an ideology that considers society to be ultimately separated into two homogeneous and antagonistic groups, 'the pure people' versus 'the corrupt elite,' and which argues that politics should be an expression of the *volonté générale* (general will) of the people." Mudde characterizes populism as a "thin" or "thin-centred" ideology, one that "can be easily combined with very different (thin and full) other ideologies, including communism, ecologism, nationalism or socialism."

To reach the pinnacles of power, Duterte "shrewdly capitalized on his image as a man-of-the people with no tolerance for the nation's political and business elite"—an image "burnished by his disdain for formal clothes, his preference for eating food with his hands and living in a simple home in Davao" (Malakunas 2016). The anti-establishment demagogue cast himself as a man of action capable of decisively and quickly solving deep-rooted problems in society. In particular, he projected himself, on the basis of his record as long-time mayor of "safe" and prosperous Davao City, as being tough on crime—one who did not hesitate to use whatever means, fair or foul, to restore and maintain law and order, a real-life version of "Dirty Harry," "The Punisher," and "The Terminator." By focusing on drugs, Duterte adroitly targeted an issue of great popular concern that could project him as an action man in busting crime and that could broaden his popular appeal.

Duterte's securitization of drugs has much more to do, however, than just projecting "Duterte Harry." For a deeper analysis into Duterte's motivations, one has to look back at his long stint as mayor of Davao City, where he had, in fact, securitized drugs and petty crimes as early as the early 1990s.

Davao City has had a long history of violence. In the 1970s and 1980s, it was reputed to be the "murder capital" of the Philippines. Military, police, and paramilitary forces engaged in many "salvagings" (summary executions) and disappearances of activists and guerrillas of the New People's Army (NPA) of the Communist Party of the Philippines (CPP). Turning Davao City into its main laboratory for urban guerrilla warfare, the NPA, through its "sparrow" and urban partisan units, hit back by "punishing" abusive soldiers and cops, and conducting *agaw-armas* operations (divesting security forces of their firearms, often shooting them down first). Just before and during President Corazon Aquino's "total war" against communist insurgents, ultra-rightist vigilante groups led by the fearsome Alsa Masa terrorized the city and engaged in a killing spree, sometimes resorting to extreme forms of violence, such as dismemberment and beheading.

Pledging to restore law and order in Davao City, Duterte was elected mayor in 1988. Going after drug pushers and other criminals was a key plank in his approach to public security. The "Dirty Harry of Davao" soon came to be. He recalls: "My hatred of criminals – that's what changed Davao" ("Rody's War" 2005).

Sunstar Davao looks back at a series of unsolved murders in Davao City:

> A long time ago, make that in the early 1990s, a man was found dead, stripped of his shirt and left with a brown carton marked: "Drug pusher *ako, huwag tularan.* – Davao Death Squad" [I'm a drug pusher, don't emulate. – Davao Death Squad].
>
> Another follower, and then another . . . and . . . even though there was no longer a carton sign stating the dead one's crime when still alive and who was claiming responsibility for his death, everyone already believes the murdered person was a pusher killed by the DDS. Those murders, too, were never solved. (Estremera 2005)

The extra-judicial killings of the DDS have been well documented by human rights groups (World Organisation Against Torture et al. 2003; Human Rights Watch 2009) as well as scholars (Kreuzer 2009, 2016; Breuil and Rozema 2009). DDS vigilantes included former NPA guerrillas, former military and police personnel, and young jobless men; their handlers were often policemen or ex-policemen, and sometimes barangay officials. Most of the victims of DDS vigilantism were alleged drug pushers, petty criminals, and street children (Human Rights Watch 2009). The killings were often perpetrated by two men without masks on a motorcycle, one serving as the hitman, the other as lookout—a pattern very similar to one NPA sparrow units had used before. According to human rights groups, some 1,400 suspicious killings have transpired in Davao since the early 1990s (Mogato 2016). Starting in 2011, while DDS vigilantes did the dirty job of killing off drug suspects, the Davao police, headed by its chief then, Dela Rosa, launched a "softer" approach of "knock-and-plead": Oplan Tokhang.

Duterte has constantly denied any involvement in extrajudicial killings in Davao, any links to the DDS, and even the very existence of the DDS. On several occasions, however, he has made slip-ups and made self-incriminating admissions. But he has quickly reverted back to denials afterwards. Sometimes, "coincidences," as in the following account of Marks (2004), strain credulity:

> [Mayor Durterte] went on local television to read out lists of alleged peddlers and addicts, warning them of dire consequences unless they left town. In the ensuing weeks, many people named were killed. Others were targeted after being picked up by police, murdered within days—or even minutes—of being released.

The Davao City government has not conducted any serious investigations or any prosecutions of extra-judicial killings said to be DDS-perpetrated. Philip Alston (2008, 16), the UN special rapporteur on extrajudicial, summary, or arbitrary executions, has commented: "The mayor's positioning is frankly untenable: He dominates the city so thoroughly as to stamp out whole genres of crime, yet he remains powerless in the face of hundreds of murders committed by men without masks in view of witnesses." Duterte has, in fact, taken responsibility for the lack of prosecutions. "I'm more interested in solving crimes against innocent people," he said. "I'm not at all interested in the killings of criminals, especially people involved with drugs" (Sipress 2003).

The clearest sign that Duterte has succeeded in securitizing drugs in Davao City is the fact that, despite all the vigilante killings, he has been a repeatedly reelected mayor.[7] Davaoeños believe that the peace and order has been restored in their city since the turbulent

1970s–80s and they feel a lot safer and secure. They can walk Davao's streets late at night without fear of getting mugged. Business leaders have praised Duterte's way of dealing with crime, saying that the elimination of criminals has created a good atmosphere for business. In 2004, Sofronio Jucutan, the president of the city's Chamber of Commerce, declared: "We don't condone summary killings, but we want society to be cleansed of its scum. These people are garbage and, just like any garbage, you have to dispose of them" (Marks 2004).

Duterte's Boss Rule and Development Strategy

Bossism, writes Sidel (1999), is a common political phenomenon in the Philippines, where warlords and powerful political clans use coercion and violence to establish and maintain power in areas under their control or influence. James C. Scott (1972, 6) describes a *boss* as follows:

> Although a boss may often function as a patron, the term itself implies (a) that he is the most powerful man in the arena and (b) that his power rests more on the inducements and sanctions at his disposal than on affection or status. As distinct from a patron who may or may not be the supreme local leader and whose leadership rests at least partly on rank and affection, the boss is a secular leader par excellence who depends almost entirely on palpable inducements and threats to move people.

Bosses such as warlords and political clan patriarchs often maintain private armies or private armed groups to ensure their coercive clout. As defined by the military and the police, a *private armed group* is "an organized group of two (2) or more persons, with legally or illegally possessed firearms, utilized for purposes of sowing fear and intimidation, and violence for the advancement and protection of vested political and economic interests" (Office of the President 2015). Although the Philippine constitution bans private armed groups, they have long existed and persisted, notwithstanding repeated calls from the public for their disbandment.

Over the years since 1988, Duterte has established and consolidated boss rule in Davao City with himself as the leader par excellence, the boss. Kreuzer (2009, 58–59) describes Davao boss rule:

> Actually Duterte is quite popular because of his determined fight against crime. However this fight is not within the limits of the rule of law, but terrorizes criminals and criminal-suspects into obedience or flight. Duterte makes abundantly clear that there can be security, but only he himself can provide it. Security is provided according to his personal ideas of justice and adequateness. In his political symbolism, Duterte clearly is above the law. It is him, who indicts, passes judgment and orders the executioners to do their job. It is a personalized fight between those who do not follow the rules and the rightful vigilante whose rules reign supreme. It is boss-rule in pure form.

It is most surprising that the DDS has sometimes not been included in the list of private armed groups (see, for instance, Mendoza 2012), even when it perfectly fits the bill. With its alleged 1,400 killings, the DDS may well be the country's most murderous private army in the post-Marcos era, rivalling that of the infamous Ampatuan political clan.[8] Whether or not direct links between Duterte and the DDS can be proven, he has long served as its inspirational beacon, as well as its virtual godfather, whose mere word is equivalent to a command.

Amid all the outrage over the hundreds of vigilante killings under his watch, one must nonetheless acknowledge the fact that Duterte's objective in establishing boss rule in Davao City, however bizarre it may seem to some, was to transform it into a peaceful, orderly, and prosperous city. During Duterte's term, the city government boasted that Davao's per capita crime rate had been reduced to the nation's lowest—from a monthly crime rate of three digits per 10,000 people in 1985 to just 0.8 cases per 10,000 persons from 1999 up to 2005—and that Davao had become the "most peaceful city in East and Southeast Asia" (Human Rights Watch 2009, 14).[9] No matter the disputable figures, Davao City indeed thrived under Duterte's authoritarian rule. Investors, traders, and tourists—local and foreign—flocked in. Under Duterte, Davao City earned plaudits from various organizations as being among the country's or Asia's most livable, most competitive, cleanest and greenest, most child-friendly, etc., and, ironically enough, even as having the country's best police force. In 2008, Davao even made it to the top ten of the "Asian Cities of the Future" of the *Foreign Direct Investment* magazine published by the *Financial Times* group. The current city government, headed by Duterte's daughter, Sara, now promotes Davao City as being a business-friendly city that has a highly skilled labor force, efficient public utilities, and a competitive cost of doing business.

Outside of his bloody anti-drug and anti-crime campaign, Duterte ran the Davao City government fairly like a well-oiled machine. In the eyes of business people, "the Duterte administration was reasonably efficient administratively and less prone to petty corruption than some other authorities" (Peel 2017). Taking pride in his work, Duterte has made it all seem very easy: "[G]overnance or whatever in public office—it's all about sense and sensibility. That is all that is needed. I am proud that I walk the extra mile to see to it that this city is peaceful" ("Rody's War" 2005).

Thanks to the "war on drugs," boss rule has gone national once again. According to Sidel (2009), the Philippines experienced over thirteen years of national boss rule after President Ferdinand Marcos imposed martial law and, together with his mafia, centralized coercive and economic powers. Kreuzer (2016), in a study on police vigilantism in the Philippines, argues that Duterte has brought back national boss rule within just a few months in office and without having to resort to martial law. He states:

> [The Duterte] administration uses police vigilantism on the national level to simulate a strong state and thereby achieve widespread public acclaim and acquiescence. By establishing the Philippine National Police as his power base,[10] the new president has within a few months successfully hollowed out democratic checks and balances and installed himself as the foremost "boss" at the national level. (Kreuzer 2016, 3)

While DDS vigilantism was instrumental to a large extent in bringing about boss rule in Davao City, the "war on drugs" has played the key role in bringing back national boss rule. The "war on drugs" bears some of the hallmarks of the anti-drug campaign in Davao—motorcycle-riding gunmen, carton signs, Oplan Tokhang, etc.—but it involves a more significant amount of *police* vigilantism. Acknowledging that anonymous vigilantes may well be responsible for most of the "war on drugs" killings, Kreuzer points out that many suspects have been killed by on-duty police officers in purportedly "legitimate encounters" justified as actions carried out in self-defense. He argues:

> [W]hile the Philippines have a strong tradition of death-squad killings, this has been complemented for a long time by a practice of "social cleansing" that did not make it necessary for agents of the state to deny complicity: official police vigilantism . . . [I]n the past such police vigilantism was a local phenomenon. This changed under the new president, who nationalized the local practice and thereby changed its dynamics. (2009, i)

With Duterte's condonation, police impunity in the "war on drugs" has been on the rise. Last November, police officers killed Albuera Mayor Rolando Espinosa, a suspected drug lord, supposedly in a firefight in his detention cell at the Leyte provincial jail. The National Bureau of Investigation recommended multiple murder charges against them, but Duterte stepped in, declaring that he would not allow the cops involved to go to jail. When they were nonetheless charged with murder, Duterte stated that he was ready to grant them absolute pardon. The number of innocent civilians killed in the "war on drugs"—"collateral damage," as Duterte puts it—has also been rising. Hardly any charges have been filed against law enforcers involved for possible negligence or recklessness.

Following the kidnap-slaying of a Korean businessman, Jee Ick-Joo, by corrupt anti-drugs police officers,[11] it seemed at first that Duterte would slow down somewhat in his "war on drugs." In late January 2017, he ordered the PNP to suspend its anti-drug operations and cleanse its ranks of "scalawags," saying that the PNP was "corrupt to the core." Shortly after, however, he called on the Armed Forces of the Philippines (AFP) to take part in the "war on drugs." The military, which has put peace and order at the top of its priorities, agreed to assist the PDEA in running after high-level drug syndicates. Then Duterte reiterated a proposal he made in September 2016 to revive the Philippine Constabulary (PC),[12] this time as a cure not only to the country's drug problem but also to corruption in the PNP. Less than a month after the suspension of PNP's anti-drug operations, Duterte ordered the "corrupt to the core" force to resume the "war on drugs."

Duterte has apparently seized openings provided by the Jee Ick-Joo killing to try to strengthen and even expand his power base. Through his plan to revive the PC, Duterte would once again centralize national police forces under the military. Through the involvement, however limited, of some AFP units in the "war on drugs," Duterte could well establish a bit more of footing in the military.

Like its Davao foregoer, Duterte's national boss rule has developmentalist ambitions. According to Socioeconomic Planning Secretary Ernesto M. Pernia, the Duterte administration, through its Philippine Development Plan for 2017–2022, aims to "lay a solid foundation for inclusive growth, a high-trust society, and a globally-competitive knowledge economy." Unlike the previous Aquino administration, which achieved high economic growth but failed to reduce poverty, the Duterte government avowedly lays stress on reducing poverty and inequality through expanded opportunities in agriculture, increased presence in the global market, quality and accessible basic education for all, and universal social protection. Sustained robust economic growth would make the Philippines an upper-middle income country by 2022, and a high-income country by 2040. In certain aspects, the Duterte government draws upon the Davao development model. In its socio-economic agenda, for instance, it seeks to increase competitiveness and the ease of doing business by learning from "successful models used to attract business to local cities such as Davao."

As a populist boss, Duterte sticks to the basic thin version of populism that is eclectic and unmixed with other ideologies. Although he has claimed to be a socialist and appointed many leftists to the Cabinet and other important posts, the officials he has appointed to craft the economic agenda of his administration are said to be neoliberals who, early on, have avowed to continue the macroeconomic policies, including fiscal, monetary, and trade policies of previous administrations. Duterte has sometimes been labeled a fascist, but his authoritarianism does not—or not yet— exhibit a totalitarian and ultranationalist bent, nor a "survival of the fittest" thinking.

For all its ostensible rationality, Duterte's national development strategy remains anchored on a perverse view of law and order. To Duterte, fighting illegal drugs and other crime is a prerequisite for achieving prosperity. Thus, the bloody "war on drugs" is his top priority and main preoccupation, and he leaves much of the governance to his Cabinet. The "war" contradicts one of the main pillars of the national development plan—*Malasakit*, or Care—which seeks "to regain people's trust in public institutions and cultivate trust among fellow Filipinos." It undermines trust in the judicial and law enforcement institutions. One newspaper reader has pointed out: "You cannot claim to be for *law and order* while at the same time bragging about flaunting [*sic*] the law" (Andrade 2016).

Prospects

Thus far, Duterte has been successful in securitizing drugs through the anti-drug "war" and in bringing back national boss rule. On the basis of his very high satisfaction, approval, and trust ratings, the populist Duterte could very well continue with the deadly "war" and national boss rule until the end of his term and possibly even beyond. Opposition, however, is growing, and it is also very possible that Duterte does not finish his term.

Opposition to Duterte since his inauguration as president has galvanized mainly on the issue of human rights, particularly in connection with the "war on drugs." All throughout his twenty-two years as mayor, Duterte managed to thwart all efforts by human rights groups, church leaders, and political opponents to have him prosecuted for extra-judicial killings in Davao. With Duterte's current popularity, domestic human rights groups would not fare any better on their own. Unlike before, however, international human rights groups have beamed much more attention on Duterte and the "war on drugs" and, working closely with domestic groups, they have been relentless in their denunciations. Moreover, Duterte has repeatedly landed in the top stories of the international media, where he has been described as the "vigilante president" and even "serial killer president." It is possible that Duterte could end up being charged and ordered arrested by the International Criminal Court for crimes against humanity. The testimonies of two self-confessed former DDS hitmen[13] could well prove very damaging to their alleged former boss. Duterte, however, has threatened to withdraw the Philippines' membership in the International Criminal Court (ICC).

Other contingencies could also becloud Duterte's future. A major economic crisis triggered by failed government policies or by extraneous factors could send Duterte's ratings plummeting. All the bad publicity generated by all the killings and violence in the country has reportedly made some foreign investors think twice. A grand corruption scandal implicating Duterte or those around him could conceivably bring him down. Two of his predecessors, Presidents Joseph Estrada and Gloria Macapagal-Arroyo, have in fact spent time in jail on corruption charges. Other possible scenarios for a shortened Duterte tenure include coup d'etat, the deterioration of his health condition, a sharp rise in terrorism or insurgency, or major mishandling of a catastrophic natural disaster.

National boss rule could take an even more authoritarian turn—dictatorship or competitive authoritarianism.[14] Duterte has several times threatened to declare martial law if the drug situation in the country becomes "virulent." Whether or not he imposes martial law, he will have to see to it that after June 2022, he will not be arrested and prosecuted for human rights violations, crimes against humanity, or other crimes. This means that either he stays on, or he makes sure that his successor is of the same mold and backs him.

The Philippines is in for interesting and uncertain times.

Endnotes

[1]   As rightly pointed out by Amnesty International (2017), the Duterte administration's "war on drugs" does not fit the definition of an armed conflict under international law.

2   In this same survey, however, a big majority of Filipinos (78 percent) said they were worried that they or someone they knew would fall victim to extra-judicial killings in the anti-drug campaign.

3   By virtue of the Foreign Relations Authorization Act, the US president determines every year which countries are to be classified as "major illicit drug producing countries" and "major drug transit countries."

4   The highest government figure being linked to the drug trade is Senator Leila de Lima, a former Secretary of Justice, who has been arrested and thrown into prison, charged with three counts of drug trafficking. Human rights groups, opposition politicians, and the European Union, however, have denounced the arrest of de Lima, Duterte's highest-profile critic, contending that the charges against her are trumped up and politically motivated.

5   The PNP has taken over much of the work of the PDEA, which by law is supposed to be the lead anti-drug law enforcement agency.

6   *Tokhang* is a play on the Visayan words *toktok* (to knock) and *hangyo* (to request or plead).

7   Duterte served as mayor of Davao City for twenty-two years from 1988 to 2016, with brief interruptions due to term limits in 1998–2001 and 2010–2013.

8   Several members of the clan now stand trial, accused of having masterminded the Maguindanao massacre of November 2009, in which Ampatuans' private army cold-bloodedly shot and killed fifty-eight people—journalists as well as relatives and supporters of a political opponent.

9   More recent data somewhat belie Duterte's "safest city" claim. PNP statistics show that from 2010 to 2015, Davao City recorded the highest number of murder incidents—1,032 killings—among the top 15 chartered cities of the country.

10   It is interesting to note that Thai Prime Minister Thaksin Shinawatra also mainly mobilized the national police force in waging Thailand's own "war on drugs" in 2003 to stop the flow of methamphetamine pills made in illicit labs along the Thai-Myanmar border. In just three months, more than 2,500 people were killed; many of them were later found to have had nothing to do with drugs. Unlike in Duterte's case, the police already served as Thaksin's power base long before he became the country's leader in 2001. Thaksin was a policeman in 1973–1987, ending his stint in the Thai Royal Police as a lieutenant colonel. (For more about the securitization of drug

trafficking and the "war on drugs" in Thailand, see Emmers 2004.)

[11] In October 2016, Jee Ick-Joo was kidnapped and strangled to death right within the grounds of Camp Crame, the PNP headquarters. Some ransom-seeking police officers, using anti-drug operations as a pretext, are believed to have perpetrated the murder.

[12] From the 1950s to the 1980s, the Philippine Constabulary was one of the four major commands of the AFP. In 1975, the dictator Marcos put together all of the country's local police units and formed the Integrated National Police (INP). He then merged it with the PC, effectively putting it under military command. Five years after Marcos's fall, the PC-INP was replaced by the PNP, which was put under civilian control.

[13] Arturo Lascañas, a retired police officer, and Edgar Matobato, a former militia man, have both testified before the Philippine Senate that they had killed scores of suspected drug pushers and criminals when they were members of the DDS, which they claim was run on Duterte's orders.

[14] "Competitive authoritarian regimes," say Steven Levitsky and Lucan A. Way (2010, 5), "are civilian regimes in which formal democratic institutions exist and are widely viewed as the primary means of gaining power, but in which incumbents' abuse of the state places them at a significant advantage vis-a-vis their opponents. Such regimes are competitive in that opposition parties use democratic institutions to contest seriously for power, but they are not democratic because the playing field is heavily skewed in favor of incumbents. Competition is thus real but unfair."

References

ABS-CBN. 2017. "Map, Charts: The Death Toll of the War on Drugs." http://news.abs-cbn.com/specials/map-charts-the-death-toll-of-the -war-on-drugs.

Alston, Philip. 2008. "Report of the Special Rapporteur on Extrajudicial Summary or Arbitrary Executions, Philip Alston, on His Mission to Philippines (12-21 February 2007)." 16 April. http://www2.ohchr.org/english/bodies/hrcouncil/docs/8session/A.HRC.8.3.Add.2_sp.doc.

Amnesty International. 2017. "'If You are Poor You are Killed': Extrajudicial Executions in the Philippines' 'War on Drugs.'" http://www.amnestyusa.org/sites/default/files/philippines_ejk_report_v19_final_0.pdf.

Andrade, Jeannette. 2016. "Duterte Admits Killing 3 Hostage-takers in Davao City." *Philippine Daily Inquirer*. http://globalnation.inquirer.net/150783/duterte-admits-killing-3-hostage-takers-davao-city.

Baldwin, Clare, and Andrew R. C. Marshall. 2016. "As Death Toll Rises, Duterte Deploys Dubious Data in 'War on Drugs.'" *Reuters*. http://www.reuters.com/investigates/special-report/philippines-duterte-data/.

Berehulak, Daniel. 2016 "They Are Slaughtering Us like Animals." New York Times, 7 December. https://www.nytimes.com/interactive/2016/12/07/world/asia/rodrigo-duterte-philippines-drugs-killings.html.

Breuil, B. and R. Rozema. 2009. "Fatal Imaginations: Death Squads in Davao City and Medellin Compared." *Crime, Law and Social Change* 52, no. 4: 405–24.

Buzan, Brenda, Ole Wæver, and Jaap de Wilde. 1998. *Security: A New Framework for Analysis*. Boulder, CO: Lynne Ruenner.

Caballero-Anthony, Mely, and Ralf Emmers. 2006. "Understanding the Dynamics of Securitizing Non-Traditional Security." In *Non-Traditional Security in Asia: Dilemmas in Securitization*, edited by M. Caballero-Anthony, R. Emmers, and A. Acharya, 1–12. Farnham, UK: Ashgate.

Diola, Camille. 2016. "How Duterte's Drug War Can Fail." *Philippine Star*, 19 September. http://newslab.philstar.com/war-on-drugs/policy.

Emmers, Ralf. 2014. "Securitisation of *Drug* Trafficking: A Study of Thailand." In *Non-Traditional Security in the Asia Pacific: The Dynamics of Securitization*, 9–34. Singapore: Eastern Universities Press.

Emmers, Ralf. 2016. "Securitization." In Allan Collins, *Contemporary Security Studies*, edited by A. Collins, 168–81. Oxford: Oxford University Press.

Estremera, Stella. 2005. "Murder Mainstreamed." *Sunstar Davao*. http://www.mapinc.org/drugnews/v05/n819/a05.html.

Human Rights Watch. 2009. "'You Can Die Any Time': Death Squad Killings in Mindanao." https://www.hrw.org/report/2009/04/06/you-can-die-any-time/death-squad-killings-mindanao.

Jordan, David. 1999. *Drug Politics: Dirty Money and Democracies*. Norman, OK: University of Oklahoma Press.

Kan, Paul. 2016. *Drug Trafficking and International Security*. Lanham: Rowman & Littlefield.

Kreuzer, Peter. 2009. "Private Political Violence and Boss-Rule in the

Philippines." *Behemoth. A Journal on Civilisation* 2, no. 1:47–63. https://ojs.ub.uni-freiburg.de/behemoth/article/view/721.

———. 2016. "'If They Resist, Kill Them All': Police Vigilantism in the Philippines." PRIF Report no. 142, Peace Research Institute Frankfurt. https://www.hsfk.de/fileadmin/HSFK/hsfk_publikationen/prif142.pdf.

Levitsky, Steven, and Lucan Way. 2010. *Competitive Authoritarianism: Hybrid Regimes After the Cold War.* Cambridge: Cambridge University Press.

Loewenstein, Antony. 2016. "How Not to Fix an African Narco-State." *Foreign Policy.* http://foreignpolicy.com/2016/01/06/how-not-to-deal-with-an-african-narco-state-guinea-bissau/.

Malakunas, Karl. 2016. "Philippines' Duterte a Controversial Anti-Establishment Firebrand." *Agence France-Press.* https://www.yahoo.com/news/philippines-duterte-controversial-anti-establishment-firebrand-044956476.html.

Marks, Kathy. 2004. "The Man They Call Dirty Harry." *The Independent.* http://www.independent.co.uk/news/world/asia/the-man-they-call-dirty-harry-563714.html.

Mendoza, Gemma. 2012. "85 Armed Groups Maintained by Politicians–PNP." *Rappler.* http://www.rappler.com/nation/politics/elections -2013/features/16706-85-armed-groups-maintained-by-politicians-pnp.

Mogato, Manuel. 2016. "Philippine Hitman Says He Heard Duterte Order Killings." *Reuters*, 15 September. http://www.reuters.com/article/us-philippines-drugs-duterte-idUSKCN11L16K.

Mudde, Cas. "The Popular Zeitgeist." *Government and Opposition* 39, no. 4:541–63.

Office of the President. 2015. "Memorandum Circular No. 83, s. 2015." http://www.gov.ph/2015/09/08/memorandum-circular-no-83-s-2015/.

O'Regan, D. 2012. "Narco-States: Africa's Next Menace." *New York Times.* http://www.nytimes.com/2012/03/13/opinion/narco-states-africas-next-menace.html.

Paoli, L., I. Rabkov, V. Greenfield, and P. Reuter. 2007. "Tajikistan: The Rise of a Narco-State." *Journal of Drug Issues* 37, no. 4: 951–79.

Peel, M. 2017. "Drugs and Death in Davao: The Making of Rodrigo Duterte." *Financial Times.* https://www.ft.com/content/9d6225dc-e805-11e6-967b-c88452263daf.

"Dirty Rudy." 2012. *Philippine Daily Inquirer, sec.* Editorial. http://opinion.inquirer.net/39666/dirty-rudy#ixzz4avgKEJ7E.

Ranada, Pia. 2016. "Duterte offers P2-M bounty for cops into drug trade."

Rappler. http://www.rappler.com/nation/144504-philippines-president-duterte-offers-two-million-bounty-police-drug-trade.

"Revisiting the World's Most Violent Cities." 2016. *The Economist.* http://www.economist.com/blogs/graphicdetail/2016/03/daily-chart-18.

"Rody's War." 2005. *Davao Today.* http://davaotoday.com/main/politics/rody%E2%80%99s-war/.

Ross, James. 2016. "Duterte and the Ghosts of Plaza Miranda." *Philippine Daily Inquirer.* http://opinion.inquirer.net/97155/duterte-ghosts-plaza-miranda#ixzz4amtfMo6p.

Scott, James. 1972. "Patron-Client Politics and Political Change in Southeast Asia." *American Political Science Review* 66, no. 1:91–113.

Sidel, John. 1999. *Capital Coercion and Crime: Bossism in the Philippines.* Stanford: Stanford University Press.

Sipress, Alan. 2003. "In Philippine City, Public Safety Has a Dark Side." *Washington Post.* https://www.washingtonpost.com/archive/politics/2003/11/27/in-philippine-city-public-safety-has-a-dark-side/b5886fff-8876-42fd-a029-a9b6c329b97e/?utm_term=.2ce72b27oaee.

Taub, Amanda. 2016. "How Countries Like the Philippines Fall into Vigilante Violence." *New York Times.* https://www.nytimes.com/2016/09/12/world/asia/the-philippines-rodrigo-duterte-vigilante-violence.html?_r=o.

World Organisation against Torture (OMCT), Preda Foundation, Task Force Detainees of the Philippines (TFDP) and Women's Education, Development, Productivity and Research Organisation (WEDPRO). 2003. "State Violence in the Philippines: An Alternative Report to the United Nations Human Rights Committee." Geneva. http://www.omct.org/files/2003/09/2437/stateviolence_philippines_03_eng.pdf.

Murder as Enterprise

Police Profiteering in Duterte's War on Drugs

Sheila S. Coronel

On 18 October 2016, a team from an elite police unit set out for Angeles City, an hour's drive from Manila. Their mission: Get Jee Ick-Joo, a South Korean businessman who was supposedly a drug dealer. They succeeded with brutal proficiency, suffocating and garroting him in the heart of the police headquarters in the country's capital.

In two Senate hearings aired live on Philippine television in January and February 2017, several police officers matter-of-factly recounted the details of that operation carried out by members of the Anti-Illegal Drugs Group. It began with the drive to Angeles City on that Tuesday morning. By late evening, Jee was dead. His murder, they said, took place at around 10 PM, at the back of a vehicle parked inside Camp Crame, the headquarters of the Philippine National Police (PNP). When asked, a sergeant who was in the team explained how the businessman was killed: A plastic bag was pulled over his head, which was then wrapped in packing tape. As Jee struggled to breathe, a policeman tied a piece of cord around the victim's neck and put the ends of the cord inside a metal device that functioned like a wheel lock. It didn't take very long, the sergeant who was there said, just one or two turns to tighten the device, before Jee expired.[1] "*Parang ginarote*," he said, referring to the garrote, an iron collar used to strangle condemned prisoners in the Philippines during the Spanish colonial era.

The policemen also recounted what happened next: the disposal of the body, the ransom the killers demanded from the family even though Jee was already dead, the botched attempt to cover up the crime. Their accounts—raw and chilling as much because of the gruesome details as for their plain, unemotional telling—provided a rare view of the planning and execution of a police killing. The policemen spoke of a place largely off limits to outsiders: the underground economy of extortion, theft, abduction, and murder in which the police are both enforcers of the law and its worst offenders. It's a place where the line between perpetrators and investigators is murky at best, and frequently crossed.

This article explores that inaccessible and uncharted terrain: the No Man's Land where policing and criminality become indistinguishable, and where the border that separates cop from criminal is constantly breached—sometimes in the pursuit of what the police believe is justice, and often in the pursuit of profit. President Rodrigo Duterte tapped into this grey zone when he unleashed his war on drugs. Using previously published research and information from interviews, court records, testimonies, oral histories, human rights reports, and journalistic accounts, this is an attempt to map that zone.

Police criminality is a long-standing problem in the Philippines. *Policing America's Empire*, US historian Alfred W. McCoy's sweeping history of Philippine policing, documents how corruption and excessive violence have been embedded in the police's DNA for more than a century and have caused recurring crises of political legitimacy. Since independence, McCoy wrote, both presidents and local strongmen have used the coercive and surveillance capabilities of the police to consolidate power, crack down on crime and dissent, emasculate political rivals, or in some cases, collect for themselves revenues from illegal gambling and other illicit activities. The police, according to McCoy, have provided the muscle and gathered the intelligence that presidents needed to exercise both legal and extralegal power (McCoy 2009, 47–56, 474–87, 506–20).

Duterte is not the first president of the republic to wield the police as a blunt instrument. His bloody purge of drug offenders was possible only because the PNP was a ready, willing, and able killing machine. A template for police killings already existed. For decades, policemen as well as vigilantes, death squads, and contract killers linked to the police have murdered criminals, journalists, lawyers, and activists.[2] It's therefore not surprising that the modes of killing employed in the anti-drug campaign—shooting by hooded gunmen riding on motorcycles or strangulation by cords or wires—are reminiscent of executions past.

Duterte himself has been accused by human rights groups and former death squad members of ordering and funding extra-judicial executions during his 22-year reign as Davao City mayor. In a sworn statement, one of his accusers, a Davao city police officer named Arturo Lascañas, provided vivid details of the murders and the burial of the victims' corpses in a quarry near the city.[3] What makes the current drug war stand out, therefore, is not the brutality of the killings but their sheer number:[4] Not in recent memory have so many members of a targeted group been killed in so short a span of time.

For the most part, academics and reformers have focused on the Philippine police as an institution crying out for reform or as a tool of local bosses and national political elites. They have not delved into the motivations and mindsets of the policemen themselves. Scant attention has been paid to the agency of individual officers. Yet Lascañas's betrayal of Duterte shows police officers can exercise autonomy. They are not merely docile tools of political bosses. Far from being passive followers, they have minds of their own. They are entrepreneurs on the hunt for moneymaking and career-advancing opportunities, or if Lascañas is to be believed, a chance to atone for past sins. Policing, therefore, is a contingent enterprise, determined as much by the police's mandate to control crime as by the calculations of individual officers as to how they and their men can profit from crime control and protection.

Duterte's anti-crime campaign opened to the police fresh

opportunities for extortion and other forms of moneymaking. Then as now, policemen weigh the continually shifting balance of incentives and risks as they seek to deter crime, advance their careers, please their political patrons, and make money while also evading exposure and prosecution. Yet in the end, these policemen often also believe they are upholding order and helping keep the peace. They are specialists in violence—practitioners in the skills of lethal force—who improvise often morally and legally questionable workarounds to the constraints of a broken justice system.

Laying the Ground for the War on Drugs

Duterte won on the promise that he would be tough on illegal drugs. He said he would wipe out drug-related crime in six months. "It's going to be bloody," he told wildly cheering crowds during the campaign. "The funeral parlors will be packed."[5] The spike in drug killings began right after the presidential election on 9 May 2016, and it was no doubt stoked by Duterte's incendiary language. By June, even before Duterte had been sworn in, an average of one person a day was being killed by either the police or unidentified assailants.[6]

Duterte's choice for PNP chief was Roland "Bato" Dela Rosa, a burly, plainspoken police officer whose first posting was Davao City in the late 1980s, when Duterte was still acting vice mayor. As Davao police chief, Dela Rosa perfected the policing technique known as *tokhang* where policemen visited the homes of *shabu* (crystal meth) addicts and street-level dealers, "pleaded" with them to surrender, and kept them under close surveillance.[7] Duterte stood as godfather at Dela Rosa's wedding, and the two men became so close that their level of understanding, Dela Rosa told an interviewer, was almost telepathic (Cupin 2016).

A graduate of the Philippine Military Academy class of 1986, Dela Rosa bypassed more senior officers when he was appointed PNP chief. He named fourteen members of his class—the first to graduate from the academy after the fall of Ferdinand Marcos—to head offices in charge of important PNP functions, including police operations, comptrollership, logistics, intelligence, and community relations. They were also put in charge of elite police units, including the Criminal Investigation and Detection Group, and of key regions, including metropolitan Manila (Dalizon 2016).

Preparations for the drug war began even before Duterte and Dela Rosa had formally assumed office. As Director Oscar David Albayalde, Dela Rosa's classmate who was named police chief of Metro Manila, said:

> We had this idea already that we'll be focusing on illegal drugs so we consolidated, integrated all our information on illegal drugs so that once we assume office, then we can start the war on drugs . . . . We have this watch list on drugs, we have all this information and our informants. We activated all our *barangay*[8] intelligence networks . . . they're the ones who actually know who are the suspected users and pushers in their *barangays*."[9]

On 1 July, Duterte's first day in office, Dela Rosa issued a circular laying out the framework for the anti-drug campaign: "Project Double Barrel" was modeled after Davao City's policing strategy. It had two prongs: one targeting big-time drug syndicates, and Project Tokhang. The circular directed "all police offices/units/stations" to "conduct massive and simultaneous operations" starting that very day.[10] Duterte reinforced that message when he addressed the police the same day and told them, "Do your duty. And if in the process you kill one thousand persons because you were doing your duty, I will protect you" (de Jesus 2016).

The police did as they were bidden. The 160,000-strong PNP mobilized nearly all its resources on the drug campaign. Unlike in the past, said Joel Napoleon Coronel, chief of the Manila Police District, "this time, we're aggressive, we go after the drug traffickers because of the directive of the Chief PNP and also because of the assessment by headquarters that these drug traffickers, pushers, are also the ones engaged in street crimes." This aggressive stance meant that controls were loosened. "We don't need to seek pre-operational clearance and approval from higher headquarters," said Coronel.[11] In the past, all drug operations needed to be approved by the Philippine Drug Enforcement Agency, the lead anti-drug body. That was also no longer the case.[12] (The new PDEA chief, Isidro

Lapeña, was a retired police general who had also served as Davao City police chief [Ocampo 2016].)

Down the line, station commanders no longer needed the district chief's nod to go after drug offenders. In fact, the circular put police station commanders in charge of "eradicating street-level distribution." In practice, this meant raiding drug dens, arresting suspected shabu users and dealers, or organizing drug busts. Station commanders, said Coronel, "are **required** to conduct drug operations and go after [those on] the watch list." In the Manila Police District, he said, 82,000 drug suspects were on the list. By the end of 2016, 42,000 of them had surrendered, 3,000 had been arrested, and 344 had been killed in police operations.

Had routine procedures been followed, the pace of anti-drug operations would have been considerably slowed. Moreover, Dela Rosa's circular instructed the police to submit reports on the anti-drug campaign every week,[13] putting pressure on commanders to show weekly progress. By the end of 2016, the police claimed that over one million had surrendered to the authorities and the crime rate was down to 32 percent ("Drug war surrenderers" 2017). Tens of thousands were crammed into already-packed jails. By December 2016, the body count was over 6,000 (Manesca 2017). In the six months before the drug war, drug-related deaths totaled only sixty-eight.[14]

"Legitimate" police actions accounted for about a third of the casualties. The death rate in these operations was unusually high. Reuters reported a 97 percent kill ratio in the fifty-one drug-related police shootings it examined, indicating, it said, that drug suspects were being summarily gunned down (Baldwin, Marshall, and Sagoli 2016). Three high-ranking police officers interviewed for this report explained that the police all over the country were instructed to conduct anti-drug operations, and in police operations, people die because suspects resist arrest or fight back in armed encounters and have to be "neutralized."[15]

The PNP attributed the rest of the killings—almost 4,000 of them—to gang rivalries, vigilantes, and rogue or "ninja" policemen coddling or extorting from drug dealers.[16] Human rights groups, however, saw the police's hand in these so-called death squad or vigilante killings. Both police and vigilante slayings, said Human

Rights Watch, used the same modus operandi: Suspected drug offenders were warned by the police or barangay officials that they were on the watch list. Before long, hooded or masked men working in groups of two, four, or a dozen barged into their houses without warrants and gunned them down. Often, uniformed policemen were nearby, securing the crime scene, and special crime scene investigators arrived within minutes of the kill.[17]

Incentives for Killing

Duterte was popular among the police who shared his passion for rooting out crime and his show-no-mercy attitude toward drugs. Morale was high in the force. "Previously, policemen get relieved if they arrest or neutralize a drug pusher who is well connected," said Albayalde. "Now it's a different thing. Our policemen are highly motivated because of the support coming from the president . . . We have full support—financial, legal." During the election campaign, Duterte dangled cash awards for policemen and promised, "P50,000 will be the bounty for a small-time drug pusher, P1 million for a 'supervisor' or a 'manager' drug pusher, and P3 million for big-time drug lord." He upped the numbers a few days later—P5 million for every drug lord killed and P3 million for a dead drug distributor (Corrales 2016). (In the second half of 2016, the peso exchange rate fluctuated between PhP 46 and PhP 49 to one US dollar.)

Once elected, Duterte set aside the entire presidential intelligence fund to fight the drug war and requested that PhP 2.5 billion be allocated to the presidential intelligence and confidential funds for 2017. Not subject to government audit, these funds were to be used for surveillance and intelligence gathering in support of the anti-drug drive (Herrera and Bencito 2016). Rewards were distributed all the way up and down the police hierarchy. Some of these were openly awarded, others given out in secret. The Dangerous Drugs Board offered sizable rewards to policemen for the seizure of illegal drugs, to be funded from the presidential intelligence fund (Mangahas and Ilagan 2016). In December 2016, the PNP chief promised bonuses of PhP 100,000–PhP 400,000 to star-rank police officers, but rescinded the offer after questions from the press and the public (Adel 2016).

Profiting from the drug war

Types of Police Activity	Typical Amounts
Extortion from drug suspects before or during arrests or while under detention.	PhP 5,000–15,000 from poor victims to as much as PhP 1 million from rich victims
Theft of victims' belongings during arrests, or during entrapment operations where drug suspects are killed	This can include cash or property worth hundreds of thousands of pesos as in the Jee Ick-Joo case; may include small amounts of cash, cellphones, jewelry, and other belongings of poor victims
Ransom demands after the abduction of so-called drug suspects, known as "tokhang for ransom"	Amounts can range from a few hundred thousand pesos to P5 million as in the Jee case
Fees or rewards paid to policemen for every person killed	PhP 5,000–20,000 for small-time drug offenders
Bonuses for police officers paid for by civilian officials	Hundreds of thousand pesos
Commissions from funeral parlors	Up to PhP 10,000 for every dead body referred

Source: Compiled by the author from interviews, news articles, and human rights reports

At the police precinct or station level, policemen were sometimes paid to kill, according to human rights and press reports. A police officer who was part of an anti-illegal drugs unit in Metro Manila described to Amnesty International "significant under-the-table payments for 'encounters'" where suspects were killed (Amnesty International 2017). The officer said members of his unit were paid PhP 8,000–15,000 for every "encounter" that resulted in the death of a drug dealer. The more notorious the drug offender, the bigger the reward. These were secret payments:

The PNP incentive isn't announced. . . . We're paid in cash, secretly, by headquarters. The payment is [split by] the unit. . . . There's no incentive for arresting. We're not paid anything. (Amnesty International 2017, 30)

The PNP denied the payments, saying the police did not have the money to fund killings, but Amnesty International said that some confidential police investigation reports it obtained referred to officers being given "appropriate rewards" for gunning down drug offenders. Some local officials provided additional bonuses. In Cebu City, Mayor Tomas Osmeña promised to reward the police PhP 50,000 for every drug lord or criminal they killed (Cuizon 2016).

There is evidence to show that the police outsourced the killings to hired guns, a practice that the police have resorted to in the past, including in Davao City, where the police were alleged to have paid slum dwellers, former communist guerrillas, and paramilitary members to kill criminals (Human Rights Watch 2009). A female contract killer interviewed by the BBC in August 2016 said that she and her team of three or four were paid PhP 20,000 for every person they killed at the behest of their boss, a police officer. She said she had killed five people, including a drug dealer who owed her police-man-boss money (Head 2017).

Two contract assassins told Amnesty International they averaged three to four killings a week:

The male paid killer said further, "When we're given an order, there's an envelope. It has the person's name, a picture, the address, what the person likes to do. It's almost a complete profile. . . . Someone else has already been assigned to do surveillance." They then watch the target and "wait for the right moment," before typically carrying out a "riding in tandem" hit and run.

When the police handler gives them an envelope with the job, payment is provided up front. "All our envelopes now give a drug link," the female paid killer told Amnesty International. "The rate depends. For a user, it's P5,000. For a pusher, P10,000 to 15,000. It depends by the person. Usually we don't have multiple targets per project, but [when we do], we're paid per head." If they work in pairs, they split the payment. (Amnesty International 2017, 37)

The Drug War as Business

The anti-drug campaign provides other opportunities for making profits at various links of the policing chain, including during arrests, while suspects are in detention, and during drug busts. The police can also get financial rewards even after suspected drug offenders have been killed. These profits are strictly off the books, generated by entrepreneurial policemen who use the drug war as a cover for their own rackets.

For example, on 30 December 2016, seven policemen barged into the home of three South Koreans in a gated community in Angeles City, and robbed them of computers, cash, golf clubs, and jewelry. Then they took the victims to the police station, put them in the firing range, and fired guns in their direction to scare them (Malig 2017). The men were accused of using drugs and kept in the station for eight hours until a friend paid the police PhP 300,000 for their freedom.

"I suspect there are many [such incidents] but most of the crimes committed against the South Koreans are not being reported," Chief Supt. Aaron Aquino, the regional police chief told journalists. "They are all afraid" ("Three Korean Golfers" 2017). Aquino relieved the police chief of Angeles City after this incident; forty-four policemen in the city's Station 5, which had become notorious for robberies and extortion of Korean businessmen, were also relieved ("44 Angeles City Cops" 2017).

In a Senate hearing in January 2017, a member of the Chinese-Filipino community revealed that there were at least eleven "tokhang for ransom" incidents involving their community, alleging that the police were setting up ethnic Chinese businessmen in Manila on false charges of drug dealing or possession so they could extort money from them. Teresita Ang-See of the Movement for Restoration of Peace and Order (MRPO) said that in all these cases, the victims paid policemen so they would not be charged even if they were innocent.

One extortion technique they used, she said, was to get search warrants and demand "ransom" from victims so their premises would not be searched. She said that in one case in November

2016, a Chinese national paid P1 million to the police. The victims, however, were afraid to prosecute. In one incident, she said, a store owner was charged with selling counterfeit goods. "When the victim proved his goods were not fake, the policemen just confiscated them and threatened to file charges of possession of illegal drugs against him, saying his store was just a front for peddling illegal drugs," Ang-See said (Felipe 2017).

Police have also extorted significant amounts from less affluent individuals detained on drug charges. In April 2017, a team from the Commission on Human Rights discovered a secret jail cell hidden behind a bookshelf at a police station in Tondo, Manila, and found twelve drug suspects who said they were being kept there until they raised money—anywhere between PhP 40,000 and PhP 200,000—for their release. The cell was dark and it had no toilet; on occasion, the police beat up the detainees with wooden paddles (See 2017).

Heart de Chavez, a small-time shabu seller, was picked up for questioning in Navotas, in the northern part of Metro Manila, on 7 January 2017. The police demanded P50,000 for her release, but her mother Elena could raise only P7,000 from pawning her pension. Elena de Chavez said she gave the cash to the policemen, who pocketed the money for themselves. Heart was released to her custody, but on the night of 10 January 2017, armed and hooded men barged into the de Chavez home, took Heart away, and then shot and killed her in a nearby house. Uniformed police and scene-of-the-crime investigators arrived just minutes later (Evagelista 2017).

Harra Kazuo's husband, Jaypee Bertes, was taken from his home by policemen in Pasay City, in Manila's Southern Police District, in the first week of Duterte's presidency. The policemen did not have an arrest warrant. They didn't have a search warrant either when they ransacked the couple's home, looking for drugs, which they did not find. Bertes was detained in the local police station, so his father, Renato, followed him there. The next day, both father and son were killed right in the police station, allegedly because they tried to grab an officer's gun. Bertes had been on the police watch list for dealing in illegal drugs. He was arrested in 2015 for illegal gambling and drug dealing. Kazuo said that at that time, she paid the police PhP 30,000 so they would release him.[18]

In a report released in February 2017, Amnesty International reported similar cases of extortion, theft, and homicide:

> A largely bedridden grandmother in Metro Manila watched as police officers stormed into the family's house and killed her grandson, who was on the "drug watch list." They proceeded to search the house. "There was a lot of money placed here," she said several months later, pointing to a particular bench. "The police pocketed the money."
>
> A 30-year-old woman whose husband was killed by police in August 2016 during a home raid similarly [said] that, "not only did they kill [my husband], they also robbed us." She works as a saleswoman on commission, and said the police stole 8,000 pesos worth of goods, 3,600 pesos she was to remit to her employer, 3,600 pesos she had set aside to pay the electric company, and "a pair of shoes we had given my child for her birthday." When she saw her husband's body at the morgue, she said she realized his wedding ring and necklace were also missing. (Amnesty International 2017, 3)

After the killings, policemen made money from the commissions they got for referring drug war victims to funeral parlors. Such commissions are a longstanding practice predating the drug war. "These policemen are naughty," Duterte joked during his election campaign. "It's true they have a contract. They call the funeral home: 'There's a body here. Claim it here. . . . I'll just drop by for the commission tomorrow'" (Macaraig 2016).

According to Amnesty International:

> The police officer with a Metro Manila anti-illegal drugs unit [said] that there is a racket between the police and some funeral homes, which drives up prices. "The police get a cut from funeral homes for every body they bring," he said. "Sometimes P10,000. . . . Sometimes if I'm the investigator, I'll bring the body to the biggest and most expensive [funeral home], because they give the biggest cuts." (43)

Murder as Enterprise: The Jee Case

Duterte's drug war, therefore, intersected with—and was bolstered by—already existing forms of routine police corruption. It also provided openings ripe for exploitation by the more ambitious racketeers within the ranks of the force. The murder of South Korean businessman Jee Ick-Joo was one such example. It so infuriated Duterte that he summoned his security chiefs on a Sunday night and said he was suspending the anti-drug campaign and abolishing the PNP's elite Anti-Illegal Drugs Group or AIDG (Lema and Petty 2017). The suspension, however, lasted only a month. Duterte ordered the police back because PDEA, the lead anti-drug agency, did not have the staff to curb street-level dealing, which was supposedly on the rise. The defunct AIDG was reorganized as the Drug Enforcement Group with a new man at the helm ("PNP Activates Drug Enforcement Group" 2017). By March 2017, the police and hooded assailants were again gunning down drug offenders, albeit at a somewhat slower pace than in the first six months of Duterte's presidency (Mendez 2017).

Jee's murder was a freelance operation by a group of rogue police and civilian officials. It showed that the PNP was not entirely under Duterte's control and that individual policemen were using the president's exhortation to go out and kill in order to advance their own rackets rather than fight the war on drugs. A key figure in the case was SPO3 Sta.Isabel, a 44-year-old sergeant assigned to the AIDG. Sta. Isabel had been a policeman for twenty years, and got good breaks in part because of his connections.[19] His *padrino* (patron) was Deputy Director General Marcelo Garbo, who headed the PNP Directorate for Intelligence, the highest intelligence-gathering unit of the police, and who recommended Sta. Isabel for a job in his unit.[20] Now retired, Garbo was one of five generals accused by Duterte of involvement in the drug trade (Ranada 2016).

Sta. Isabel himself was accused in 2007 of complicity in the kidnap-for-ransom of an ethnic Chinese businesswoman, but the charges were dropped. Despite his low rank—the monthly base pay of a police sergeant is in the PhP 25,000-range—he was fairly wealthy. In 2015, he declared some PhP 17 million worth of assets, including five houses and a four-story commercial building. He and his wife also run several businesses, including lotto and Western Union franchises.

Sta. Isabel's appointment to the AIDG was for that of chief clerk,[21] a position that would not have given him the power to plan a police operation. But on 4 October 2016, he put together a surveillance team from the AIDG and the National Bureau of Investigation (NBI) to monitor Jee. Two team members later told investigators that Sta. Isabel recruited them to be part of an operation targeting a "big drug lord" in Angeles City (National Bureau of Investigation 2017, 2). SPO4 Roy Villegas, a cameraman assigned to the AIDG's Technical Support Unit, recalled that Sta. Isabel showed him an arrest warrant for the drug lord. He said that Sta. Isabel was getting instructions from Supt. Rafael Dumlao, a colonel who headed the AIDG's Special Interdiction Unit 2. Villegas also claimed that Dumlao himself instructed him to join the operation. Dumlao, however, has denied authorizing any such operation. He said the arrest warrant was fake, and blamed two NBI officials for masterminding the murder with Sta. Isabel's complicity.

On 18 October 2016, Sta. Isabel and his team headed to Angeles City, trailing Jee from his office to his home. They grabbed Jee as he was preparing to return to his office after lunch at home and shoved him into the back seat of his black Ford Explorer SUV. They kept him there while Sta. Isabel went inside the house supposedly to search for drugs. A subsequent investigation showed he stole PhP 300,000 worth of jewelry and PhP 250,000 in cash (National Bureau of Investigation 2017, 6).

The policemen drove back to Manila with Jee, who was sitting blindfolded and handcuffed inside the SUV. They went to Camp Crame and waited for hours in various parking lots for further instructions. At around 10 PM, Sta. Isabel knocked on the side of the vehicle and handed the police team a plastic bag containing surgical gloves and packing tape and ordered the men to put on the gloves. "I was starting to have doubts, sir, I was becoming afraid," Villegas told the senators in a public hearing on the case. "Even the driver [of the vehicle] who was seated next to me was also getting nervous. But we wore the gloves, sir, hoping that this would just be a TI [tactical interrogation]."[22]

At that point, Jerry Omlang, a "striker" or civilian agent who was also part of the team, entered the vehicle. Omlang was the one who wrapped the businessman's head in packing tape, said Villegas,[23] but it was Sta. Isabel who tightened a cord around the victim's neck and killed him. Both Omlang and Sta. Isabel denied this account and said they were not in the vehicle when Jee was killed. Omlang said that he went with the other policeman to withdraw money from Jee's account, using the businessman's ATM card. Jee's wife later reported to the police that four withdrawals of PhP 20,000 each were made on her husband's card that night.

At around midnight, Sta. Isabel brought Jee's body to Gream Funeral Services in Caloocan City, a business owned by Gerardo Santiago, a former policeman and a barangay captain who had worked with Sta. Isabel in the past.[24] Santiago agreed to clean up the body for PhP 30,000, which Sta. Isabel paid. The body was given a false name and address and Gream employees sent it to a nearby crematorium the next day. Gream staff kept the ashes in the funeral home until mid-January, when the story of the killing broke in the press, and the frantic owner told them to dispose of the remains. The panicked staff flushed Jee's ashes in the toilet.[25]

Sta. Isabel said he disposed of the body on the orders of two police colonels, Dumlao from the AIDG and the other from the PNP Anti-Kidnapping Group. Dumlao, however, said this was entirely Sta. Isabel's operation. Sta. Isabel, for his part, believes that he is being used as a fall guy for the killing to shield the two officers, who were the masterminds of the murder.

Less than two weeks later, on 30 October, Jee's wife got ransom demands by text message and dropped off P5 million at a parking lot near a mall in Angeles City, not knowing her husband was already dead. A second demand for P3 million more was made but she refused to pay unless the abductors provided proof of life. She found out her husband was dead only later, after police investigators questioned the officers and civilians involved. The acting head of the Anti-Kidnapping Group, Supt. Glenn Dumlao (not related to

Rafael Dumlao of the AIDG), was one of those who interrogated Jee's abductors. His theory of the case, one shared by the top brass of the PNP, is this: Jee was killed because he refused to pay protection money to the police preying on the many South Korean businesses that had set up shop near the former US–run Clark Air Force base, now a bustling industrial park, in Angeles City. Jee also dissuaded his friends from succumbing to extortion demands.[26]

Whoever was ultimately responsible for killing Jee, the South Korean's strangulation right in the heart of the PNP headquarters showed how deeply embedded criminality is in the police, making it difficult to distinguish legitimate police operations from extra-judicial killings, policing from profiteering. The abductors were policemen and a civilian asset. Police resources and police personnel were used to conduct surveillance of the victim. And policemen also covered up the crime.

Blurring the Lines: Police as Criminals

In the aftermath of the Jee case, an angry Duterte said that about 40 percent of the police were using their power to commit crime and ordered his police chief to rid the PNP of "scalawags" (Andolong 2017). The irony, of course, is that if the manual of police operational procedures were followed strictly, then Duterte's incitements to kill would have been exhortations without action. The binary view of the police—that there is a clear line that separates scalawags in uniform from all the rest—does not conform to the facts on the ground. The police almost always operate in a grey zone, where rules and procedures are honored mostly in the breach. In the end, government—and society—have no choice but to rely on a police force of rogues and scalawags to uphold order and keep the peace.

One of the most telling examples of this is in the credentials of the people who exposed the murder of Jee. Glenn Dumlao was the police colonel who cracked the case. In 1995, he was one of the accused in the summary execution of eleven suspected members of the Kuratong Baleleng, a kidnap gang that had its origins in Mindanao. The charges were eventually dismissed for various reasons, including that four of the five witnesses retracted their testimonies after visits from the accused (McCoy 2009, 464–65). Dumlao was then a police captain assigned to the Presidential Anti-Crime Commission headed by Chief Supt. Panfilo Lacson, who was also charged for the killings. Lacson was elected senator in 2001 and is now on his third Senate term. As chair of the Committee on Public Order and Safety, he led the inquiry on the Jee murder case, asking pointed questions of the police and telling them to clean up their act.

In 2000, Dumlao and Lacson were implicated in another murder, that of Salvador "Bubby" Dacer, a well-connected publicist who was believed to have evidence that then President Joseph Estrada made illegal profits from insider trading. Lacson was Estrada's police chief at that time. According to court records, three police officers, including Dumlao, abducted Dacer and his driver, brought them to Cavite, and interrogated them there. Witnesses said that Dacer and his driver were later strangled with an electric cord and their bodies burned (McCoy 2009, 503). Dumlao was charged, and he implicated both Lacson and Estrada in the murder. He escaped from police detention in 2003, then fled to the United States. He was extradited in 2009.[27] Lacson was indicted the next year and went into hiding, saying President Gloria Macapagal-Arroyo was persecuting him for exposing her husband's corruption. Dumlao, meanwhile became state witness against Lacson, and was dropped from the charge sheet. But during the trial, Dumlao withdrew his earlier testimony, saying he was pressured to implicate Lacson in the murder ("In the Know" 2013).

In 2011, the Court of Appeals dismissed the charges against Lacson. Dumlao was reinstated in the PNP in 2012, and in 2013 he was back in the news, this time as director of the Regional Public Safety Battalion for southern Luzon. Investigators alleged that he had authorized a "rubout" of thirteen people at a police checkpoint in Quezon province. Twenty-five policemen and soldiers were charged, but not Dumlao (Sauler 2013).

The reality is that illegal behavior is embedded in the way the police operate. The police routinely violate procedures and just as routinely get away with it. In their pursuit of criminals, policemen resort to criminal methods, justifying this as the only way they can realistically curb criminality in the face of a dysfunctional justice system. In 1988, Edmundo R. Fernandez surveyed fifty-seven randomly selected police investigators from eight police stations in what was then the Metropolitan Police Force. Forty of the fifty-seven admitted to using "third-degree methods" on hardened criminals. These included "water therapy" ("submerging the head of the suspect under water or putting a cloth over the face of the suspect and slowly administering water over the covered face to prevent the suspect from breathing"), electric shock, and what the police called the whipping board, i.e., repeatedly beating a suspect with truncheons (Fernandez 1988, 74–76).

An unspecified number of the respondents in the survey also admitted to summarily executing criminals, communists, and killers of law enforcers. The methods used in these executions included strangulation, stabbing, or staged shoot-outs. "Some of the respondents were of the idea that this summary execution is a substitute for capital punishment," the study said. Policemen justified the killings as the only way to get incorrigible criminals or suspects who have connections that would allow them to escape punishment (Fernandez 1988, 76–77). Yet most these police officers also saw themselves as doing good. They described their role as that of "fact finder," "discoverer of truth," and "instrument of justice" (Fernandez 1988, 85).

In 1995, the Philippine Center for Investigative Journalism sent a photographer and reporter to spend six months at the downtown Manila headquarters of the Western Police District (now the Manila Police District), the country's premier police post. Their book, *Brother Hood,* found that policemen and criminals were so tightly bound, it was difficult to tell them apart. They reported on anti-narcotics agents who were themselves drug users and dealers, and homicide policemen who killed criminals in secret executions (Baluyut and Corotan 1995). A homicide detective told journalist Gemma Luz Corotan that the executions were not done on a whim. Before each killing, the police investigated and assessed the gravity of the victims' crimes. The detective believed the executions were necessary because the legal system was incapable of delivering justice.

One of Corotan's informants, Rudy Jacinto, was an assassin-for-hire who once ran a protection racket in the nightclub row along Manila Bay. He recounted how the police tamed gang violence in Manila's notorious Tondo district by executing the gangsters. These executions, he said, were "usually done by policemen so doped they would be crazy enough to kill." Once the gangsters were gone the police took control of vice dens and hired former hoodlums to run them, with the police getting half of the profits from the operations.

> One hoodlum provides illegal electricity to sidewalk vendors in a public market . . . Another hoodlum runs the protection racket at the Lawton Parking Area for buses and sidewalk vendors . . .
>
> A member of a notorious holdup and snatchers gang operating in Blumentritt in Sta. Cruz and Tondo claims that a cop actually heads the gang . . . A certain percentage of the take, he says, goes to the fund for expenses. The cop gets the lion's share while the rest of them divide the remaining proceeds.
>
> If they could help it, many hoodlums wouldn't hook up with cops, says Rudy. Because the hoodlums are at the frontline and do the dirty work for policemen, they usually take the heat and are therefore considered dangerous to the organization. Once a hoodlum, he says, has learned the ropes of the operation and has outlived his usefulness, he is disposed of in the usual gangland execution.
>
> "*Magtiwala ka na lang sa sampung hoodlum. Huwag lang sa pulis* [Put your trust in ten hoodlums, but not on a single cop]," is the philosophy of most hoodlums, says Rudy. (Baluyut and Corotan 1995, 72–73)

Law Enforcer/Lawbreaker

Policemen, therefore, operate in a continuum of illegality—from investigative and crime-control methods that include torture and summary execution to extortion from suspects to protecting or controlling organized crime syndicates. The latter is particularly true of illegal drugs. Historically, government anti-drug campaigns have been hobbled by the complicity of police officers with drug dealers. In 1990, undercover agents from the US Drug Enforcement Agency and the NBI shot a businessman in the country's biggest drug entrapment operation. The businessman turned out to be a police colonel, the deputy chief of the Northern Luzon Command who had previously been charged with kidnapping, extortion, and smuggling. His killing led to a standoff between the NBI and the Narcotics Command, the elite anti-drug unit of the police. At one point, armed Narcom officers circled the NBI headquarters. Ten days later, NBI agents with Uzi submachineguns killed two Narcom members. The NBI chief at that time, police general Alfredo Lim, who later became Manila mayor, went overseas to escape what seemed an imminent showdown. Lim had aggressively pursued drug dealers, killing them in shootouts that investigators said were more like summary executions. As the *Los Angeles Times* reported, this was a battle for control between two factions of law enforcers over the spoils of the drug trade (Drogin 1990; McCoy 2009, 446–47).

The extent of the police's current involvement in the drug trade is not known. The PNP said it was monitoring nearly 600 police personnel for involvement in drug-related crimes.[28] According to the PNP's Internal Affairs Service, nearly 300 police officers, including forty lieutenant colonels, eleven colonels, and one general, were suspected drug protectors or "coddlers"[29] as of the end of 2016. These figures are very rough approximations and the PNP has used them to point to the culpability of "ninja cops" in some of the killings in the drug war. Like other aspects of police criminality, there is much we don't know.

What we do know is that Filipinos have consistently judged the police the most corrupt of all government agencies.[30] In 1964, amid a surge in crime and widespread perception of the breakdown of law and order that was destabilizing the presidency of Diosdado Macapagal, the US Agency for International Development sent a team to look into what can be done about the police. The team found that the police suffered from lack of training, inadequate disciplinary procedures, low pay, and scant resources (Walton 1964).

The team also found that patrolmen's salaries, PhP 3,500 a month, was not a living wage but an inducement to misbehavior:

> Where salaries are too low to meet living requirements, the police officer is not likely to resist when opportunities to make additional money come his way. Such opportunities range from another job

in addition to his police job . . . to payoffs for permitting illegal operations to flourish, shakedowns of motorists and truck drivers in lieu of traffic arrests, and participation as members of criminal gangs. (Walton 1964, 68–69)

Forty years later, in 2005, Macapagal's daughter, President Gloria Macapagal-Arroyo, was being hounded by allegations of police malfeasance somewhat similar to those her father had faced. In response, the government set up a commission to draft a report on reforming the police. The commission found a low level of professional training, massive human rights abuses, corruption, and low conviction rates. It found that only 15 percent of crime victims reported to the police because they thought the process was too cumbersome and they did not trust law enforcers. In addition, the resources for investigation and building cases were inadequate, forcing policemen to take shortcuts. Low pay continued to be a problem as 60 percent of the police force lived below the poverty line.[31]

Since then, significant amounts of money from the United States and the European Union have been invested in training and upgrading the capacity of the PNP. But like previous reform efforts, these programs failed to change the culture of the police force and to sever the police's links to politics, crime, and corruption. As in the past, erring officers were rarely sanctioned, and wrongdoing often not penalized. Although police salaries were raised—a patrol-man's 2017 base salary was in the PhP 15,000-per-month range, above the poverty threshold—these did not compare to the profits that could be made from extortion and other rackets.

Why Do the Police Kill?

There are many reasons why the police have resorted to excessive force. One is that this is the only type of policing they know. The organizational culture of the PNP, as described above, is one where questionable practices are tolerated and normalized. Lack of training and policing resources as well as a dysfunctional criminal justice system have made these practices part of routine procedure: Instead of gathering forensic evidence and eyewitness testimony that would support a criminal charge, the police resort to torture to elicit confessions. They stage sting operations where suspects are killed because surveillance and investigation are too time-consuming. Summary executions delivering instant justice take the place of long drawn-out trials by possibly compromised judges.

This situation is not unique to the Philippines. The human rights community began to be concerned about the police's use of excessive force in the late 1980s, when the police or groups linked to them were found to be responsible for unauthorized killings, mainly of criminals, in some countries transitioning from authoritarianism. "Across Latin America, death squads and paramilitary/parapolice groups, made up of off-duty police, military, and civilians, torture and murder as if they were the embodiment of law, order, and security," said Martha Huggins, who has studied "vigilantism" in the region. She saw vigilantism as the product of weak or "peripheral" states where the "war on crime" or the "war on drugs" had replaced the national security ideology that justified authoritarian rule (1991).

Paul G. Chevigny, a US law professor who took part in human rights investigations in Latin America in the late 1980s, found that police killings in Jamaica, Argentina, and Brazil shared the same patterns. The victims were uniformly poor, much of the violence took place in cities, and the killings were seen as a necessary deterrent to crime (Chevigny 1990, 407). These killings were different from the political killings during dictatorships. They were "not outright political repression in the partisan sense" but were nonetheless a way of keeping the poor in line, especially in countries where cities were swelling with migrants and rife with crime.

"Police violence," said Chevigny, "can serve as an instrument of coercive social control as long as it can be characterized as a justifiable response to violent crime." He found that citizens and opinion makers thought that police use of deadly force was "an inescapable consequence" of poverty, inequality, and underdevelopment. In Jamaica, for example, the consensus was that "the police, like the criminal justice system as a whole, are not competent enough to deal with crime through legal methods and that extralegal measures, including homicide, are required" (Chevigny 1990, 411).

In India, Jyoti Belur, a former officer in the Indian Police

Service, found vast public support for "encounters," supposedly unplanned shootouts with the police where criminals are invariably killed. Police use of deadly force, she said, was not seen as a form of deviance. On the contrary, policemen who killed suspects in encounters were considered heroes and rewarded with promotions, medals, and in some cases, public adulation. "Encounters" were seen as a way to get around the problems of the criminal justice system (Belur 2010).

Filipinos share the same frustration with delays, corruption, and incompetence in the justice system. They distrust the police and yet many of them accept that police violence is a necessary deterrent to crime. This partly explains the popularity of Duterte's drug war. As in India, police violence is viewed as a form of informal or street punishment for breaking the law, and policemen see themselves—and are often seen—as upholding law and order even when they torture and kill. American ethnologist Beatrice Jauregui studied police violence in the Indian state of Uttar Pradesh and noted the ambivalence of both the police and citizens about the "moral virtue and instrumental necessity" of "providing violence as a service that is at once required and reviled" (Jauregui 2016, 89).

> Rather than presuming that police violence is categorically destructive, oppressive, or evil, people may see it as a resource, a positive provision, a public service geared toward realizing something like order or justice (even if some might call it vengeance or harassment) when other more or less "legal channels" fall short. (92)

Duterte's drug war was waged by a police force accustomed to extortion and execution. While Duterte may see his war on drugs as a way to achieve political control, the policemen fighting that war saw it in different lights. To police officers, the drug war was many things: a golden opportunity to crack down on street-level drug dealing, a shot at getting a promotion, a profitable business prospect, a chance to eliminate rivals in syndicate crime, or maybe all of the above. The police were acting not always as loyal executioners for their political patrons but as entrepreneurs looking for maximum gain.

Nowhere is this clearer than in the life story of SPO4 Arturo Lascañas, a Davao City policeman who was one of Duterte's most trusted police officers. In a handwritten memoir made available by his lawyers, Lascañas said he grew up in the slums of Davao City. He dreamed of becoming a lawyer or businessman, "but the love of gun and police uniform prevailed in my mind." As a young cop in 1982, he got into trouble for killing a bystander. With the help of Duterte, then Davao City assistant prosecutor, the charges were dropped. But Lascañas got into trouble again in 1985, for his role in a shootout with Philippine Constabulary troopers.

With the help of his mentor, a police intelligence officer, Lascañas fled to Manila, working as a bodyguard for a Forbes Park millionaire until 1989, when his case was dismissed, again with Duterte's help, and he was reinstated. By then Duterte was mayor, and Lascañas was assigned to the city's Anti-Organized Crime Task Force. At around that time, Duterte is alleged to have formed the Davao Death Squad to target criminals. City funds paid for the policemen's salaries, they used police vehicles, and operated right within the police's anti-crime group.[32]

Lascañas said he was one of the leaders of the death squad and was paid a fee for every kill, usually PhP 20,000 or PhP 50,000 per head, depending on the target's status. In addition, he got a monthly allowance from the city government, starting at P25,000 before it was raised to P50,000, and more recently, P100,000.

Lascañas said he went into business for himself, including selling real estate, and also freelanced as a gun for hire. For a time, he provided "protection" for rice smugglers and illegal gambling operators in Davao City; he also supplied security for "VIP person-alities." He was Duterte's man but he was also a police entrepreneur, a provider of security services who leveraged his connections and access to lethal force in order to generate substantial extra income. At the same time, he was awarded medals for his performance.

Lascañas operated in two realms: In the realm of legal policing, he thought of himself as an "achiever" because he conducted inves-tigations, made arrests, filed cases, and saw the cases through in court. But he also operated in the shadows, where he was, in his words, a "performer," one who "had the courage" to kill hardcore criminals. He was proud of having "cleaned" the city of both "small and big drug personalities" and considered himself an honorable man. "I choosed [*sic*] or favored no one, relatives and friends alike, in the enforcement of the law against illegal drugs," he wrote in his memoir.

Lascañas left the police force in late 2016 for various reasons, including, he said, a serious illness, a falling out with other members of the Davao police over money and rackets, and his refusal to follow orders to kill the intelligence officer who was his mentor. Parts of his story have been confirmed by human rights reports and an investigation by the Commission on Human Rights, and by Edgar Matobato, another self-confessed death squad member, but other parts have not been corroborated. Lascañas went public in March 2017, in a press conference sponsored by a senator who is one of Duterte's most vociferous critics. Duterte has so far remained silent about the allegations, although his press secretary has dismissed them as "political drama" staged by the president's enemies.

Lascañas's life story, however, shows how much more we need to learn about the police. We know how they are used as instruments of political power and are cognizant of the societal and structural reasons why they resort to violence. But we know less about the moral disengagement that allows them to kill, the processes that transform a young officer into a murderer, and the calculations that take place when a policeman crosses into the twilight zone where policing melds into criminality. And that enables the mobilization of a murder machine that works on an unthinkable scale and impunity.

Endnotes

1   Villegas's and others' account of how Jee Ick-Joo was killed comes from the transcript of the hearing of the Committee on Public Order and Dangerous Drugs held at the Philippine Senate on 26 January and 23 February 2017. Villegas's account is on pages 104–23 of the 23 February transcript. Other details of Jee's killing are in the Resolution filed by the Senior Assistant Prosecutor of the Department of Justice, Philippine National Police-Anti-Kidnapping Group-Kungjin Choi vs. SPO 3 Ricky Sta. Isabel y Molabola et al., 17 January 2017.

[2]   See, for example, Alston 2008; Parreño, 2011; and Sales, 2009, 321–36.
[3]   Affidavit, Arturo Bariquit Lascañas, 19 February 2017, Makati City.
[4]   News reports quoting the PNP said the number of deaths in eight months of the Duterte presidency exceeded 8,000. See Mogato 2017. But in March 2017, PNP chief Roland Dela Rosa said that the numbers released by the PNP in previous months included nondrug-related killings. He said there were over 6,000 homicides in the country from 1 July 2016 to 26 March 2017. Of this number, 1,398 were confirmed to be drug-related while 828 were not drug related. The rest—3,785 cases—remained under investigation. See Tubeza 2017.
[5]   "Kill the Criminals! Duterte's Vote-Winning Vow" 2016.
[6]   From January to April 2016, the four months before the election, drug-related casualties averaged only two a week. In the seven weeks between Election Day and Duterte's inauguration, the kill rate for drug-related crimes more than tripled (Mogato and Chalmers 2016).
[7]   *Tokhang* is a contraction of two Bisaya words, *toktok-hangyo*, meaning knock and plead.
[8]   The barangay is the smallest unit of local government in the Philippines, and its officials are elected.
[9]   Author's interview with Police Director Oscar David Albayalde, chief of the National Capital Region Police Office, 3 January 2017.
[10]   Command Memorandum Circular No. 16-2016, 1 July 2016. This circular outlined the administration's operational plan against illegal drugs. It said "the actual house to house visitations of suspected drug personalities shall be the highlight of Project Tokhang. It shall be simultaneously conducted nationwide on the first day of the Office of the CPNP [Chief PNP]." The purpose of the visitations, the circular said, was "to persuade suspected illegal drug personalities to stop their illegal drug activities."
[11]   Interview with Senior Supt. Joel Napoleon Coronel, 8 January 2017.
[12]   Interview with Coronel.
[13]   Command Memorandum Circular No. 16-2016, 1 July 2016, 6.
[14]   See Human Rights Watch 2009, 38.
[15]   Interviews with Albayalde, Coronel, and Quezon City Police District chief, Sr. Supt. Guillermo Eleazar, 9 January 2017.
[16]   Interview with Albayalde.
[17]   Human Rights Watch 2009, 8. Journalists have reported similar

accounts of policemen in the vicinity of death squad killings. See, for example, Evangelista 2017.

[18]   Interview with Harra Kazuo, 21 December 2016.

[19]   This account of Sta. Isabel's career is from his testimony and that of PNP Chief Roland Dela Rosa before the Senate Committee on Public Order and Dangerous Drugs held at the Philippine Senate on 26 January 2017.

[20]   See Cupin 2017 for explanation on Garbo connection.

[21]   PNP Personal Data Sheet for Ricky Sta. Isabel, submitted to the Angeles City Regional Trial Court.

[22]   Villegas's and others' account of how Jee Ick-Joo was killed comes from the transcript of the hearing of the Committee on Public Order and Dangerous Drugs held at the Philippine Senate on 23 February 2017. This quote is translated from Tagalog. Other details about the killing are in the Resolution filed by the Senior Assistant Prosecutor of the Department of Justice, Philippine National Police Anti-Kidnapping Group-Kungjin Choi vs SPO 3 Ricky Sta. Isabel y Molabola, et al., 17 January 2017.

[23]   In their Senate testimony and affidavits submitted to government prosecutors, both Omlang and Sta. Isabel said they were part of the operation against Jee, but they denied they killed him.

[24]   Sta. Isabel's testimony before the Senate Committee on Public Order and Dangerous Drugs held at the Philippine Senate on 26 January 2017. In his testimony, Sta. Isabel said he brought Jee's body to the funeral home on the orders of his superior, Supt. Rafael Dumlao. In the same hearing, Dumlao denied giving such an order.

[25]   From the testimony of Director Augusto Marquez Jr. of the PNP Directorate for Investigation and Management, before the Senate Committee on Public Order and Dangerous Drugs held at the Philippine Senate on 23 February 2017, p. 46 of the transcript. Marquez cited sworn affidavits of Gream employees as the source of this information.

[26]   Interview with Supt. Glenn Dumlao, by phone, 21 March 2017. This theory was also articulated by Director Augusto Marquez Jr. of the PNP Directorate for Investigation and Management before the Senate Committee on Public Order and Dangerous Drugs held at the Philippine Senate on 23 February 2017, 156–57 of the transcript.

[27]   Carina Dacer et al. vs Joseph Ejercito Estrada et al., "Action for Compensatory and Punitive Damages for Cruel, Inhuman and Degrading Treatment, Torture and Extrajudicial Killing of Plaintiffs'

Father, Decedent Salvador 'Bubby' Dacer," United States District Court, Northern District of California.

28 "Internal Cleansing: Period Covered: July 1 to November 30, 2016," Philippine National Police.

29 Numbers from the PNP Internal Affairs Service as of 31 December 2016.

30 For some examples of public perception surveys on the police, see Romero 2013; and European Country of Origin Information Network, Reports of corruption and bribery within the police force; government response; frequency of convictions of members of the police force accused of criminal activity (2004–2006) [PHL101564.E], http://www.ecoi.net/local_link/191373/309682_de.html.

31 A summary of the commission's findings can be found in "Realities in the PNP" (2005), by the Center for Police Strategy Management, http://www.cpsm.ph/pnp-challenges.xml.

32 Lascañas's handwritten memoir. See also Human Rights Watch 2009.

References

"44 Angeles City Cops Transferred Over Koreans' 'Hulidap.'" 2017. *ABS-CBN News*, 31 January. http://news.abs-cbn.com/news/01/31/17/44-angeles-city-cops-transferred-over-koreans-hulidap.

Adel, Rosette. 2016. "Bato: No cash bonuses for top police officials." *Philippine Star*, 20 December. http://www.philstar.com/headlines/2016/12/20/1655273/bato-no-cash-bonuses-top-police-officials

Alston, Philip. 2008. "Report of the Special Rapporteur on Extrajudicial, Summary or Arbitrary Executions, Mission to the Philippines." United Nations General Assembly.

Amnesty International. 2017. "If You Are Poor, You Are Killed: Extrajudicial Executions in the Philippines' 'War on Drugs.'" 1 February.

Andolong, Ina. 2017. "Duterte Seeks PNP Revamp to Get Rid of Corrupt Cops." *CNN Philippines*. 30 January. http://cnnphilippines.com/news/2017/01/30/rodrigo-duterte-seeks-pnp-revamp-to-get-rid-of-corrupt-cops.html.

Baldwin, Claire, Andrew R. C. Marshall, and Damir Sagoli. 2016. "Police Rack Up Almost Perfect Deadly Record in Philippines Drug

War." *Reuters*, 5 December. http://www.reuters.com/investigates/special-report/philippines-duterte-police/.

Baluyut, Alex, and Gemma Luz Corotan. 1995. *Brother Hood*. Pasig City: Philippine Center for Investigative Journalism.

Belur, Jyoti. 2010. *Permission to Shoot? Police Use of Deadly Force in Democracies*. New York: Springer.

Chevigny, Paul G. 1990. "Police Deadly Force as Social Control: Jamaica, Argentina, and Brazil." *Criminal Law Forum* 1, no. 3.

Corrales, Nestor. 2016. "Duterte Raises Bounty for Killing Drug Lords to P5 M." *Philippine Daily Inquirer*, 5 June. http://newsinfo.inquirer.net/789225/duterte-raises-bounty-for-killing-drug-lords-to-p5-m.

Cuizon, Razel V. 2016. "Osmeña To Give P50,000 for Every Drug Lord Killed." *Sun-Star Cebu*, 17 May. http://www.sunstar.com.ph/cebu/local-news/2016/05/17/osmena-give-p50000-every-drug-lord-killed-474002.

Cupin, Bea. 2016. "Duterte's 'Bato': Who is Ronald dela Rosa?" *Rappler*, 19 May. http://www.rappler.com/nation/133519-ronald-dela-rosa-duterte-pnp-chief.

———. 2017. "Sta. Isabel: Garbo Friend Helped Me Enter Intel Directorate." *Rappler*, 26 January. http://www.rappler.com/newsbreak/inside-track/159605-sta-isabel-garbo-friend-help-intelligence-directorate.

Dalizon, Alfred. 2016. "Rally Behind My Team, 'Bato' Tells Men, Public." *Journal Online*. 3 July. http://www.journal.com.ph/editorial/opinion/rally-behind-my-team-bato-tells-men-public.

De Jesus, Julliane Love. 2016. "Duterte Tells Cops: Will Die For You If You Fulfill Your Duty." *Philippine Daily Inquirer*, 1 July. http://newsinfo.inquirer.net/793794/duterte-tells-cops-will-die-for-you-if-you-fulfill-your-duty.

Drogin, Bob. 1990. "An Asian Drug War Backfires." *Los Angeles Times*, 1 October. http://articles.latimes.com/1990-10-01/news/mn-1228_1_dea-agent.

"Drug War Surrenderers Breach 1 Million Mark." 2017. *Philippine Star*, 1 January. http://www.philstar.com/headlines/2017/01/01/1658665/drug-war-surrenderers-breach-1m-mark.

Evangelista, Patricia. 2017. "Impunity: Welcome to the End of the War." *Rappler*, 7 February. http://www.rappler.com/newsbreak/in-depth/158886-impunity-end-drug-war.

Felipe, Cecille Suerte. 2017. "Tokhang For Ransom: 11 More Cases Bared," *Philippine Star*, 20 January. http://www.philstar.com/

headlines/2017/01/20/1664322/tokhang-ransom-11-more-cases-ba
red.

Fernandez, Edmundo R. 1988. "The Police Investigation System of the
Metropolitan Police Force: A Study." MA thesis, National Defense
College of the Philippines.

Head, Jonathan. 2017. "Philippines Drug War: The Woman Who Kills
Dealers for a Living." *BBC*, 16 August. http://www.bbc.com/news/
world-asia-37172002.

Herrera, Christine F., and John Paolo Bencito. 2016. "Du30 War Chest
VZs Narcs Raised." *Manila Standard*, 25 August. http://manilastan-
dard.net/news/top-stories/214292/du30-war-chest-vs-narcs-
raised.html.

Huggins, Martha K. 1991. *Vigilantism and the State in Modern Latin
America: Essays on Extralegal Violence*. New York: Praeger.

Human Rights Watch. 2009. "'You Can Die Any Time': Death Squad
Killings in Mindanao."

"In the Know: Ex-Senior Supt. Glenn Dumlao." 2013. *Philippine
Daily Inquirer*, 11 January. http://newsinfo.inquirer.net/338701/
in-the-know-ex-senior-supt-glenn-dumlao.

Jauregui, Beatrice. 2016. *Provisional Authority: Police, Order, and Security
in India*. Chicago: University of Chicago Press.

"Kill the criminals! Duterte's Vote-Winning Vow." 2016. *Philippine
Daily Inquirer*, 16 March. http://newsinfo.inquirer.net/774225/
kill-the-criminals-dutertes-vote-winning-vow.

Lema, Karen, and Martin Petty. 2017. "Death of a Businessman:
How the Philippines Drug War Was Slowed." *Reuters*, 13
February.   http://www.reuters.com/article/us-philippines-drugs
-southkorea-idUSKBN15R121.

Macaraig, Ayee. 2016. "Funeral Parlor Workers' Misery on Frontlines
of Philippines' Drug War." *GMA News Online*, 9 December. http://
www.gmanetwork.com/news/news/specialreports/591880/funer-
al-parlor-workers-misery-on-frontlines-of-phl-s-drug-war/
story/.

Malig, Jun A. 2017. "Angeles City Police Chief Axed Over Men's Crimes
vs Koreans." *Rappler*, 25 January. http://www.rappler.com/
nation/159470-angeles-police-chief-relieved-koreans.

Manesca, Thomas. 2017. "Duterte's Controversial Drug War: 6
Months, 6,000 Deaths in the Philippines." *USA Today*, 6 January.
http://www.usatoday.com/story/news/world/2017/01/06/
rodrigo-duterte-philippines-drug-war/96062066/.

Mangahas, Malou, and Karol Ilagan. 2016. "Cash for Drugs, Drug Kills: How Will Duterte Pay Up?." *Philippine Center for Investigative Journalism*, 20 September. http://pcij.org/stories/cash-for-drugs-drug -kills-how-will-duterte-pay-up/.

McCoy, Alfred W. 2002. *Policing America's Empire: The United States, the Philippines, and the Rise of the Surveillance State*. Madison: The University of Wisconsin Press.

Mendez, Christina. 2017. "Duterte Vows Brutal Drug War." *Philippine Star*, 20 March. http://www.philstar.com/headlines/2017/03/20/1682910/duterte-vows-brutal-drug-war.

Mogato, Manuel. 2017. "Four Drug Suspects Killed as Philippine Police Resume Drugs War Operations." *Reuters*, 7 March. http://www.reuters.com/article/us-philippines-drugs-idUSKBN16E0HI.

Mogato, Manuel, and John Chalmers. 2016. "As Duterte Takes Over Philippines, Police Killings Stir Fear." *Reuters*, 29 June. http://www.reuters.com/article/us-philippines-duterte-k illings-idUSKCN0ZE300.

National Bureau of Investigation. 2017. "Jee Ick Joo Investigation Report." 20 February.

Ocampo, Yas D. 2016. "New President's Men." *Mindanao Times*, 1 June. http://mindanaotimes.net/new-presidents-men/.

Parreño, Al A. 2011. "Report on Extrajudicial Killings 2001–2010." Supreme Court of the Philippines.

"PNP Activates Drug Enforcement Group; Double Barrel Reloaded, Tokhang Revisited." 2017. Press release from Philippine National Police, 7 March. http://www.pnp.gov.ph/news-and-information/news/773-pnp-activates-drug-enforcement-group-double-bar-rel-reloaded-tokhang-revisited.

Ranada, Pia. 2016. "Duterte Names Alleged Police Generals in Drug Trade." *Rappler*, 5 July. http://www.rappler.com/nation/138704-duterte-names-police-generals-drugs.

Romero, Alexis. 2013. "PNP Most Corrupt Agency – Survey." *Philippine Star*, 11 July. http://www.philstar.com/headlines/2013/07/11/96408 4/pnp-most-corrupt-agency-survey.

Sales, Peter M. 2009. "State Terror in the Philippines: The Alston Report, Human Rights and Counterinsurgency under the Arroyo Administration." *Contemporary Politics* 15 (3): 321–26.

Sauler, Erica. 2013. "Murder Raps Filed vs 25 Cops, Soldiers in Atimonan Rubout Case." *Philippine Daily Inquirer*. http://newsinfo.inquirer.net/372021/murder-raps-filed-vs-25-cops-soldiers-in -atimonan-rubout-case.

See, Aie. 2017. "Inside Secret Cell: 'You're Like Pigs.'" *Philippine Daily Inquirer.* http://newsinfo.inquirer.net/892868/inside-secr et-cell-youre-like-pigs.

"Three Korean Golfers Also 'Tokhang-for-Ransom' Victims." 2017. *Philippine Daily Inquirer*, 25 January. http://newsinfo.inquirer. net/865216/3-korean-golfers-also-tokhang-for-ransom-victims.

Tubeza, Philip. 2017. "PNP Says Media Sensationalized Figures of Drug Kills." *Philippine Daily Inquirer*, 28 March. http://newsinfo.inquirer. net/884351/pnp-says-media-sensationalized-figures-of-drug-kills.

Walton, Frank et al. 1964. "A Survey of the Manila Police Department." Office of Public Safety, Agency for International Development, Department of State: Washington.

A MANDATE FOR MASS KILLINGS?
PUBLIC SUPPORT FOR DUTERTE'S WAR ON DRUGS

Jayson S. Lamchek

The public's acquiescence to Rodrigo Duterte's bloody war on drugs is as concerning, if not even more so, than the daily slaughter of suspected drug dealers. Seven months since Duterte took office, over 7,000 people have been shot dead as part of the drug war, more than 2,500 by on-duty police. At the same time, the president registered a public approval rating of 83 percent (Pulse Asia Research Inc. 2016). For Duterte's spokespersons, these numbers are not surprising. Filipinos care more about decisively solving the drug problem than protecting individual rights (Ramos 2017). Duterte is popular, as his spokespersons and allies claim, because he delivered on his promise of delivering peace and order, and this comes at the cost of cadavers piling up in the morgues.

If the government were to be believed, then human rights campaigners are in very big trouble. They may put together a robust record of the human costs of Duterte's drug war, but this will matter little to a nation where killing seems to be an acceptable solution to an everyday problem. One could not help but draw parallelisms with the United States during President George W. Bush's

War on Terror. Pollsters reported that as many as 40.8 percent of Americans supported the use of torture as means to prevent a terrorist attack. American support for torture exceeded opposition to it in June 2009, six months after Obama's inauguration (Gronke et al. 2010). This was a blow to human rights organizations who gathered evidence on America's torture techniques that violate the UN Convention Against Torture. What use are data on human rights violations if the public cares little about this issue?

The lack of outrage over the killings and the apparent support for Duterte's war on drugs provoke some challenging questions. Did Filipinos ever consider human rights important? Were people actually harboring murderous contempt for criminals all this time? Were citizens just waiting for a strongman unshackled by political correctness to speak against the tyranny of human rights?

We ought to re-examine what popular support for Duterte's war on drugs means. In this chapter, I argue that the public is, at best, ambivalent toward killings. Their knowledge and judgment of the killings are being muddled by the haze Duterte and his allies created over the question of killings, thereby allowing the president to distance himself from responsibility for these crimes. It also permits the supporters of his war on drugs to be equally in denial that the killings are wrong. However, the public's ambivalence or acquiescence toward killings can change for the worse, i.e., toward open support which can make killings of truly genocidal proportions happen. Thus, the stakes of human rights advocacy are therefore very high indeed, requiring advocates to respond with better society-focused initiatives.

A Popular War?: Mixed Messages from Polling Data

Survey data provides some clarity to the questions I raised above. Highlights from a Pulse Asia survey conducted in December 2016 are as follows:

- Duterte has an 83 percent approval rating. This is the highest among elected officials.
- "Fighting criminality" received the highest performance

rating of 84 percent among twelve issues listed by the polling firm. "Controlling inflation" and "improving/increasing the pay of workers" received more modest approval ratings of 44 percent and 51 percent, respectively.

- "Fighting criminality" is also identified as among the most urgent national issues. While "improving/increasing the pay of workers" landed on the top spot of most pressing issues (45 percent), "fighting criminality" as well as "reducing poverty" made it to the top 3 (both at 33 percent).

Based on these statistics alone, one could infer that Duterte's popularity is underpinned by public approval for his performance in "fighting criminality," more than any other issue deemed urgent by respondents. But it is also important to unpack these numbers. Caution is warranted when making inferences about these numbers (see Holmes, in chapter 3). We ought to examine, for example, whether supporting the fight against criminality means open endorsement of extrajudicial killings of suspected criminals.

Data from Social Weather Stations (SWS) provides further insight into public opinion on the war on drugs (Social Weather Stations 2016). Here are the highlights:

- 84 percent express satisfaction with the Duterte administration's campaign against illegal drugs.
- 69 percent of respondents think that extrajudicial killings (EJKs) are a serious problem
- 71 percent of respondents say it was very important that drug suspects be captured alive.
- 78 percent express concern that they or someone they know could become a victim of EJKs. When asked "How worried are you that you or anyone you know will be a victim of 'Extra-Judicial Killing or EJK'?" 45 percent answered very worried, 33 percent answered somewhat worried, 10 percent answered not too worried, and 12 percent answered not worried at all.

How can one make sense of this data? First, one can infer that the public does not openly endorse EJKs. With the huge majority saying that it is important that drug suspects are kept alive, one can argue that the public does put a premium ("very important") on averting the violent deaths of drug suspects. It is also revealing that the public is concerned about being a victim of EJKs. None of these affirmations of the value of life and concern for one's own safety, however, translate to dissatisfaction with Duterte's war on drugs.

Some of the SWS survey's other findings give clues why this might be so. First, 88 percent of respondents thought the drug problem declined in their area since Duterte became president. This indicates that the public views the drug war as effective, bloody and dirty it may be. People may be able to rationalize the killings as cost for the increased sense of overall security. This explanation, however, doesn't illuminate why people appear to accept even the risk that they could be the next victims of EJKs.

Second, respondents had a split opinion about the police. Forty-two percent were undecided on whether they believe the police's allegation that suspects got killed because they had resisted arrest ("nanlaban"). Such indecision may be a function of ignorance about who does the killings and how they are undertaken, or, possibly, a willful disregard for the extent to which the police are involved in the killings.

Denial, Recalibration, and Deflection: State's Response to Criticisms

The state's response to criticisms against the war on drugs has fostered a situation where public knowledge and judgment about the killings are muddled.

The responses have been a combination of **denial, recalibration, and deflection**, coupled with thin legal justifications for the president's actions in inciting them. President Duterte denies the reports from media and human rights organizations on the killings, suggesting that these reports are exaggerated. He argues that the police only kill suspects to defend themselves. The Philippine National Police (PNP) has justified most killings attributed to the police as the result of "legitimate operations" against armed

suspects who resisted arrest while classifying killings by unidentified assailants as "deaths under investigation." In his speeches,
Duterte always underscores his support for police officers, saying
that "Do your duty, and if in the process you kill one thousand
persons because you were doing your duty, I will protect you"
(Mendez 2016).

Not all police killings, of course, were outcomes of violent
encounters with drug suspects resisting arrest. The Senate
Committee investigation on EJKs, for example, reveals cases of
unarmed suspects getting killed while already in police custody.
For example, Jaypee and Renato Bertes, arrested for drug offenses,
were killed while in the custody of the Pasay City police. Victims'
relatives underscored that in 2015, before Duterte was president,
police have arrested the two for peddling drugs but police have
released them after demanding and receiving bribe money (Senate
of the Philippines 2016, 11–13). Recalibration is the response in this
context. The Philippine National Police chief responded to these
reports by saying that investigations have been conducted against
erring police officers, though the Commission on Human Rights
chair said none of these investigations have so far led to punish-
ments being levied against them.

Aside from denial and recalibration, the state has also been
masterful in deflecting responsibility in the most heinous cases of
EJKs. Duterte and his PNP Chief Roland Dela Rosa have disavowed
police responsibility for shocking cases of EJKs, in which victims'
faces were wrapped in masking tape. Duterte remarked:

> We do not do that. It's a dirty job. It is unmanly to tie them up;
> wrap them—it's a form of torture. . . . That's not the work of the
> police or the soldier even. Why the trouble of wrapping them up if
> you can just kill 'em? We are not producing mummies. (Aben and
> Casayuran 2016)

Duterte and Dela Rosa lead in the speculation that apparent
vigilante killings might actually be the handiwork of drug lords
silencing small fry, without substantiating such allegation through
serious investigation. Deflection is a key government strategy in
distancing itself from the most troubling realities of the drug war.

Will Human Rights Fact-finding
and Campaigning Matter?

Debunking official denials requires a lot of heavy lifting on the part
of human rights campaigners. Amnesty International and Human
Rights Watch have been at the forefront of independent fact-finding
investigation on the drug war. Using a different approach, a report
by the Peace Research Institute Frankfurt on "police vigilantism"
also offers many valuable insights. These organizations released
their reports in early 2017, the highlights of which are as follows:

> Amnesty International (Report released on 31 January 2017):
> - Data is based on twenty police operations and thirteen
>   cases involving unknown and armed persons.
> - PNP Headquarters had been exerting pressure on police
>   officers to show results in terms of "neutralizing high value
>   and street level targets" (pp. 29–30).
> - Witnesses testify to police officers receiving "under-the-
>   table cash payments" from PNP Headquarters for each
>   "encounter" (pp. 29–30).
> - Witnesses also testify to police disguising themselves as
>   paid assassins to undertake the killings, when there is a
>   high risk of complaint from victims' relatives (p. 37).
> - Police officers collude with funeral parlors who charge
>   exorbitant fees from the relatives of the victims. Police
>   also stole property from victims as they worked on crime
>   scenes (p. 42).
>
> Human Rights Watch (Report released on 1 March 2017):
> - Data is based on twenty-four incidents in and around the
>   NCR involving the police, resulting in 32 deaths; the victims
>   are poor, with irregular or no employment.
> - Witnesses provided testimony on police planting handguns,
>   spent ammunition and packets of *shabu* (crystal metham-
>   phetamine) on suspects to stage a "legitimate encounter."
> - Days before a killing, the victim may receive a visit from
>   a barangay official to inform her/him that s/he is in the
>   "drug watch" list.

- Later, masked assailants enter the victim's dwelling unannounced, and witnesses testify that they saw or heard the victim being beaten and killed while begging for his/her life.
- Police reports in nearly all of these incidents claimed they were "buy bust" operations, and no one was prosecuted for these killings.

Peace Research Institute Frankfurt (Report released on 20 January 2017):
- The report suggests the implausibility of the PNP's claim that suspects were killed in "legitimate encounters." The report assembled data on killings by on-duty police per million population before and during Duterte's war on drugs, and compared data in Philippine cities, provinces and regions with those in foreign cities and countries. Killings by on-duty police per million population under Duterte shot up by as much as ten times compared to before Duterte. Philippine killings by on-duty police per million population under Duterte was seventy times more than those in the United States. The ratio of suspects killed to police killed from 1 July to 3 November 2016 in the Philippines was 223 suspects killed for each police officer killed. This rate is twelvefold more than for Rio de Janeiro (17.9). The ratios for the United States and South Africa were 8.7 and 4.6, respectively.
- "Encounter" killings—killings by on-duty police where the threat of harm to police was very low but were justified as "legitimate encounters"—were practiced before Duterte, though relatively sparingly. Duterte has elevated "encounter" killings into a new tool of law and order. "Encounter" killings differed from death squad killings in that the state did not deny authorship in the killings but merely that they were wrongful or illegal. While death squad killings afforded the state deniability for murders, "encounter" killings allowed the state to take credit for the killings as furthering law and order.

- Local elites play a mediating role in realizing Duterte's national vision, and Duterte uses coercive means to get local bosses in line. The Duterte government has wrested control of local police from mayors and governors. Statistics on EJKs illustrate a disproportionate rise in provinces, cities, or municipalities where local bosses have aligned or failed to resist pressure from Duterte. Within the National Capital Region (NCR), for example, the number of EJKs in Quezon City spiked in August 2016 when the mayor was forced to cooperate with Duterte after he mentioned two of its high ranking police officers as drug protectors, and named the mayor's brother as drug user. In contrast, Manila, which accounted for 40 percent of EJKs in the NCR, recorded a spike in killings as early as May 2016 after Mayor Joseph Estrada chose immediately to ingratiate himself with Duterte (Kreuzer 2017, 15–16).

Will any of these reports matter? Yes, potentially they can help clarify muddled public judgments about the police's responsibility for the killings, including "deaths under investigations" from which police have distanced themselves. They also articulate how official explanations of the killings, particularly the "nanlaban" theory, do not make sense. While Duterte has dismissed human rights groups as "out of touch" with the public and asked them to "go to hell," it is fair to say that these groups' criticisms of the war on drugs can also have traction with the public in the long run, if they haven't already started doing so.

SWS data indicates that the "nanlaban" theory has few adherents among the public (9 percent believed it and 19 percent said it was probably true) despite Duterte's total endorsement thereof (Social Weather Stations 2016). These reports can help the undecided (42 percent) take sides. Moreover, public awareness of human rights organizations' claims that innocents have been killed is reflected in the SWS data that people are afraid they might be the next victims. Significantly, the influential Catholic Bishops' Conference of the Philippines (CBCP) has broken its silence on the war on drugs, citing, among others, the reality of innocents getting killed (Legarde

2017). The Victims Against Crime and Corruption, a civil society group supportive of Duterte's anti-drug initiatives and which initiated drug charges against Sen. de Lima, has also responded to the argument that innocents are getting killed in the war on drugs, and urged Duterte to address the matter ("Duterte Urged" 2017).

Human rights organizations' arguments putting a spotlight on corruption and demonstrating how the war on drugs abetted corrupt practices by police can have resonance with the public. The public wrestles with corrupt practices by police in daily life. Even Duterte was compelled to admit that police corruption was rampant and their low credibility jeopardized his war on drugs when he reacted to the "tokhang for ransom" case of the South Korean businessman Jee Ick-Joo.[1] Though not prompted by human rights campaigning, Duterte suspended police operations to pave the way for "internal cleansing" of the PNP. This move creates expectations, which human rights organizations can monitor and, if not realized, expose.

The suspension also effected the replacement of the PNP with the Philippine Drug Enforcement Agency (PDEA) in the lead role. The chief of the Armed Forces of the Philippines (AFP) Eduardo Año has also stepped up to announce a plan to create a special task force that will concentrate on higher-level drug syndicates. (Reuters 2017) Duterte brought the PNP back in with the promise that only a "select" group of police officers "with no cases and history of corruption" can participate in anti-drug operations (Romero 2017).

While addressing corruption, especially in the police ranks, is always a welcome development, the changes to the war on drugs introduced post–Jee Ick-Joo can quickly turn, if not intended precisely, to produce even more haze about the killings. In the first place, Duterte has not recognised that EJKs are a serious problem and has not committed to stop them, instead vowing to continue the killings of suspected drug offenders. Second, removing the PNP from the lead role and introducing specialized bodies like the PDEA and an AFP special task force will allow Duterte to represent his war on drugs to the public as being carried out by persons with more professionalism and discipline. This can bolster his depiction of killings as principled acts, perhaps as acts of patriotism. In turn, this will allow his supporters to continue denying that killings are wrongful.

Duterte's Direct Role in the Davao Death Squad

Even more explosive than evidence of police misdeeds, evidence has surfaced on Duterte's direct participation in forming and operating the Davao Death Squad (DDS). While Duterte has boasted of his murderous record in Davao, he never admitted responsibility for DDS killings. He said he inspired the killings but did not order them. His supporters have excused statements like "I will kill you" as part of his playful macho language. President Duterte advances the dubious theory that his statements like "I will kill you" are mere threats against wrongdoers, which he is legally allowed to make as chief enforcer of law and order. Even his controversial statement "I am the death squad" was made in the context of challenging human rights organizations to find evidence and file a case against him while he was still Davao mayor. In short, the DDS killings have been enveloped in a thick haze.

There have been attempts to expose the DDS in the past. UN Special Rapporteur Philip Alston's report on EJKs in the Philippines in 2008, while focused on the killings of leftist activists, contained a brief section on the killings in Davao (Alston 2008, 39–44). In 2009, Human Rights Watch issued a report which featured, among others, evidence that death squad killings have victimized innocents, including people mistaken for others (Human Rights Watch 2009). The Commission on Human Rights also investigated Duterte but no prosecution came out of it.

The game changer midway in Duterte's presidency has been the testimonies of Edgar Matobato and Arthur Lascañas. Matobato, the first to testify, said he was an original member of the death squad. Matobato said he was an illiterate member of the paramilitary when then Mayor Duterte recruited him in March 1988 to be part of a small group called "Lambada Boys" that undertook killings of suspected petty criminals. The group evolved into the DDS, whose members were drawn from the heinous crimes unit of the Davao police and former NPA rebels who have surrendered. In his

Senate testimony, Matobato detailed a few of the at least 50 murders he confessed to committing as a death squad member. He claimed that he is revealing his knowledge of the operations of the DDS after his decision to leave the group making him a "loose cannon." The threat he posed by leaving the DDS led his own former colleagues to frame him up for a murder he said his DDS colleagues committed. Matobato claimed that the DDS murdered businessman Richard King on the order of Duterte's son Paolo because King was a rival of Paolo over a woman he was courting. Matobato said the DDS tortured him to confess to the murder, but that he escaped from the clutches of his torturers and he now denounces them. Lascañas, who was tagged by Matobato as a DDS leader and Duterte's trusted aide, first denied Matobato's allegations but later came out to confirm his testimony (ABS-CBN Investigative and Research Group 2017). Lascañas, a police officer who studied law, also said he killed his own siblings for their involvement in drugs out of a sense of total loyalty to Duterte. He felt betrayed when Paolo Duterte intervened to stop Lascañas from entrapping a smuggler believed to be shipping illegal drugs to Davao (Gonzales 2017). The details of their testimonies thus far are too many and complicated to summarize here. Suffice it to say that they paint a picture of the DDS as less like the heroes of society that supporters of killings might have imagined them to be and more like the private army of a political family.

Testimonies from Matobato and Lascañas provide a clear narrative that counters the denials that the DDS ever existed. They also provide an inside view of how killings are done, who gets targeted, and so on. For some of Duterte's critics in the government, the Matobato and Lascañas testimonies pave the way for Duterte's impeachment or filing of charges at the International Criminal Court.

As evidence against Duterte continues to pile up, tactics of deflection are put to work. Senator Leila de Lima, for example, conducted an inquiry into the extra-judicial killings, and gave Matobato the national spotlight to reveal Duterte's role in the DDS. The government, in turn, filed a case against her, which pins her down for being in cahoots with drug cartels in the National Penitentiary when she was Secretary of Justice. De Lima is in jail today. The vice-president has also been a target of attack. Timed during the Senate hearing featuring Lascañas, a website that claims to "leak" information about the vice-president and her late husband's link to the drug trade in their hometown surfaced. By discrediting the vice-president's integrity, there is less appetite for impeaching or deposing Duterte, for his constitutional successor has questionable credentials. These actuations further the politicization of the drug problem so that those who oppose his anti-drugs campaign are cast as destabilizers of his government.

Participatory Surveillance and Community-Sourced Death Sentence

I have argued so far that the muddled perception of killings permits people to remain ambivalent or to acquiesce toward killings.[2] How can this ambivalence or acquiescence change?

One way mere ambivalence or acquiescence could change for the worse, i.e., to open support for mass killings, is if people themselves are given more direct roles in the killings.[3] Duterte himself has envisioned a "final solution" to the drug problem when he intimated in a notorious speech that he'd be happy to slaughter three million people, his estimate of the total number of drug addicts in the country (Lema and Mogato 2016). The term "final solution" is used with approval by his representative to the United Nations Teddy Locsin in reference to Hitler's own "final solution" to the "Jewish problem" (Lui 2016).

Civilians do not openly engage in vigilante-style killings. But Duterte has urged them to do so, just as he has encouraged the police. Speaking to a crowd of 500 people in an urban poor community in Manila on the evening of his inauguration, Duterte said: "If you know of any addicts [sic], go ahead and kill them yourself as getting their parents to do it would be too painful." If coordinated killings of three million people, a truly genocidal scale, are to be carried out, Duterte will very likely have to enlist large segments of society to take on more direct roles in killings. As Duterte's war on drugs went from Davao to the national stage, the form of killings shifted from death squad killings (with people not knowing exactly

who's doing the killings and how) to "encounter" killings plus killings by unidentified assailants (with people knowing police were
killing thousands of people but shrugging their shoulders). This
may yet change to also include riots or some other forms of violence
with civilians openly embracing and themselves acting on Duterte's
"final solution." That is the looming scenario that human rights
advocates will have to prepare for.

The signs are dire. The marching orders on Duterte's drug war
is not only limited to the police and drug enforcement agencies.
Increasingly, ordinary citizens are tasked to perform surveillance
on their neighbors and families. Take the case of drawing up the
"drug watch" list, which essentially serves as a blacklist of targets in
the war on drugs. These lists may have predated the Duterte administration, but this regime has intensified its utilization (Amnesty
International 2017, 19). In 2015, for example, a circular from the
Department of Interior and Local Government (DILG) revitalized
the Barangay Anti-Drug Abuse Council. It called on barangay officials to support police "drug clearing" operations. It envisioned the
formation of an operations committee, tasked to "prepare a confidential list of users, pushers, financiers and/or protectors of illegal
drug trade" in every barangay to be submitted to the PNP. Chaired
by a barangay *kagawad*, the committee also includes the chief *tanod*
and ideally twenty-five auxiliaries for every 2,000 barangay population. They were tasked to conduct pre-operations "identification
of drug affected house clusters, work places, streets, puroks and
sitios"; assist police during operations; and provide "post-opera-
tions" support such as execution of affidavits as witnesses to police
operations (Department of the Interior and Local Government 2015).

Duterte's drug watch list has an eerie resemblance to Gloria
Macapagal-Arroyo's "Order of Battle" lists (OB lists), which played
a role in the EJKs in the counterinsurgency context, and which
continued to be used in Benigno Aquino III's term. During the Arroyo
administration, the Philippine military engaged in a grassroots
campaign to "weed out" left-wing civil society actors from the barangays, leaving hundreds of activists killed. In what were called "OB
lists," persons believed to be armed combatants of the Communist
Party of the Philippines-New People's Army (CPP-NPA) were drawn

up in the same list with supporters or members of "front organiza-tions" like Bayan Muna and Gabriela. Barangay residents provided names to be included in OB lists, often but not always because they were coerced to do so (Alston 2008, 20). In theory, individuals who make it to the list are encouraged to "surrender" (Alston 2008, 20). In practice, however, they often ended up abducted and/or killed, often in broad daylight. EJKs conveyed the message that those in the list who do not "cooperate" with the counterinsurgency campaign will suffer the same fate. Because the military did not distinguish between legal activists and armed rebels, leftist activists had their guilt predetermined. So when villagers supplied names to the "OB lists," they were not merely providing intelligence to the military but meting out punishment on enemy-others.

What we are seeing in the current "drug watch" lists is similar. "Drug watch" lists do not appear to attach particular importance to distinguishing among addicts and pushers and financiers/protectors. On the contrary, the emphasis is on making the lists as inclusive as possible. Already, this indicates an encouragement by authorities for people not to weigh the relative faults of different categories of drug offenders. A *purok* leader who participated in drawing up a "drug watch" list said police instructed him to include names of people "who are using drugs, even if it was in the past." He also included names not only of people he knew personally to be drug users but also those given to him by other community members even though he couldn't verify if they were indeed drug users (Amnesty International 2017, 19–20).

The DILG under the Duterte regime has also put forward changes in the conduct of the war on drugs that ostensibly give the anti-drug campaign more legitimacy by involving more civilian actors at the barangay level. In what is termed "MASA MASID" (Masses Observe) program,[4] the DILG aims to "heighten commu-nity involvement" and volunteerism in the anti-drugs campaign. MASA MASID Teams, composed of representatives of civil society and faith-based organizations in barangay-level bodies, will lead local residents to report on drug-related incidents in their neigh-borhood. It also aims to set up a local hotline and other reporting systems for people to directly report information on addicts, etc., to authorities (Department of the Interior and Local Government 2016). Further, the DILG Secretary announced the use of "Drug-Free Household" stickers in order to mark out households that are, according to barangay authorities, certifiably "drug-free" from those that are not. The stickers are designed to put pressure on families themselves to police their ranks (Ongkiko 2017).

Outsourcing surveillance directly to barangays and volunteers increases the opportunities for citizens to directly take part in identifying undesirable others for targeting by executioners. Mapping out "drug-free" households make visible to everyone where the problematic others are located in space. This "knowledge" in turn can be exploited for crafting means for containing, managing, or bringing "help" to them, and possibly, neutralizing and eliminating them (the "final solution").

Many—including those who have stopped using drugs for a long time or have been wrongly identified as drug users—have given themselves up to authorities upon learning that they were included in "drug watch" lists. They had hoped that "surrendering" would spare them from "encounter" killings. Nonetheless, Human Rights Watch (2017) reports that those who have surrendered ended up dead in the custody of authorities or soon after being released. The lack of protection from being killed, or indeed, the increased risk of being killed that accompany "surrendering" underlines the fatal character of "drug watch" lists. These blacklists assume the quality of final judgments of guilt, despite being merely community-sourced intelligence information.

A Genocide in the Making: What Can Be Done?

None of the foregoing discussion should lead us to the conclusion that the battle to uphold human rights is already lost. If human rights are not the internalized beliefs that we supposed Filipinos widely shared, neither is Duterte's vision of a "final solution" to the drug problem foreordained. If anything, the realization that the people's belief in human rights is so tenuous and shouldn't be taken for granted should spur advocates to find new society-focused modes of operation that grow and deepen rights. Whether or not Duterte has merely stepped in to give voice to a deep longing in Filipino society, and whether or not Duterte is soon persuaded or forced to stop the killings, we will still have to deal with society's fraught relationship with the right to life.

There are spaces for improvement of advocates' strategies. On the part of human rights advocates, they must persevere to fight apathy, ignorance, or misinformation. They must expose the folly of aiming for "zero tolerance" for drugs and fight the sentiment that drug users' lives are worthless. Such efforts have to be brought to the barangay and household levels where the Duterte regime has already started recruiting volunteers for his campaign.

A counter-campaign at the community level may well involve families and neighbors organizing to pressure barangay officials not to cooperate in assembling "drug watch" lists. It is instructive, for example, that in Makati City, there was zero recorded EJKs from 10 May to 10 October 2016 when local villagers refused to submit "drug watch" lists to the PNP (Kreuzer 2017, 18). Further campaigning may demand that all "drug watch" lists be made public and be subjected to judicial or community scrutiny in order to shift the burden of proof to those who accuse others of offenses under the anti-drug law. To counter the use of villagers for surveillance of drug addicts, families and neighbors may also witness and record abuses in anti-drug operations through cellphone cameras and the like. Local parishes may assume their traditional function as refuges for the persecuted in relation to those already listed in "drug watch" lists. Some of them are already doing so (McPherson 2017).

Countering the dehumanization of drug users is most needed in neighborhoods where anxieties about crime and drug use easily lend themselves to conversion into assent to "final solution"-type scenarios. There is certainly a void for new types of society-focused initiatives underlining the commonalities between drug users and the rest of society and strengthening the familial and neighborly connections between drug users and non-drug users. There may already be pockets of resistance to dehumanization expressed in terms of simple acts of kindness from private individuals,[5] which advocates can model and scale up into resistance strategies. These ideas are of course easier to conceive of than to actualize. The stakes for human rights advocacy are very high indeed. We need all our imagination and courage to take on the task of avoiding a looming genocide.

Endnotes

1   See the chronology of events in Placido 2017.
2   My view is the opposite of putting the public's "ambivalence toward 'democracy'" prior to "populist politicians," see, e.g., the comments of Webb in Webb et al. 2016.
3   Change could also take place for the better, i.e., toward rejection of killings. Being directly involved in mass killings, as opposed to merely (mis)perceiving the operations of mass killings from the outside, could result in a shock or sudden realization of the moral disaster that one has all the while denied.
4   The acronym stands for Mamamayan Ayaw Sa Anomalya, Mamamayan Ayaw Sa Iligal na Droga (Citizens against anomalies, citizens against illegal drugs).
5   For example, Patricia Evangelista writes about a former Vietnamese refugee who lived in the Philippines who raised money for the burial of two victims on the conviction that burial humanized the brutalized dead (Evangelista 2016).

References

Aben, Elena L., and Mario B. Casayuran. 2016. "Duterte Disowns EJKs, Calls Them a 'Dirty Job'; Lacson Urges Probe." *Manila Bulletin*, 13 December. http://news.mb.com.ph/2016/12/13/duterte-disowns-ejks-calls-them-a-dirty-job-lacson-urges-probe/.

ABS-CBN Investigative and Research Group. 2017. "Retired SPO3 Lascañas: What He Said before, What He Now Says." News. *ABS-CBN News*, 20 February. http://news.abs-cbn.com/news/02/20/17/retired-spo3-lascanas-what-he-said-before-what-he-now-says.

Alston, Philip. 2008. "Report of the Special Rapporteur on Extrajudicial, Summary or Arbitrary Executions, Addendum, Mission to the Philippines." A/HRC/8/3/Add.2.

Amnesty International. 2017. "'If You Are Poor, You Are Killed': Extrajudicial Killings in the Philippines' 'War on Drugs.'" https://www.amnesty.org/en/documents/document/?indexNumber=asa35%2f5517%2f2017&language=en.

Department of the Interior and Local Government. 2015. "Memorandum Circular No. 2015-63 Re Revitalization of BADAC and Their Role in Drug Clearing Operations." http://dpcr.pnp.gov.ph/portal/images/downloads/PPD/PNP%20MC%202015-63%20re%20Revitalization%20of%20BADAC%20and%20their%20role%20in%20Drug%20Clearing%20Operations.pdf.

———. 2016. "Memorandum Circular No. 2016-116 Re Implementation of MASA MASID Program." http://www.dilg.gov.ph/PDF_File/reports_resources/dilg-reports-resources-2016927_aefb2696d6.pdf.

"Duterte Urged: Create Task Force on 'Collateral Victims' of Drug War." 2017. *ABS-CBN News*, 2 January. http://news.abs-cbn.com/news/01/02/17/duterte-urged-create-task-force-on-collateral-victims-of-drug-war.

Evangelista, Patricia. 2016. "Impunity: Let Them Sleep." *Rappler*, 30 November online edition. http://www.rappler.com/nation/152477-impunity-let-them-sleep-jerico-angel-ejks.

Gonzales, Yuji Vincent. 2017. "Lascañas: Paolo Duterte Stopped Arrest of Drug Suspect in 2014." *Philippine Daily Inquirer*, 6 March. http://newsinfo.inquirer.net/877823/lascanas-paolo-duterte-stopped-arrest-of-drug-suspect-in-2014.

Gronke, Paul, Darius Rejali, Dustin Drenguis, James Hicks, Peter Miller, and Bryan Nakayama. 2010. "U.S. Public Opinion on Torture, 2001–2009." *PS: Political Science and Politics* 43 (3). /core/journals/ps-political-science-and-politics/article/div-classtitleus-public-opinion-on-torture-20012009div/D2F34C40D2945A2547A4F0664118E0FB.

Human Rights Watch. 2009. "'You Can Die Any Time': Death Squad Killings in Mindanao." New York: Human Rights Watch.

———. 2017. "'License to Kill': Philippine Police Killings in Duterte's 'War on Drugs.'" New York: Human Rights Watch. https://www.hrw.org/report/2017/03/01/license-kill/philippine-police-killings-dutertes-war-drugs.

Kreuzer, Peter. 2017. "'If They Resist, Kill Them All': Police Vigilantism in the Philippines." PRIF Report No. 142. Frankfurt, Germany. https://www.hsfk.de/fileadmin/HSFK/hsfk_publikationen/prif142.pdf.

Legarde, R. 2017. "Pastoral Letter on Drug War Grounded in Truth—Bishop." *CBCP News*, 6 April. http://www.cbcpnews.com/cbcpnews/?p=91250.

Lema, Karen, and Manuel Mogato. 2016. "Philippines' Duterte Likens Himself to Hitler, Wants to Kill Millions of Drug Users." *Reuters*, 1

October.   http://www.reuters.com/article/us-philippines-duterte
-hitler-idUSKCN1200B9.

Lui, Kevin. 2016. "New Philippine U.N. Ambassador 'Invoking Nazis on
Twitter.'" *Time*, 4 October. http://time.com/4516275/teddy-locsin-
philippines-un-ambassador-nazi-twitter-drug-war-duterte/.

McPherson, Poppy. 2017. "'Open the Doors': The Catholic Churches
Hiding Targets of Duterte's Drug War." *The Guardian*, 28 February
online edition, sec. World news. https://www.theguardian.com/
world/2017/feb/28/catholic-churches-hiding-targets-of-dutertes
-drug-war.

Mendez, Christina. 2016. "Duterte to PNP: Kill 1,000, I'll Protect
You." *Philippine Star*, 2 July 2, online edition. http://www.phil-
star.com/headlines/2016/07/02/1598740/duterte-pnp-kill-1000-ill
-protect-you.

Ongkiko, Renz. 2017. "Household 'Drug-Free' Stickers to Replace
'Tokhang' - DILG." *InterAksyon.Com*, 24 February. http://inter-
aksyon.com/article/137272/household-drug-free-stickers-to-re
place-tokhang---dilg.

Placido, Dharel. 2017. "'Tokhang-for-Ransom': Timeline of South
Korean Businessman's Abduction, Killing." *ABS-CBN News*, 20
January. http://news.abs-cbn.com/focus/01/20/17/tokhang-for-ran-
som-timeline-of-south-korean-businessmans-abduction-killing.

Pulse Asia Research Inc. 2016. "December 2016 Nationwide Survey
on Urgent Personal and National Concerns and National
Administration Performance Ratings." Pulse Asia. http://www.
pulseasia.ph/december-2016-nationwide-survey-on-urgent-per-
sonal-and-national-concerns-and-national-administration-per-
formance-ratings/.

Ramos, Marlon. 2017. "Palace: CBCP 'Out of Touch' with Sentiments
of Faithful." *Philippine Daily Inquirer*, 5 February. http://news-
info.inquirer.net/868378/palace-cbcp-out-of-touch-with
-sentiments-of-faithful.

Reuters. 2017. "Philippine Army to Join Duterte's Drug War: Military
Chief." *ABC News*, 19 February. http://www.abc.net.au/news/2017-
02-19/philippine-army-to-create-task-force-to-chase-drug-syn-
dicates/8284494.

Romero, Alexis. 2017. "Duterte Brings Back Police into War on Drugs."
Philippine Star, 28 February. http://www.philstar.com/headlines
/2017/02/28/1676660/duterte-brings-back-police-war-drugs.

Senate of the Philippines. 2016. "Joint Committee Report on

Extra-Judicial Killings." Committee Report No. 18. Senate of the Philippines.

Social Weather Stations. 2016. "Fourth Quarter 2016 Social Weather Survey." Social Weather Station. http://www.sws.org.ph/swsmain/artcldisppage/?artcsyscode=ART-20161219110734.

Webb, Adele, Christine Milne, Henrik Bang, James Loxton, Jan-Werner Muller, John Keane, Laurence Whitehead, Mark Chou, Nick Rowley, and Stephen Coleman. 2016. "We the People: The Charms and Contradictions of Populism." *The Conversation*. 2 November. http://theconversation.com/we-the-people-the-charms-and-contradictions-o f-populism-63769.

CELEBRITY POLITICS AND TELEVISUAL MELODRAMA IN THE AGE OF DUTERTE

Anna Cristina Pertierra

Rodrigo Duterte's election to President of the Philippines in 2016 has attracted tremendous international attention. His controversial character, apparent disregard for protocol, and the wave of deaths in his "war on drugs," including extra-judicial killings, have garnered extensive coverage in the global media—and rightly so. But to understand Duterte's success, it is important to extend analysis of Duterte as a political figure, to also explore the nature of his relationship to members of the public who voted for him (Curato 2016). In this chapter, I focus in particular on the role of media and celebrity in the national electoral machine, and the entertainment media's constitutive role in the cultural context that has enabled his success. I argue that Duterte is a beneficiary of a political culture where policies and processes have been less electorally effective than the glitz of showbusiness and success of personal charisma. His ongoing political popularity rests not only on his deployment of media in his own political performance, but also more broadly on the convergence of entertainment and politics as it is experienced in the Philippines (and in other parts of the world) through emotional connections with audiences who are also publics.

The Celebrity Factor

Duterte's colorful public persona is highly mediated. As with any contemporary national politician, engagements with the press corps are a daily occurrence and Duterte's relationship with news journalists has often been tense. Yet his frequent outbursts and public gaffes do not diminish his popularity and seem only to reinforce his outsider status, despite being one of the country's longer serving bearers of political office. Public performance and "tabloid-style communication" has been an essential part of his process of building support and outlining a position; among other things, Duterte has long used the media to name his enemies, publicly revealing those placed on his infamous lists on television and radio programs (Curato 2016, 94; Reyes 2016, 7).

Duterte's reputation as a tough-talking man who takes no hostages echoes the imagery and language of Philippine and Hollywood action film heroes, as reflected in some of his many nicknames: "The Punisher" and "Duterte Harry." But Duterte's success in evoking a macho cinematic style is by no means a new feature of Philippine politics. Such a formula has been successful since at least the 1960s, when Ferdinand Marcos and his glamorous wife Imelda rose to power using film-star looks and flashy performances to generate popular appeal. The Marcoses frequently sang together on stage during electoral campaign events and "turned their private lives into a public spectacle, staging a stylized version of their intimacy" that was a crucial element in their popularity during the early years of the Marcos presidency (Rafael 1990, 284; see also Espiritu 2015). After the ousting of the Marcoses—which was in itself a highly melodramatic set of events worthy of a television drama—succeeding politicians have also drawn from the repertoire of images and personalities that showbusiness provides, with both Mayor Lim in Manila and President Joseph Estrada enacting a cinematically inspired macho style in their public pronouncements against lawbreakers (Reyes 2016).

The intertwining of politics and showbusiness celebrity is not merely seen in the ways that Filipino politicians adopt the look and style of celebrities to generate votes. In many cases, as is common knowledge in the Philippines, politicians actually were media celebrities before they became elected politicians. Actors, singers, comedians, and news anchors frequently win political office across the country. In the 2016 elections alone, forty-four show business celebrities ran as candidates at the national or local level. The 2016 Philippine senatorial winners included Manny Pacquiao, a world champion boxer who recently reclaimed his welterweight title belt in Las Vegas while on a short break from his senatorial duties. Vicente "Tito" Sotto III, one of the country's most famous stars, who for more than thirty years has hosted a high-rating noontime variety show, was also re-elected to the Senate, and joins a long list of current and former actors, newscasters, and children of films stars to have forged careers in public office. In a political scene that continues to be dominated by dynastic families—many of whom control whole provinces or regions—celebrities are often the only candidates who can generate enough momentum to be elected. Such momentum is generated from their longstanding interactions with members of the public through media entertainment, and it is no coincidence that the viewers who achieve high ratings for broadcast television stations and Philippine film distributors are the same demographic of working-class Filipinos whose votes decide elections. As I have argued elsewhere, media celebrities and elected politicians both build upon longstanding traditions of chains of vertical loyalty between the rich and the poor that are frequently described as "patron-client" relations in scholarly literature (Pertierra 2016; Doronila 1985). It is not so much the case that media celebrity and electoral politics have converged in the Philippines; rather, both media figures and politicians evoke positive versions of vertical relationships to generate followings that are easily translated between the screen and the ballot box. Such an integration of popular media and populist politics results in a sort of televisual politics that assumes both the political leaders and their audiences of viewer-voters are adept at embracing the emotional elements of melodrama that figure centrally in both the entertainment and the electoral mode.

Melodrama in Televisual Politics

Rather than entertaining audiences on comedy shows or at sporting events, in late 2016 senators Sotto and Pacquiao were on television screens across the nation cross-examining witnesses in a televised inquiry investigating the killing of an arrested mayor in his jail cell. Across the country, many Filipinos were transfixed by daily proceedings that resembled a courtroom drama. For several weeks, the private life of Senator Leila de Lima, who is a rare voice of opposition against Duterte, was discussed in lurid detail in both congress and the senate, where investigations were being conducted on the drug trade and corruption in prisons.

De Lima had previously served as the Secretary of the Department of Justice, and had been accused of heading a drug trade through prisons with the aid of her driver, with whom she admitted to having had a romantic relationship. This driver, after much evasion and complication, was brought to testify at the house and senate hearings and claimed that he received bribes from drug dealers—de Lima and her defenders insisted such claims were fabrications. The televised senate proceedings also featured dramatic testimony from an arrested drug-lord, Kerwin Espinosa, who wanted to atone for the death of his father by testifying against corrupt officials, and from the charismatic National Chief of Police Ronald Dela Rosa. A close Duterte ally whose nickname is "The Rock," Dela Rosa was moved to tears while speaking to the senate, having heard testimony about corrupt police. At the same time, a parallel set of speculations surrounded the hurried and controversial burial of former President Ferdinand Marcos in the National Heroes' Cemetery. The adult Marcos children, themselves seasoned political personalities, had pushed for their father's long delayed burial to be authorized in the military-operated cemetery. When the burial took place on 18 November 2016, no public notification had been made, and the public was taken unawares. Duterte himself denied prior knowledge of the burial—but commentators noted that a prominent wreath placed next to the grave bore Duterte's name and condolences.

It is no coincidence that these political intrigues read like soap opera storylines. Such melodramatic scandals are watched with great interest by everyday Filipinos, who follow the storylines as if they were from a television serial. Daily revelations and entanglements are discussed while people watch the live streams or television broadcasts in living rooms, malls, or restaurants, or listen on the radio while traveling on public transport. Such conversations mix with celebrity gossip and conversations about television as part of the fabric of daily life; people speculate about the twists and turns of each day's revelations and consider the personal enmities and family histories behind political disputes.

The overriding themes of betrayal, revenge, secret love, and complex family histories are the sorts of plot lines that frequently feature in the *teleserye* soap operas—originally inspired by Latin American *telenovelas*—that play on Philippine television channels at night (Sanchez 2014; Allen 2002). Soap operas, *telenovelas,* and related global serialized television genres rely heavily on precisely the dramatic elements that make political intrigues in the Duterte era such good television. Consider, for example, how esteemed media scholar Ien Ang describes at length the hallmarks of soap opera as found in the US series *Dallas,* the reception of which formed the basis of Ang's pioneering study of television audiences:

> The multiple storylines revolve around the complicated mutual relations between the characters, and focus on emotive states of affairs and incidents that are quintessential to soap operas: the struggles between love and hate, loyalty and betrayal, greed and compassion, hope and despair. While . . . the constant subject of grandiose narrative plots including murder attempts, kidnappings, dubious billion dollar business deals, political machinations, mistaken identities and so on, the hub of the story—and the key anchor for the intense audience involvement—were the "ordinary human" dimensions of personal and family relationships, marked by age old rituals such as births, marriages and deaths, the intimacies, disappointments and petty jealousies of romance and friendship, and the moral dilemmas brought about by conflicting interests and values. In short, it is at the intimate level of *feeling* that *Dallas* resonated. (Ang 2007, 19)

In televised Senate hearings in the month of November 2016

alone, murder attempts, illegal business deals, and political machinations were featured, as were former lovers in scandalous circumstances, former allies turned enemies, and figures on both sides of the fence, whether drug lords or police chiefs, who had to face their own betrayal of loved ones or the betrayal of their comrades. In these and other storylines, feelings of honor, loyalty, and love were in conflict with the temptations of corruption and the fear of retribution. For viewers of the Philippine Senate proceedings, as for the viewers of *Dallas* studied by Ang, it is the human dimension of the politicians and witnesses brought before the Senate to tell their stories and determine the truth that captures attention.

As Ang notes, despite the grandness of scale upon which many storylines play out, viewers engage "at the intimate level of *feeling*." Soap operas have frequently been derided for their unabashed exploration of feeling, and it is no coincidence that such derision bears a strong resemblance to the ways in which Duterte's mass supporters have sometimes been characterized: as lacking in culture or knowledge, low in status, or "trashy" (Allen 2002, 4). In her call for a more complex approach to unpacking the nature of Duterte's popular support, Curato has come from a different angle to note the important role of feelings in explaining the motivations of many Duterte voters, arguing that "impoverished publics view consideration and kindness as constitutive of 'good politics'" (2016, 96), and that their support of Duterte is "a product of constant negotiation between the politics of anxiety and the politics of hope" (92). The centrality of feelings in the formation of moral and political worldviews, whether in the embracing of popular cultural forms like soap opera or in the embracing of populist candidates like Duterte, does not sit well with traditional conceptions of how an effective public sphere in a modern nation state should operate. Just as educated viewers are expected to develop refined tastes that value "quality" television, educated voters are expected to make political choices based on rational debate. In the following section, then, I suggest how the parallel explorations of popular audiences and populist politics might be fruitfully brought into conversation to understand the success of Duterte in a highly mediated era.

Audiences and Publics

Following Curato's call to better understand the nature of Duterte's voting public, I suggest that some cues can be taken from the early work of media and cultural studies scholars on soap opera and other forms of mass entertainment, which argued for popular culture as an important site for the study of social life. Studies of audiences like those of *Dallas* or similarly derided forms of culture argued that mass entertainment cannot be dismissed as an inferior or misplaced set of tastes. Such work rejected the notion of popular audiences as "cultural dupes" being manipulated by the media; audiences' genuine identifications with, and feelings for, television storylines were explored as a serious expression of sentiments, values, and ideologies—even when viewers themselves may not take their programs of choice entirely seriously (Ang 2007; Fiske 1987).

Since it first flourished in the late 1980s, audience studies have received their fair share of critique and pushback within the world of media scholarship. Arguing for the capacity of audiences to appropriate the media contents they consume and defending popular tastes as something more than media manipulation have at times veered too far into assuming that the consumption of popular entertainment is inherently positive and perhaps even empowering for audiences (Parameswaran 2013). Certainly, in the case of the Philippines, there is little evidence that viewers who engage enthusiastically in both the television programs that fill the airwaves and in the elections that bring their leaders to power have experienced any significant cultural or economic mobility as a result. Acknowledging the validity of popular preferences in cultural forms or politics and exploring the motivations of viewers and voters, therefore, do not mean that these expressions of popular enthusiasm automatically result in serious sociopolitical transformation.

Over the past two decades, media scholars have turned from demarcating the audience as a discrete realm of practices and tastes related to media consumption toward a broader examination of how people interact with media texts and technologies as part of their everyday lives. No longer seen as "just" audiences, viewers have been variously defined as users, participants, *produsers* (producer-users), cultural citizens, or increasingly, as publics. Audiences and publics have traditionally been conceived from different disciplinary traditions, perhaps most simplistically being associated with the fields of media studies and political science, respectively. As Sonia Livingstone has noted, audiences and publics have sometimes been understood in opposition: "in both popular and elite discourses, audiences are denigrated as trivial, passive, individualised, while publics are valued as active, critically engaged and politically significant" (2005, 18). Audiences have historically been associated with the private realm of entertainment, family, and emotion, while publics are associated with politics, citizenship, and rational debate. Yet audiences and publics are made up of the same people, and increasingly in both media studies and political science, audiences have been productively studied as publics, and publics as audiences. Seeing audiences as publics, made up of viewer-voters or citizen-consumers, is particularly relevant in an age of multiple media platforms and interactive technologies, in which people engage in public and private dialogue while engaging with entertainment and political content in digitally mediated contexts, sometimes simultaneously and frequently on the same device (Livingstone 2005).

Drawing from Anderson's notion of the *imagined community*, ethnographies of media production and consumption have also investigated the central role that popular media can play in the construction of national publics. Around the world, scholars have shown how television programs make use of melodrama to convert their audiences into national communities. In China in the 1990s, the popular soap opera *Yearnings* took the country by storm and viewers were "heatedly debating the qualities of the heroes and villains" at a time when the Chinese state was undergoing a transition to market socialism that was transforming everyday life (Rofel 1994, 700). In Egypt, too, melodramatic serials have been studied by Lila Abu-Lughod as an important mechanism by which women were able to engage with discourses of modernity that were shaping the nation-state (Abu-Lughod 2004). The emotional impact of daily soap operas and other melodramatic programs connect viewers at home to a public world in which political leaders and advertisers compete for their loyalty. But the Philippines has gone one step further in bringing together dramatic entertainment and national publics. There, politics makes use of television melodrama to keep citizens following the storylines.

Concluding Comments

Although at first glance a Senate full of television stars and sports-people may seem to be amusing buffoonery, this chapter has sought to demonstrate that melodrama is in fact very serious business. In a context where few politicians have ever delivered genuine reform to improve the lives of Filipinos through actual policies, the emotional dimension of following the ups and downs of political players in their television senatorial courtroom drama at least offers some kind of connection for everyday viewers.

Observers note that pursuing Senate investigations that explore the details of a senator's sexual life and televising testimony from alleged drug-lords is distracting politicians and the public from more serious issues. Within the Philippines, the cycles of news stories created by senatorial investigations and presidential pronouncements occupy at least as much airtime as stories of extra-judicial killings. They also generate further discussion—and dispute—on social media. Yet the melodramatic dimensions of Philippine politics cannot be dismissed as a sideshow in the national political scene; the melodrama of Senate hearings and other mediated political encounters is important to understand because these moments generate the emotional ties that push people to support politicians in times of tension and transition.

The Philippines offers an extreme example of an evolution of electoral politics that has been noted around the world, with the mixing of entertainment media and political movements. Silvio Berlusconi's media empire was an essential part of his domination of Italian politics (Campus 2010). Most recently, Donald Trump was able to parlay his mastery of reality television into political success, a culmination of the growing presence of what Elisabeth Anker has described as "melodramatic political discourse" in US politics (2014). While mastering the art of public performance is part of any politician's job, populist leaders who rise to power as symbols of change have an especially good talent for melodrama. They thrive on conflict, and they don't shrink away from the twists and turns of changing loyalties and personal vendettas. Politics is a world for which showbusiness celebrities are perfectly adapted, and their predominance in the Philippines offers a glimpse of what televisual populism could look like in other countries.

References

Abu-Lughod, Lila. 2004. *Dramas of Nationhood: The Politics of Television in Egypt*. Chicago: University of Chicago Press.

Allen, Robert C., ed. 2002. *To Be Continued . . . Soap Operas Around the World*. London and New York: Routledge.

Ang, Ien. 2007. "Television Fictions Around the World: Melodrama and Irony in Global Perspective." *Critical Studies in Television: The International Journal of Television Studies* 2 (2):18–30.

Anker, Elisabeth R. 2014. *Orgies of Feeling: Melodrama and the Politics of Freedom*. Durham NC: Duke University Press.

Campus, Donatella. 2010. "Mediatization and Personalization of Politics in Italy and France: The Cases of Berlusconi and Sarkozy." *The International Journal of Press/Politics* 15 (2):219–35.

Curato, Nicole. 2016. "Politics of Anxiety, Politics of Hope: Penal Populism and Duterte's Rise to Power." *Journal of Current Southeast Asian Studies* 3:91–109.

Doronila, Amando. 1985. "The Transformation of Patron-Client Relations and Its Political Consequences in Postwar Philippines." *Journal of Southeast Asian Studies* 16 (1):99–116.

Espiritu, Talitha. 2015. "The Marcos Romance and the Cultural Center of the Philippines: The Melodrama of a Therapeutic Cultural Policy." *Journal of Narrative Therapy* 45 (1):141–62.

Fiske, John. 1987. *Television Culture*. London and New York: Routledge.

Livingtone, Sonia. 2005. "On the Relation Between Audiences and Publics." In *Audiences and Publics: When Cultural Engagement Matters for the Public Sphere*, ed. Sonia Livingstone, 17–41. Bristol, UK: Intellect Books.

Parameswaran, Radhika. 2013. "Studying the Elusive Audience: Consumers, Readers, Users, Viewers in a Changing World." *International Encyclopedia of Media Studies* 4:1–24.

Pertierra, Anna Cristina. 2016. "Re-locating the Spaces of Television Studies." *Media and Communication* 4 (3):123–30.

Rafael, Vicente L. 1990. "Patronage and Pornography: Ideology and Spectatorship in the Early Marcos Years." *Comparative Studies in Society and History* 32 (2):282–304.

Reyes, Danilo A. 2016. "The Spectacle of Violence in Duterte's "War on Drugs."" *Journal of Current Southeast Asian Studies* 3:111–137.

Rofel, Lisa. 1994. "Yearnings: Televisual Love and Melodramatic Politics in Contemporary China." *American Ethnologist* 21 (4):700–722.

Sanchez, Louie Jon. A. 2014. "Koreanovelas, Teleseryes and the 'Diasporization' of the Filipino/the Philippines." *Plaridel* 11 (10):66–85.

The Rise of Trolls in the Philippines (And What We Can Do About It)

Jason Vincent A. Cabañes
Jayeel S. Cornelio

The promise of social media is to democratize public participation. But accompanying it is the curse of hate.

There are, regrettably, no signs that social media will be any less virulent any time soon. Still recovering from the battlefield that was the 2016 presidential race, social media in the Philippines continues to be a site for animosity and spite. This is far from the ideal of a digital public sphere that can be a site for critical yet engaging discussions. Mainstream media in the Philippines—and some foreign media outlets as well—have linked the emergence of this phenomenon to Duterte's rise to power (see Almario-Gonzales 2017; Caruncho 2016a; Ressa 2016; see also Lamble and Mohan 2016; Williams 2017). As observers have pointed out, some of the key perpetrators of this virulence are President Rodrigo Duterte's supporters. They are social media users—with both verified and suspicious accounts—who seem to take every opportunity to attack Duterte's critics. They are collectively referred to as trolls, which, as our discussion below will show, is not an unproblematic category. Their attacks range from a simple rebuttal to a concerted assault on prominent figures by shaming them. These entities have caused anxiety and panic among not just other online users but also journalists and commentators.

Political trolling in itself is neither new nor unique to the Philippines. Political communication strategists have long been "weaponizing" various media platforms to generate for their clients a competitive advantage over their political opponents (Burroughs 2013, 260). Even before the advent of Internet 2.0, strategists from the early 1990s right up to the 2000s were already using, amongst other tactics, mudslinging stump speeches and negative television ads (Ansolabehere and Iyengar 1995; Scammell and Langer 2006). In the Philippines, these activities began appearing not soon after, starting as well in the early 1990s and further ratcheting up by the early 2000s with the lifting of the ban on political advertisements in the mainstream media (Bionat 1998; Perron 2008). Emblematic of these trolling activities was the campaign to label the late Senator Miriam Defensor-Santiago "Brenda" (which was short for brain-damaged). Although this label was first concocted to undermine her status as one of the leading contenders during the 1992 presidential elections, it was an attribute that continued to hound her subsequent attempts to run for public office.

What the Philippine and foreign mainstream media have gotten right, however, is the newness of the intensity that has come to characterize the online version of political trolling in the country. This is a trend that one can also see in many other contexts, from similar transitional democracies like Turkey to relatively more mature democracies like the United States (see Ozsoy 2015; Pew Research 2016). By paying particular attention to contemporary developments in the Philippines, this chapter contributes to efforts at establishing a more general account of the increasingly vitriolic online political trolling coming out of many democratically inclined societies. In the ensuing discussion, we provide sociological explanations for the rise of online political trolling in the Philippines and assess whether and how online political trolls play a role in fostering a democratic media in the country. We also caution against the use of trolling in our political vocabulary, for we find this term problematic.

We begin by considering the definition of an online political troll. We argue that in the Philippines, as in many other contexts, one needs to be careful in approaching such a contested term. We then look at the role of the online political troll in Philippine politics. We attend to how they have gained unprecedented popularity through the distinct dynamics of the country's democracy but also to how they have undermined the possibility of making better this very same democracy. We conclude by turning to normative frameworks that might help the public sphere move away from the pernicious predominance of toxic online political trolling. We suggest two particular approaches to re-imagining the country's media so that it could move toward a more democratic future.

Defining the Online Political Troll

Before examining how online trolls matter in today's Philippine politics, it is important to reflect on the ways in which this concept has been defined. This is crucial insofar as we need to understand "why and how trolls, what they are and what they do, and what is discursively legitimate and what isn't, have come to preoccupy us" (Fuller et al. 2013, 6).

Today's popular conception of the online political troll is an amalgam of two distinct ideas that have preceded it. One is political trolling. This idea, as we have mentioned earlier, was established even before the arrival of Web 2.0. It pertains to how political communication strategists employ negative campaign tactics in harnessing media for political gain (Burroughs 2013). The other idea is online trolling. It has its origins in the 1990s, when its use was, at the time, not necessarily related to political activities. It instead pertained to any individual's attempt to generate a reaction from others by posting provocative or offensive online messages on what was then known as Usenet boards (Bishop 2014).

Drawing on these two ideas, today's online political troll is often understood to be someone who uses the practices of online trolling as part of negative political campaigns. According to the most up-voted definition in the Urban Dictionary—the so-called "crowdsourced mirror of the vernacular" (Fuller et al. 2013, 2)—these tactics are characterized by

The art of deliberately, cleverly, and secretly pissing people off, usually via the Internet, using dialogue. Trolling does not mean just making rude remarks: Shouting swear words at someone doesn't count as trolling; it's just flaming, and isn't funny. Spam isn't trolling either; it pisses people off, but it's lame. The most essential part of trolling is convincing your victim that either a) truly believe in what you are saying, no matter how outrageous, or b) give your victim malicious instructions, under the guise of help. Trolling requires decieving [*sic*]; any trolling that doesn't involve decieving [*sic*] someone isn't trolling at all; it's just stupid. As such, your victim must not know that you are trolling; if he does, you are an unsuccesfull [*sic*] troll.

Characterized as they are by deception, provocation, and futile conversation, online political trolls are branded in primarily negative terms (see Schwartz 2008; see also Donath 1996; Herring et al. 2002). Calling out someone as an online political troll can be a power-laden exercise. It is often the case that this is used polemically, as a way to indicate that someone is acting in a manner that transgresses and harms the shared values of an online community. As the invocation "Do not feed the trolls!" makes clear, this act of labeling involves recognizing "who ought or ought not to speak or be listened to" (Fuller et al. 2013, 1) and consequently "shutting down debate and self-reflection amongst community members" (Bergstrom 2011, online). It is clearly important to be careful in labeling someone as an online political troll.

In the Philippines, the label of "online political troll" has been tacked on to a broad swathe of people. The country's experience in the recent 2016 elections demonstrates how liberally this term has been used. On one end of the spectrum are the paid professional trolls. They are the ones who most closely resemble the conceptual definition we have fleshed out above, in that their work involves the three elements of deception, provocation, and futile conversations. These trolls are said to be behind fake social media accounts that advance the cause of particular political candidates by "infiltrat[ing] online conversations, specifically on Facebook, to promote causes or candidates, and in the [2016 Philippine] elections succeeded in using this organization to disparage political opponents, among others" (Almario-Gonzales 2017, online).

At the opposite end of the spectrum, there are real individuals who happen to believe in and, consequently, participate in propagating the concerted messages laid out by the professional trolls. While they are not motivated by a desire for deception or futile conversation, they are also labeled trolls or, at the very least, part of the infrastructure of the so-called Philippine troll army (see Caruncho 2016b). It is important to note here that when individuals label other individuals a troll, they depend heavily on their political loyalties; a troll for one person might be a reasonable person for another. For instance, those who support President Duterte refer to other supporters as "Ka-DDS" (that is, a fellow Diehard Duterte Supporter). Meanwhile, those who oppose the president would be inclined to think of his supporters as trolls and call them a "Dutertard" (that is, a retarded supporter of Duterte). Unfortunately, once an individual is labeled a Dutertard—and by implication, a troll—then that individual is put "beyond the pale" (Fuller et al. 2013, 1). The insidious consequence of this is that some quarters use this label as a

> reassertion of the "table manners" of liberal civility; like any such insistence it can be a way of forestalling political demands made outside the current limits of acceptability in political contention. It can also be used to redefine these demands as so much unintelligible noise. (Fuller et al. 2013)

In other words, labelling those who do not agree with one's political leanings "trolls" is saying that they are not worth engaging, thereby completely closing the possibility of any meaningful dialogue.

What complicates all these categorizations is that there are people who occupy the gray area in between professional trolls and real individuals expressing their own political beliefs albeit in ways that might resemble trolling. Take the case of Mocha Uson, who has emerged as a key figure in contemporary Philippine social media. Mocha rose to fame as the lead singer of an all-girl group known for its risqué performances. Contrary to depictions of her as a political opportunist, she was in fact an advocate of various social issues even before Duterte campaigned for the presidency. For instance, she had previously campaigned for breast cancer awareness and for what was then the Reproductive Health Bill (Carpio 2016). During the elections, Mocha was one of Duterte's most vocal supporters. For Mocha's own supporters, her Facebook page now serves as a credible source of information about Duterte and his detractors. Her claim on her Twitter account that she is "not a journalist" takes a swipe at mainstream reporters whom she believes are paid to attack the president (Cornelio 2016). As a result, Mocha is lionized as a hero. For these presidential supporters, she maintains "the most enlightening website out there" (Dizon 2016). But she is at the same time reviled by the president's critics and dismissed as a professional troll. For these critics, Mocha is "a national troll, a laughing-stock, a 'Dutertard'" (Dizon 2016).

As we carry on with our discussion, it is important to keep in mind the complexity of delineating the boundaries of those who can be usefully called trolls. In the next section, we attempt to explain the rise of professional trolls as key actors in contemporary Philippine politics. We focus on the vitriolic brand of trolling that they have brought into online political discussions. To do this, we talk about how they have risen precisely because of the dynamics that predominate in the country's democracy. We also discuss how they risk hindering the further development of this very same democracy.

Reflecting on the Rise of the Online Political Troll

Today's prominence of the online political troll in the Philippines—most especially of the vitriolic kind—cannot be easily reduced to the crucial role of political machineries and their operations. In order to make sense of the rise of this phenomenon, we suggest a sociological approach that attends to the prevailing public sentiments that have embraced the provocative message of trolls.

To be sure, the political campaign strategists in the 2016 elections hired advertising agencies to create a buzz around their candidates. Communication campaign plans were drafted and implemented by these offices that operated like call center agencies. Part of these plans was to use professional trolls to respond to targeted individuals, with prepared responses that were simply copied and pasted. The ultimate objective of marshalling these trolls was to hijack conversations of legitimate social media account owners. As a strategist involved in using trolls put it, the aim was to make ordinary individuals "become a servant of the ideology that these fake trolls have injected you with" (Caruncho 2016a). This professional troll work was a financially rewarding job, which could reportedly earn a keyboard warrior as much as PhP 3,000 a day.

An ongoing study[1] has discovered that even beyond the 2016 election cycle, campaign strategists have continued to work with similarly structured "black ops" projects. These are led by consultants, most of whom are professionals previously employed by advertising agencies, PR firms, and/or media organizations. They would gather a small team of about five individuals to create and maintain troll accounts on social media, primarily on Facebook. These troll accounts, originating primarily from Manila, would chat one-on-one with individuals, with the aim of orchestrating a unified "campaign message" about particular political figures or issues. This campaign message would then be amplified by click farm workers based in the regions, who are employed to like, share, and follow a script in commenting on relevant social media posts. Apart from these real individuals manning troll accounts, the ecology of trolls has also relied on automated bots on social media that generate roughly 20 percent of troll posts. In concert with manned troll accounts, these programs could be activated to make particular messages trend.

Trolling has become readily associated with Duterte's supporters, who defend him against his critics and exalt him "as the father of the nation deserving the support of all Filipinos" (Serafica 2016). Trolls and bots have reportedly come together to sow fear and uncertainty by threatening Duterte's critics. In spite of the president's call for his supporters to temper themselves, some of his critics have been bullied and threatened with rape and murder (Rappler 2016). Journalists reporting on Duterte have also been attacked for being biased and corrupt.

It is easy to relate the vitriol of trolls against Duterte's critics to the demeanor of the president, who is seen to be unforgiving toward his own adversaries. Some commentators have argued that his cursing has engendered a following that is equally angry. We suggest, however, that the process is not as straightforward. This view is one-sided, with attention given to the power of trolls to influence public opinion, often through fear and misinformation.

Our view is that much of the message of trolls could not have gained traction if they did not resonate with public opinion, especially those that mainstream news media, whether wittingly or otherwise, did not adequately acknowledge and engage. Interrogating their emergence means looking at the mainstream media's capacity to balance the often-contradictory demands of representing public opinion in a way that promotes shared values but that, crucially, also represents diverse voices (Scammell 2003). Beyond this, such an interrogation is also as much about the "culture in which trolls thrive" (Phillips 2015, 12). For the message to become viral, it had to, one way or another, speak to the felt experiences of many people that were being neglected in broader public discourses. Contra the generally elite-driven reportage of the mainstream news media then (Ong 2015), the dummy accounts professional trolls made imbibed realistic characters such as the "concerned netizen" or the "struggling OFW" (Caruncho 2016a). And these personae pointed to the gut issues that remain important for the ordinary Filipino aspiring for the good life. They also pointed to the disillusionment of many Filipinos about their current living conditions.

Duterte's rise to power did not happen overnight. His message was carefully deployed around his own credentials, personality, and record. His campaign strategy identified the single issue of criminality and made it the pillar even of his entire presidency. Although this approach was unusual relative to the broad advocacies of other candidates, he tapped into an issue that mattered to local communities. There is no doubt that in previous years, criminality and drug abuse were perennial concerns at the level of the community. But surveys show that Duterte turned it into the top national concern as his campaign progressed, effectively dislodging the predictable issues of employment, inflation, and wages (Holmes 2016).

If there was anything that trolls effectively took advantage of for Duterte, it was his ruthless attitude to criminality that made the public reimagine the new enemies of the state. Duterte, after all, embodied a game-changer in the recent elections: political will and discipline. In fact, the way he cursed and talked about corruption, the bureaucracy, and justice resonated with an electorate looking for a figure who understood their plight and had the track record to back it up. This explains why trolls and legitimate online users could readily dismiss critics of the president as enemies of the state and the nation at large. In fact, even journalists have also been attacked for their perceived bias against the administration. Although journalists have reframed their objectivity as a struggle for truth and justice, professional trolls have accused them of being paid, for example (Dangla 2016). As a result, trolls and prominent figures for Duterte, like Mocha Uson, have become alternative sources of information and criticism and they even frame their statements as such (see Cornelio 2016).

The virulence of trolling and the rise of professional trolls are not simply a consequence of Duterte's gutter language. Trolling relies on the aspirations of both the "struggling OFW" and the fears of the ordinary Filipino affected by crime, both of which have been perceived to be largely ignored until recently by mainstream news media. The moral panic about Duterte's aggressive speech and the rise of trolling misses out on the implicit discontent of the public and the desire for a game-changer who would finally recognize and act on their concerns. We then agree with Curato's (2016, 92) argument that the massive support for Duterte is a product of "constant negotiation between the politics of anxiety and the politics of hope." Virulence, in other words, is not only about anger, frustration, and disillusionment. In a counterintuitive manner, it is also a figurative language that points to a better world. It revolves around Duterte and comes against his enemies.

To sharpen our point: The virulence of trolls would not have gone viral if it were simply reliant on campaign strategies. Trolls and the legitimate online users who passed on their message found a language in which they could articulate people's disappointments and aspirations. It is by surfacing shared public sentiments that we offer a corrective to the concept of "mediated populism," which for the most part focuses on how the candidate with "the best-told narrative" wins "media attention, and ultimately voter support" (McCargo 2016, 189). The narrative involves populist themes that play on, among others, people's fears and anxieties, desire for a political redeemer, and rejection of traditional politicians. In our view, trolls and their messages that go viral online demonstrate how the mediation of populism does not only emanate from the top. It relies on timely sentiments shared (actively, in many cases) by the public who support the populist candidate. In the Philippine experience in 2016, the "populist publics," as Curato (2016, 95, 97) refers to Duterte's supporters, cut across "classes, generations, gender and geography." In other words, Duterte's support base is not only the poor or the Visayan-speaking regions. This explains why the message of vitriolic trolling has resonated with different kinds of online actors: from Manila's everyday commuter to longtime overseas Filipino workers.

There is, however, a caveat on the pervasiveness of trolling. In the same manner that the rise of Duterte did not happen overnight, sustaining his popularity is not going to be an easy feat. Much of it lies in following through on his promises, not least of which is his commitment to eradicating illegal drugs and criminality. It also lies in his ability to bridge massive divides in society and politics (Habito 2017). If it were to come, the decline of Duterte's popularity can spell the limit of trolling in defense of the president. In other words, there is an end to the vitriol. But if there is any lesson to be learned from Duterte's rise, it is that trolling could make a comeback insofar as it gives mediated expression to the repressed discontent of a public left out by economic progress and a government seen to favor only those it wishes to favor. This is the promise of trolling. It is also its pitfall.

Thinking of a Future Beyond the Online Political Troll

The final contribution of this piece lies in thinking about the ethical implications of trolling in relation to politics in the Philippines, in general, and to media democratization, in particular. There are two areas that we need to revisit in light of the discussions above: *how we understand trolling and who constitutes trolls* and *how we might imagine a more democratic media that can move beyond the need for trolls.*

Much of the discourse on contemporary trolling has depicted it as a massive enterprise that hijacks the quality of democratic conversations. To those who are affected by professional trolls, for example, their anger and frustration are understandable. But at the same time, we need to emphasize that not all those who are portrayed as trolls are paid to deliver a scripted message against Duterte's opponents. Many of them are also legitimate owners of social media accounts, which they use to engage in the public sphere. But because they are associated with Duterte, they are altogether readily dismissed as uncritical supporters of the president. It is in this manner that we wish to rethink how discourse about trolling could also be a form of moral panic—that is, a fear of an attack on an idyllic social order—conjured by Duterte's critics (Bishop 2014; Fuller et al. 2013).

A sense of moral panic is discernible, for example, in Renee Juliene M. Karunungan's response to the threats she received when she campaigned against Duterte in 2016: "More than the need to re-evaluate and change the government and the system, it's time we re-evaluate ourselves, check our values, and start becoming human again."[2] Karunungan's brief commentary is as much about society as it is about trolling. One problem though is that it is not clear what "becoming human again" means and whether it refers to a condition that existed before trolls arose. The other problem is that it is also not clear whether the attacks she received came from professional trolls, legitimate account owners, or both. The brief commentary, heartfelt as it might be, reinforces the moral elitism that was perpetuated by the Liberal Party's depiction of Duterte (and by implication his supporters) as indecent (see Office of Mar Roxas 2016). It is not the first time that we have seen this move, of course. In the past, populist publics who supported such figures as Joseph Estrada and Jejomar Binay were also framed as unintelligent, fanatic voters by their opponents (Curato 2016). In this light, it is crucial for commentators and the wider public to make a clear distinction between professional trolls, automated bots, and those who are readily dismissed as trolls even if they are legitimate social media account users. The conflation of these different entities is not helpful especially in trying to understand the logics of a particular support base.[3]

Our other ethical concern has to do with how we might imagine a more democratic media. At the level of the individual, it is important for online users to rethink how they respond to those whom they perceive to be trolls. The easy way out for many is to block them immediately. But the distinction we made above has to be made first. We are convinced that although one of their primary tasks is to exploit fear and uncertainty, trolls have a contribution to deepening the quality of conversations in the public sphere. Inasmuch as professional trolls, for example, are paid to incite other users, their contrarian views can sharpen public opinion about issues. Some of these issues are Duterte's war on drugs, extra-judicial killings, the death penalty, and the burial of Marcos in the Libingan ng mga Bayani. Political parties in the Philippines, because of shifting allegiances, are unable to provide clear ideological lines that guide or shape public opinion (Hicken 2015).

But there is a caveat here. Inasmuch as they sharpen people's opinions, the presence of trolls can also give the impression (and thereby distraction) that democratic participation is alive and well, especially when online actors are fired up to respond. What reinforces this impression is that content that is widely circulated—trending, in Twitterspeak—makes it to primetime news. Media companies aim for their information to trend and at the same time perpetuate its impression of success by reporting them. Therefore, inasmuch as there are discussions of how the online environment fosters the participation of citizens, political and business elites can dominate them and shape what comes out of these platforms (Harder, Paulussen, and van Aelst 2016). In fact, that business interests, in the form of advertising agencies, collude with political machineries exemplifies how "communicative capitalism" or the celebration of online spaces as the success of democratic participation can be taken to the extreme (Dean 2009). What happens in communicative capitalism is that a message proliferates without being engaged in a meaningful conversation or aiming for action that affects politics at the level of institutions (see also Golumbia 2013).

We must therefore be concerned about the management of trolls and ensuring the quality of conversations on the Internet. The democratic sphere on the Internet is a space for individuals to engage especially with those who hold differing beliefs. Threads, online forums, and comment sections are spaces for the sharing of diverse opinions. But in the spirit of democratic discourse, these spaces call for "mutual accountability" such that when an opinion is challenged, individuals have an ethical responsibility to respond using rationalities and values that are generally understandable (see discussion in LaFont 2009). Trolls, as paid professionals, are not in these spaces for discussions (Golumbia 2013). There is thus no doubt that professional trolls (including automated bots) do not deserve any public engagement. We need structures and online systems that ensure that bots and professional trolls are discouraged from hijacking online spaces. But the other issue has to do with the vigilance of legitimate online actors who may echo the message of trolls. It is they who deserve engagement even if their response may not be forthcoming.

Beyond people's individual engagements with trolls then is a broader arena that needs to be considered. Here we are talking about how Philippine mainstream media might be able to provide spaces that could accord recognition to a wider array of public perspectives on the issues that shape the country's political life. Recall that one key point we have raised in the previous section is that trolls have gained currency because of how they have managed to articulate and amplify the disgruntled sentiments of the public.

It is in this light that we suggest that mainstream news companies in the Philippines—including those operating in the space of social media—are now at a crossroads concerning how they are to engage opinion makers whose views differ from their own. To us, the conventional debate on handling trolls is no longer tenable. It cannot simply be about encouraging a libertarian approach that fosters unregulated free speech or pursuing a strict communitarian model that maintains the integrity of social media at the expense of dissent (Herring et al. 2002).

To us, the situation calls for mainstream news media to reconsider the debates about how one might arrive at the truth, a value that constitutes "the most longstanding and pervasive normative understanding of journalism" (Ryfe 2017, 108). Here we suggest two ways of moving forward. One is that the media can continue to assert their claim to neutrality and objectivity, a news principle that the Philippine media primarily has imbibed from the US media (and something that is not necessarily predominant in other democratic media) (Tandoc 2016). This impels journalists to adopt an attitude of detachment and impartiality as well as to develop practices such as building stories from facts, checking the credibility of sources, verifying information, and ensuring balanced views (Kovach and Rosenstiel 2001). We argue, however, that the media should do this better. They particularly need to maximize the ideal of promoting internal diversity, which is about "a situation in which a single media outlet comprises all relevant viewpoints without favoring a particular position" (Voltmer 2010, 144). In concrete terms, this means opening spaces wherein public perspectives, such as those espoused by the so-called trolls who support and undermine President Duterte, can be aired alongside other perspectives. This also means taking pains to regulate this space so that it fosters meaningful dialogues across competing political beliefs.

The second, and perhaps bolder, approach that we suggest that the mainstream news media can take is to recast the way they understand how the truth is arrived at. As in the case with the news media in some European democracies and, recently, in some quarters of news media in the United States as well, they can emphasize transparency over neutrality and objectivity (see Hanitzch et al. 2014). This would require journalists to be reflexive about their biases and for mainstream media outlets to be clear about their partisan leanings. Take, for instance, how the *Guardian* took a clear pro-Remain stance during the 2016 EU referendum, running an editorial that laid out why they thought that key to the UK's future was to "keep connected and inclusive" and "not [be] angry and isolated" (The Guardian Editorial Board 2016). There was also the *New York Times* taking a strong stand against the candidacy of President Donald Trump, with an editorial that spelled out their reasons for "why

Donald Trump should not be president" (New York Times Editorial Board 2016). The barrier in reimagining the Philippine media along these lines, however, is that it will necessitate tremendous structural change. It will mean the entire media infrastructure shifting toward promoting external diversity, which is about "a plurality of perspectives to be evident across media markets and a wide range of outlets, without major restrictions or censorship limiting freedom of expression" (Voltmer 2010, 260). Concretely, this will entail legitimate media outlets that would each clearly align with those who support different political personalities and political positions, such as those who back and critique President Duterte and other positions in between. The point here is to have legitimate media platforms, rather than trolls, articulate these different positions.

In a time of increasing vitriol in our social media, we would like to push mainstream news media companies in the Philippines to reimagine what journalism could be, both in terms of how they deliver information and how they engage the public (see Zelizer 2017). We contend that they should experiment with fresh and more compelling ways of harnessing the space of the social media to guide the audience to think through and act on salient issues that trolls bring up. The point therefore is that social media becomes an authentic space for critical exchange and political action. The proposals we have offered are ways of moving forward to render media spaces more flexible, thus avoiding the temptation to build boundaries that end up creating echo chambers instead. We are of the view that "a retreat into one's local enclave, while effective at preventing attack, is not effective for building a robust modern democratic public" (Forestal 2017, 158).

Widening the opportunity for the sharing of different opinions by the media can enhance the political participation of online actors who otherwise would be isolated in their own echo chambers (Vromen 2017). A plurality of voices on various issues can weaken well-rehearsed messages of online political trolls that essentialize dissenters as being uncritically loyal or opposed to certain figures or parties.

At this point, however, online political trolls have hijacked much of the space. News companies and other social media actors are left with little choice but to play the crucial but inadequate role of reclaiming it. But simply reclaiming the space will no longer do. The task is to reimagine it.

Endnotes

[1]   As part of the Newton-funded Tech4Dev Network, Cabañes is a co-researcher in an ongoing study that assesses the state of digital labor in the Philippines. Amongst other kinds of digital workers, this research looks at the working lives of individuals who staff online political troll accounts. The other co-researchers in this research are Cheryll Soriano and Jonathan Corpus Ong.

[2]   Based on the Facebook photo posted by Renee Julienne M. Karunungan: www.facebook.com/photo.php?fbid=1015363859612886 5&set=a.70760843864.66430.635843864&type=3

[3]   This assessment also parallels the findings from Vote of the Poor 2016, a study in which Cornelio is involved. The other investigators are Filomeno Aguilar Jr., Jowel Canuday, and Lisandro Claudio. A monograph is being prepared for the Institute of Philippine Culture.

References

Almario-Gonzales, Chi. 2017. "Unmasking the Trolls: Spin Masters Behind Fake Accounts, News Sites." *ABS-CBN News*, 20 January. http://news.abs-cbn.com/focus/01/20/17/unmasking-the-trolls-spin-masters-behind-fake-accounts-news-sites.

Ansolabehere, Stephen, and Shanto Iyengar. 1995. *Going Negative: How Attack Ads Shrink and Polarize the Electorate*. New York: Free Press.

Bergstrom, Kelly. 2011. "'Don't Feed the Troll': Shutting Down Debate About Community Expectations on Reddit.com" *First Monday* 16: 8. http://firstmonday.org/article/view/3498/3029.

Bishop, Jonathan. 2014. "Representations of 'Trolls' in Mass Media Communication: A Review of Media-Texts and Moral Panics Relating to 'Internet Trolling.'" *International Journal of Web Based Communities* 10, no. 1:7–24.

Bionat, Marvin. 1998. *How to Win (or Lose) in Philippine Elections: The Dynamics of Winning or Losing in Philippine Electoral Contests*. Pasig City: Anvil.

Burroughs, Benjamin. 2013. "Obama Trolling: Memes, Salutes and an

Agonistic Politics in the 2012 Presidential Election." *The Fibreculture Journal* 22:257–76.

Carpio, Audrey. 2016. "Who's Afraid of Mocha Uson?" *Esquire.* http://www.esquiremag.ph/long-reads/profiles-and-features/mocha-uson-full-text-a1521-20161202-lfrm4/.

Caruncho, Eric. 2016a. "Confessions of a Troll." *Inquirer*, sec. Lifestyle. http://lifestyle.inquirer.net/236403/confessions-of-a-troll/.

———. 2016b. "The Infrastructure of the Philippine Troll Army." *Inquirer*, sec. Lifestyle. http://lifestyle.inquirer.net/244554/infrastructure-philippine-troll-army/.

Cornelio, Jayeel. 2016. "So What if Mocha Uson Is Not a Journalist?" *Rappler.* http://www.rappler.com/thought-leaders/154936-mocha-uson-not-a-journalist/.

Curato, Nicole. 2016. "Politics of Hope: Penal Populism and Duterte's Rise to Power." *Journal of Current Southeast Asian Affairs* 35 (3):91–109.

Dangla, Demerie. 2016. "What Journalists Say on 'Bias' Tag, Attacks." *ABS-CBN News.* http://news.abs-cbn.com/news/09/30/16/what-journalists-say-on-bias-tag-attacks.

Dean, Jodi. 2009. *Democracy and Other Neoliberal Fantasies: Communicative Capitalism and Left Politics*. Durham and London: Duke University Press.

Donath, Judith. 1999. "Identity and Deception in the Virtual Community." In *Community and Identity in Cyberspace*, ed. P. Kollock and M. Smith. London and New York, NY: Routledge.

Dizon, Irish Christianne. 2016. "A Night with Mocha Uson." *Philippine Star.* http://www.philstar.com/supreme/2016/06/11/1591614/night-mocha-uson.

Forestal, Jennifer, 2017. "The Architecture of Political Space: Trolls, Digital Media, and Deweyan Democracy." *American Political Science Review* 111 (1):149–61.

Fuller, Glen, Christian McCrea, and Jason Wilson. 2013. "Troll Theory?" *The Fibreculture Journal* 22:1–14.

Golumbia, David. 2013. "Commercial Trolling: Social Media and the Corporate Deformation of Democracy." https://papers.ssrn.com/sol3/papers.cfm?abstract_id=2394716.

Habito, Cielito. 2017. "Badly Divided." *Philippine Daily Inquirer*, A11.

Hanitzsch, Thomas, Folker Hanusch, and Corinna Lauerer. 2014. "Setting the Agenda, Influencing Public Opinion, and Advocating for Social Change." *Journalism Studies* 17 (1):1–20.

Harder, Raymond, Steve Paulussen, and Peter van Aelst. 2016. "Making Sense of Twitter Buzz." *Digital Journalism* 4 (7):933–43. doi: 10.1080/21670811.2016.1160790.

Herring, Susan, Kirk Job-Sluder, Rebecca Scheckler, and Sasha Barab. 2002. "Searching for Safety Online: Managing "Trolling" in a Feminist Forum." *The Information Society* 18 (5):371–84.

Hicken, Allen. 2015. "Party and Party System Institutionalization in the Philippines." In *Party System Institutionalization in Asia: Democracies, Autocracies, and the Shadows of the Past*, ed. Allen Hicken and E. Martinez Kuhonta, 307–27. Cambridge and NY: Cambridge University Press.

Holmes, Ronald. 2016. "The Early Duterte Presidency in the Philippines." *Journal of Current Southeast Asian Affairs* 35 (3):15–38.

Kovach, Bill, and Tom Rosenstiel. 2001. *The Elements of Journalism: What Newspeople Should Know and the Public Should Expect.* New York, NY: Crown Publishers.

Lamble, Kate, and Meghan Mohan. 2016. "Trolls and Triumph: A Digital Battle in the Philippines." *BBC.* http://www.bbc.com/news/blogs-trending-38173842.

LaFont, Cristina. 2009. "Religion and the Public Sphere: What Are the Deliberative Obligations of Democratic Citizenship?" *Philosophy and Social Criticism* 35 (1–2):127–50.

McCargo, Duncan. 2016. "Duterte's Mediated Populism." *Contemporary Southeast Asia: A Journal of International and Strategic Affairs* 38 (2):185–90.

NYT Editorial Board. 2016. "Why Donald Trump Should Not Be President." *New York Times.* https://www.nytimes.com/2016/09/26/opinion/why-donald-trump-should-not-be-president.html.

Office of Mar Roxas. 2016. "Roxas kay Duterte: Ang Pangulo Dapat Disente." http://blog.marroxas.com/2016/04/11/roxas-kay-duterte-ang-pangulo-dapat-disente/.

Ong, Jonathan. 2015. "The Television of Intervention: Mediating Patron-Client Ties in the Philippines." In *Television Histories in Asia: Issues and Contexts*, ed. G. Turner and J. Tay. Abingdon. New York, NY: Routledge.

Ozsoy, Duygu. 2015. "Tweeting Political Fear: Trolls in Turkey." *Journal of History School* 8, no. 22:535–52.

Perron, Louis. 2008. "Election Campaigns in the Philippines." In *The Routledge Handbook of Political Management*, edited by D.W. Johnson, 360–69. New York, NY and Abingdon: Routledge.

Pew Research Center. 2016. "Partisanship and Political Animosity in 2016." http://assets.pewresearch.org/wp-content/uploads/sites/5/2016/06/06-22-16-Partisanship-and-animosity-release.pdf.

Phillips, Whitney. 2015. *This Is Why We Can't Have Nice Things: Mapping the Relationship Between Online Trolling and Mainstream Culture.* Cambridge, Mass. and London: MIT Press.

Ressa, Maria. 2016. "Propaganda War: Weaponizing the Internet." *Rappler.* http://www.rappler.com/nation/148007-propaganda-war -weaponizing-internet.

Ryfe, David. 2017. *Journalism and the Public: Key Concepts in Journalism.* Cambridge and Malden, MA: Polity.

Scammell, Margaret. 2003. "Citizen Consumers: Towards a New Marketing of Politics?" In *Media and the Restyling of Politics: Consumerism, Celebrity and Cynicism*, ed. J. Corner and D. Pels. London: Sage.

Scammell, Margaret, and Ana Ines Langer. 2006. "Political Advertising in the United Kingdom." In *The Sage Handbook of Political Advertising*, ed. L.L. Kaid and C. Holtz-Bacha, 65–82. London: Sage.

Schwartz, Mattathias. 2008. "The Trolls Among Us." *New York Times.* https://www.nytimes.com/2008/08/03/magazine/03trolls-t.html? pagewanted=all&_r=0.

Serafica, Raisa. 2016. "'Sana Ma-rape Ka': Netizens Bully Anti-Duterte Voter." *Rappler.* http://www.rappler.com/move-ph/128602-viral-du terte-supporters-harass-netizen.

Tandoc Jr., Edson. 2016. "Country Report: Journalists in the Philippines." Singapore: Nanyang Technological University. https://epub.ub.uni-muenchen.de/30119/1/Country_report_Philippines.pdf.

The Guardian Editorial Board. 2016. "The Guardian View on the EU Referendum: Keep Connected and Inclusive, Not Angry and Isolated." *The Guardian.* https://www.theguardian.com/commen-tisfree/2016/jun/20/the-guardian-view-on-the-eu-referendum-keep-connected-and-inclusive-not-angry-and-isolated.

Vromen, Ariadne. 2017. *Digital Citizenship and Political Engagement: The Challenge from Online Campaigning and Advocacy Organisations.* London: Palgrave Macmillan.

Voltmer, Katrin. 2010. "The Media, Government Accountability, and Citizen Engagement." In *Public Sentinel: News Media and Governance Reform*, ed. P. Norris. Washington, D.C.: The World Bank.

Williams, Sean. 2017. "Rodrigo Duterte's Army of Online Trolls: How Authoritarian Regimes Are Winning the Social Media

Wars." *New Republic*. https://newrepublic.com/article/138952/
rodrigo-dutertes-army-online-trolls.
Zelizer, Barbie. 2017. *What Journalism Could Be*. Cambridge and Malden,
MA: Polity.

QUEERING RODRIGO DUTERTE

John Andrew G. Evangelista

The Philippines is one of the region's top performers when it comes to indicators of gender equality. The country consistently lands in the top ten of gender equality indices, alongside Sweden, Switzerland, and Norway (World Economic Forum 2016). A few years ago, feminist movements were finally victorious in passing the Reproductive Health Law—a bill that languished in Congress for decades because of the strong Catholic Church lobby. Catcalling is now a punishable offense in some jurisdictions. There are anti-discrimination policies against sexual discrimination in key cities and private companies. In 2016, the Philippines elected its first transgender woman to the Congress of the Philippines. And, after two decades, the Anti-Discrimination Bill on the Basis of Sexual Orientation and Gender Identity and Expression (SOGIE) finally has a shot at getting passed.

But 2016 is also the year when the Philippines voted a sexist president into office. Rodrigo Duterte—the man who catcalled a female reporter, kissed his attractive supporters on the lips, boasted of his Viagra-powered sexual conquests, joked about raping a dead

251

Australian missionary, and called the US ambassador a gay son of a bitch—won by a landslide. His sexism was not only excused. It was embraced by the large crowds that laughed at his misogynistic remarks, defended by his supporters on social media, and justified by his feminist allies.

What accounts for this seeming disconnect between the Philippines' inroads to gender justice and the election of a misogynistic politician to the highest position in the land? Has the Philippines become a misogynistic nation as Duterte rose to power?

It is important to take a long and broad view of gender relations in the Philippines to answer these questions. I argue that Duterte's misogyny is not a new phenomenon, but one that is deeply anchored on the culture of macho politics in the Philippines. Duterte did not make politics sexist—it was already sexist to begin with. What Duterte brings to the table is his hyper-masculine performance of a strongman/father/womanizer politician as part of his narrative of tough governance. To make sense of these observations, I draw on queer theory to bring into sharp focus the complexity of gender performances underpinning Philippine politics, in general, and Duterte's leadership, in particular.

A Queer Reading

When Duterte makes jokes about lusting after beautiful women, one can easily brush this off by saying that "boys will be boys." This has been one of the more popular responses among his supporters, even from Congresswoman Pia Cayetano—the feminist politician responsible for the passage of the Magna Carta for Women. Others, on the other hand, appeal for understanding. In an event Malacañang organized to conclude the International Women's Month, Assistant Communications Secretary Marie Banaag appealed to the public:

> I don't want to be defensive about all these, but for women's month, if we can have a forgiving heart. We voted for a president, we did not vote for a priest, we did not vote for a saint.

Both approaches to Duterte's sexism—the acceptance that boys will be boys, and the appeal for forgiveness for his imperfections—exemplify the underlying social structures that perpetuate sexism in the country. These social structures can be described as hetero-patriarchal.

A hetero-patriarchal system is one where political practices are understood through hierarchical dichotomies between sexes. These are dichotomies because sexes are "biologically" understood as a heterosexual binary: male or female. They are hierarchical because male subjectivities are valorized for their physical strength, rationality, and emotional toughness. These virtues are prized in nation building because these are necessary resources to protect the state from external aggression. Women, on the other hand, are depicted as physically inferior, emotional, and temperamental—therefore citizens of a lower status. Queer citizens are invisible in this discussion, as if they are not legitimate political actors.

The hetero-patriarchal system derives its strength from the assumption that this order is "natural." As Chris Weedon puts it, the "appeal to the 'natural' is one of the most powerful aspects of common-sense thinking, but it is a way of understanding social relations which denies history" (Weedon 1987, 3). So when we say that it is "natural" that boys will always sexualize women, or that it is only "normal" that tough men make good presidents, or that women should be forgiving toward the men's indiscretions, we are using the vocabulary of a hetero-patriarchal system. We think it is "normal" to do these things because we are socialized to think that these are the expectations from good citizens. The task of critical citizenship is to reflect on the reasons why we think some things are normal, and, more importantly, to ask who benefits from this particular social order.

Queer theory provides a lens by which we can critically analyze the hetero-patriarchal system in the Philippines. There are, of course, many ways of interpreting queer theory. For the purposes of this chapter, I focus on Judith Butler's work on performativity. For Butler (1990), gender is not natural or pre-given. Instead, gender is a performance—something we act out to conform to expectations on how we should act in accordance with our identities. One way of understanding Butler's theory of performativity is to use the metaphor of the wardrobe. We may be free to choose our clothes everyday, but we are constrained by the number of costumes that allows us to curate our gender style.

Take Hillary Clinton as an example. When she was First Lady of the United States, Clinton was the subject of heterosexist judgments. She was parodied for appearing to usurp power from her husband, with cartoons and sketch comedy portraying her as a "radical feminist emasculator" (Templin 1999, 25). This makes Hillary "a failed woman." She is not fulfilling the expectations of a hetero-patriarchal system, which is to stay away from political matters as First Lady and instead stay home, make tea, and bake chocolate chip cookies. Such portrayal of Hillary Clinton as a power-hungry, therefore un-feminine, personality was carried on until she made her own bid for the White House.

The same analysis can be made with presidential contender Grace Poe. Poe was at the top of the polls before Duterte took the lead. A neophyte senator, Poe's political brand was immaculately curated by portraying her as a compassionate politician who took after her parents who are the most beloved royalties of Philippine cinema. Poe assumed the role of a dutiful daughter and a caring mother. Her signature style is a combination of a white collared shirt and jeans to portray simplicity with pearl earrings to communicate female middle class respectability. She appeared presidential in the televised debates. She dazzled audiences with memorized statistics and eloquently articulated her point using plain and dignified Filipino. But Poe's brand was disrupted when Duterte, in a one-on-one segment in the presidential debate, asked her about what she would do in the event China attacked the Philippines. Poe stumbled in her answer, struggling to place her motherly persona in the context of external aggression. This, when read using the lens of queer theory, was a no-win situation for Poe. If she performed her femininity, she would look ill-prepared to keep the country safe, and if she performed an aggressive behavior, she would breach the boundaries of acceptable conduct for a woman. Duterte, meanwhile, had an easy time sticking to the script of his masculine performativity: he said he would jet-ski to disputed territories and plant the Philippine flag.

Macho Politics

Duterte's aggressive response to a foreign policy question works well in a context where macho politics is deeply engrained in the country's political culture. There are various ways in which macho politics is performed. Let me cite two examples.

On one end of the spectrum are the so-called statesmen—those who engage in gentlemanly discourse that approximate the ideals of Enlightenment. Claro M. Recto, Jovito Salonga, and Benigno "Ninoy" Aquino Jr. are some examples. Statesmen are "proper gentlemen." They use words, not fists. They draw from a legal vocabulary and elegant prose to make their arguments. They dress well. Their speeches are immortalized in textbooks on political rhetoric. But they can also be elitist. As feminist and queer scholars argue, the privilege accorded to gentlemanly rules of discourse disadvantages alternative forms of claim-making, such as the emotional, colloquial, folksy, and sometimes playful forms of speech. Even though statesmen can make nationalist speeches that champion the causes of the poor, they do not necessarily speak with the poor.

This leads us to the other end of the spectrum—the politicians of the masses. Former President Joseph Estrada is the exemplar of this gender performance, where he uses the simple, aggressive, yet relatable "masa" language—the machismo of the street. Estrada's speech during his inauguration is perhaps one of the best examples of how a speech in Filipino can effectively send a message that resonates with the masses. "Walang kaibigan, walang kumpare, walang kamag-anak, o anak na maaring magsamantala ngayon . . . Huwag niyo akong subukan" (No friends, no mates, no relatives, no sons can take advantage now . . . Do not test me) was a powerful line that is reminiscent of Estrada's roots in Philippine cinema. In his films, Estrada fulfills the masculine hero. He was a savior, a protector of the masses. He defends the defenseless. He is physically strong as he is compassionate and merciful. Unlike the ideal statesman, Erap was not divorced from the masses. In fact, he is one of them. In his films, he works like them. He speaks like them. He looks like them. He defends them because he knows how to be them. So while his cinematic image stands out as a hero, he was also ordinary in some respects.

His persona as a masculine protector who comes from the masses allowed Estrada to construct his image as public servant, anchored on the tagline, "Erap para sa mahirap" (Erap for the poor). He was portrayed as the public servant who eats with farmers in boodle fights or drives public utility jeepneys. Capitalizing on his popularity, these portrayals draw the relationship between his persona as an actor and as a public servant. They intend to show the masses that Erap, like those characters in his film, is their typical savior. Unlike statesmen who are a cut above the rest, Estrada did not claim superior intelligence. He admitted being kicked out of high school, and made no secret of his extra-marital affairs.

How can he get away with this? Because Estrada's gender performance still comfortably fits the script of masculinity in politics. He still performs masculine virtues of toughness and virility. While he was ousted in office through a popular uprising due to a series of corruption scandals, Estrada remains well-entrenched in Philippine politics today. After he received pardon for the crime of plunder, he returned to politics, this time as Manila mayor—and one of Duterte's closest allies in the war on drugs.

Estrada's masculinity continues to be performed in the national scene. World boxing champion Manny Pacquiao now holds a seat in the Philippine Senate. Following Estrada's brand of masculinity, Pacquiao takes pride in his broken English and folksy appeal, but derives his masculinity from his background as a boxer who has a heart for the poor. Pacquiao is one of the most vocal opposition against women's and LGBT rights in the Senate, calling gays "worse than animals." This is part of his gender performance as an upright senator/pastor who draws the boundaries of acceptable gender performances.

Where is Duterte located in this spectrum? I argue that his entry to the national political scene merely extends this spectrum of macho politics in the Philippines and foregrounds a disruptive yet familiar form of hyper-masculinity. Duterte performs the role of a strongman and protector, a father ("Tatay Digong") who knows what's best for the nation, and a womanizer who can be forgiven because he is a bachelor anyway.

To a certain extent, Duterte's brand of masculinity is

comparable to Estrada's. Both portray themselves as ordinary and authentic personalities who are relatable to the masses. Duterte, however, pushes the boundaries of "street masculinity" farther than Estrada. While Estrada did attempt to conform to norms of elite respectability such as wearing a barong in formal events, reading his prepared speeches in English, and, indeed, showing interest in finer things in life (such as top shelf whiskey), Duterte's masculinity rejected these norms. He goes to official functions wearing his most comfortable clothes. He rarely reads his prepared speeches and instead goes on a free-flowing commentary peppered with cuss-words, as though having a drink with his mates at the corner store. Some compare him to Venezuela's Hugo Chavez who has little care for elitist norms, and instead places more value in connecting to their constituencies.

During the campaign, Duterte's political style was called out by his most vocal critic, the Secretary of Interior and Local Government Manuel Roxas. In the spectrum I have identified, Roxas approximates the category of the statesman. In his speeches and interviews, he speaks of policy proposals and puts forward evidence to back his claims. He belongs to one of the most illustrious clans of the Philippines, and boasts of his achievements as an investment banker, cabinet secretary, and senator. He sometimes gets baited by Duterte's tough talk, such as the time when he dared Duterte to a fist fight when the Davao mayor cast doubt on his degree from the Wharton School of Economics. Nevertheless, Roxas sets his masculinity apart by performing respectability. In the final stretch of the campaign, he made his case to the people by appealing to their decency. "In the Philippines, it's so hard to be decent," he said, in his closing statement in the presidential debate. "Usually, the decent ones finish last. . . . Let's give the country back to decent people." A seeming swipe at Duterte's indecency, Roxas draws a line between acceptable forms of hetero-patriarchy and those that go beyond the norms.

"Decent masculinity," however, did not gain traction. It seemed too soft, too inappropriate for the kinds of evils the country is facing. Part of Duterte's masculinity is his performance of a crisis (Curato 2017), where his street machismo is essential to cure the country's ills. His masculinity became the major tool through which his campaign gained recognition and credence. He is the tough father of the nation who is willing to beat his children up—or even kill them—for the sake of the common good. He is the punisher who enforces curfews for minors and limits the sale of cigarettes and alcohol as a way of implementing discipline to the nation. He is the strongman who expects full obedience once he says "stop it." He is also the charmer—the man who will not apologize but acknowledge the naughtiness of his sexual escapades. He is, in other words, the intersection of many forms of strong masculinity—the strongman leader, the disciplinarian father, the punisher, the womanizer.

Macho Publics

A macho president, of course, can only win office if there is a constituency that is ready to accept, if not celebrate, his hyper-masculinity. Even though the country has gained inroads in achieving gender equality, there are still broader social practices that make Duterte's masculinity familiar and acceptable.

"The Bisaya are really like that" is one of the most common remarks people make when asked to make sense of Duterte's appeal. The Bisaya are often stereotyped for their brash language and aggressive tone. Others would say "go to the provinces, you'll see that people talk like that." Indeed, Duterte's rhetorical style is consistent with how local electoral campaigns are held in some municipalities, where mayoral candidates also speak in crass language and some even take part in lewd dancing with skimpily clad female performers. Political cultures in small towns, of course, are not homogeneous. There have been some push back against Duterte's ill manners, such as those coming from rural areas who prize respectful conduct.

Nevertheless, Duterte's entry to the political scene no longer surprised many, as he is already a familiar personality. His tirades against gays are the jokes we hear from macho stand-up comedians in comedy bars or television shows. His stories about his masculine prowess are the anecdotes we hear from male friends in drinking sessions. His stern and disciplinarian ways are recognizable to us because, in one way or another, we had male figures in our lives who took on that role. His threatening comments are the same remarks we hear in street fights among gangs and fraternities.

Duterte may be new to the national political scene but his masculinity has always been known to us. To single out Duterte is to misrecognize the broader systems of hetero-patriarchy in the country, and act as if what he is doing are transgressions rather than articulations of already-existing norms.

This, to a certain extent, explains why a number of renowned feminists have thrown their support behind Duterte. Irene Santiago, for example, described as "the lead convenor of the global peace initiative Women Seriously," is a vocal Duterte supporter. "There are things that are done in Davao City that are not done in any other city—policies and procedures, benefits for women you can't find anywhere else," she argues. She cites the legal support the city provides for rape victims, which is in line with Duterte's peace and order agenda (Sabillo 2016). Congresswoman Pia Cayetano makes a similar testimony, this time lauding Davao City's ban on bikini contests in beauty pageants. She shares the anecdote of Duterte calling out men who harass women in Davao, suggesting that in practice, Duterte can traverse the spectrum and imbibe the gentle-manly form of masculinity. Mocha Uson—perhaps Duterte's most popular and controversial supporter—tells the story of Duterte being a gentleman to sexy dancers like herself, unlike other politicians who demand a "courtesy call" whenever her all-girl group performs in different parts of the country. Testimonies like these productively fracture Duterte's hyper-masculinity. He is sexist in words but not in action, thereby creating spaces for engagement with a range of allies.

For others, Duterte's masculinity sources its appeal from his promise of redemption. His supporters bowed down to the patri-arch because only he, they believe, could save our society from the perils of criminality. They have excused and tolerated bigoted speech in exchange for a better future that they think only the misogynist could deliver. Viewed this way, Duterte's hyper-masculinity is multi-faceted, but it nevertheless works within the paradigm of hetero-patriarchy.

Disruptions

What then are the prospects for gender politics in the Philippines? By putting forward a queer analysis of Duterte's political style, I do not mean to excuse his sexism. Instead, it is important to understand how his masculinity is performed, to better understand spaces for engagement. I offer two examples of the ways in which hetero-patriarchal politics can be destabilized.

One form of disruption is the emergence of a strong queer movement or movements in the Philippines. The weak political representation among women and LGBT reveals the deeply rooted hetero-patriarchal design of our national politics. Political institutions are taken for granted as masculine. The intolerance of non-conforming identities reveals an implied hierarchy protecting the power and privileges afforded to heterosexual men. It follows the logic of patriarchy—men are for politics, women are for reproduction, and LGBTs are for neither.

The political fortune of Ang Ladlad (Out of the Closet) is illustrative of this marginalization. Ang Ladlad is a political party that aims to promote the human rights of the LGBT community in the country. In 2009, the party was denied its application by the Commission on Elections (COMELEC) as a viable organization to run for office. Basing its decision on the Constitution, the Bible, and the Qur'an, COMELEC asserted that the party promotes immorality because it carries LGBT causes. Such absurd decision exposes prejudices that homosexuality is not only immoral but also politically unworthy. Ang Ladlad filed an appeal to the Supreme Court to contest this decision. The party won the legal battle. However, it failed to muster votes that would have afforded it congressional seats. But there is room for hope. The election of Geraldine Roman in the Congress is a welcome step toward better representation of the LGBTQ community in the Philippines. The queer movement outside spaces of party politics is also thriving, suggesting that there is room for negotiation of hetero-patriarchal norms, if not in parliament, then in the streets.

Another opening has to do with the pushback against Duterte and his allies' misogyny. The highlight of sexism in the Duterte administration, so far, has been the slut-shaming of Senator Leila de Lima. The former chairperson of the Commission on Human Rights and Justice Secretary, de Lima led in the senate investigation of extra-judicial killings. Part of the political ploy to discredit de Lima was to expose her affair with her driver and bodyguard who was accused of being part of the drug trade. Newspapers and online media made a circus of de Lima's love affair. "Love affair led to corruption" was the headline of *Manila Times*. "Leila's driver was her lover," the *Manila Standard* printed in big bold letters. In congressional enquiries, representatives grilled de Lima's driver, asking him to rate the intensity of their love affair as though it were an earthquake. When asked for his opinion on whether de Lima should be detained in a special facility, Congressman Harry Roque said, "Why does she want to be detained at the Armed Forces of the Philippines? Is it because there are many men there?" The conduct of the proceedings is an exemplary case of how locker room banter is transposed in the "dignified halls" of Congress.

But there is pushback against such kind of behavior. In social media, calls against slut-shaming have emerged, effectively questioning the double standard imposed on women's sexuality, compared to the tolerance the public extended to Duterte's affairs. The hashtag #Everywoman trended on Twitter, a campaign that expresses solidarity not only with de Lima but with all women who have been shamed because of their sexual conduct. This particularly took off when the House of Representatives considered showing an alleged sex video of de Lima in their investigations. These micro-protest actions may seem mundane, but they do destabilize hetero-patriarchal norms in politics, where women are discredited for their sexuality while men only serve to benefit from displays of their sexual prowess.

Conclusion

There is no doubt that Duterte's street masculinity deserves critical engagement. But to do this meaningfully, we need to look beyond the president. Beyond his misogyny and homophobia, we must begin reflecting on the broader hetero-patriarchal discourses from which his gender performance draws recognition and legitimacy.

Duterte's rise to power played around stereotypical and misogynistic forms of manhood. Some have found his performance familiar and amusing while others find it offensive. The challenge today, I argue, is not to demand that Duterte conform to gentlemanly norms of respectability. This too can be oppressive, as in the case of Mar Roxas who called for decency but nevertheless rejects the legalization of same-sex marriage, as if gay couples are second-class citizens. Sexism has insidious manifestations. They are not always as brusque and confrontational as Duterte's style.

And this is why we need to look beyond the person and focus our attention on the system. As critics of hetero-patriarchal discourses, we must be wary of all forms of gender performances and narratives that reify the gender hierarchy. We must be pessimistic hyper-activists (Foucault 1984). We must always reflect on discourses that result in different forms of subjugation especially when these discourses are embedded in our own actions or speech.

References

Butler, Judith. 1990. *Gender Trouble: Feminism and the Subversion of Identity*. London: Routledge.

Curato, Nicole. 2017. "Flirting with Authoritarian Fantasies? Rodrigo Duterte and the New Terms of Philippine Populism." *Journal of Contemporary Asia* 47 (1):142–53.

Foucault, Michel. 1984. *The Foucault Reader*, edited by Paul Rabinow. New York: Pantheon Books.

Sabillo, Kristine Angeli. 2016. "Feminist on Duterte: I Can Work With That." Philippine Daily Inquirer. http://newsinfo.inquirer.net/789435/feminist-on-duterte-i-can-work-with-that#ixzz4esmqjzU9.

Salih, Sara 2004. "On Judith Butler and Performativity." In *The Judith Butler Reader*, ed. Sarah Salih, 55–68. London: Routledge.

Templin, Charlotte. 1999. "Hillary Clinton as Threat to Gender Norms: Cartoon Images of the First Lady." *Journal of Communication Inquiry* 23 (1):20–36.

Weedon, Chris. 1987. *Feminist Practice and Poststructuralist Theory*. Oxford: Basil Blackwell.

World Economic Forum. 2016. *The Global Gender Gap Report*. http://reports.weforum.org/global-gender-gap-report-2016/.

DUTERTE'S OTHER WAR

THE BATTLE FOR EDSA PEOPLE POWER'S MEMORY

Cleve Kevin Robert V. Arguelles

Stone walls bearing the words of General Douglas MacArthur stand guard over a 103-hectare cemetery complex named Libingan ng mga Bayani (Heroes' Cemetery): "I do not know the dignity of his birth, but I do know the glory of his death." The sprawling complex houses the remains of more than 49,000 Filipino soldiers, politicians, and martyrs. All of them were buried by a nation grateful for their service, with one striking exception.

The new and markedly different resident, interred only in November 2016, is the man who took the nation to its darkest periods in contemporary history. He declared Martial Law in 1972, which resulted in almost 4,000 deaths, and his family looted over 10 billion US dollars from the national coffers. His grave can be found in the dignitaries' section. It is topped with a black granite slab and marked with the simplest of inscriptions: "Ferdinand E. Marcos 1917–1989 Filipino."

How to Bury a Memory

On the morning of 18 November 2016, the Marcos family took the nation by surprise. Martial law victims were busy preparing for a protest outside the Supreme Court to contest its ruling that allows the burial of the late dictator at the Heroes' Cemetery. As this happens, military helicopters carrying Marcos's body, together with the dictator's immediate family, were on their way to Manila. By three in the afternoon, a twenty-one gun salute was heard from the gates of the national cemetery. Police and navy officers lined the streets leading to the cemetery, preventing protesters from coming close to the site.

The dictator's daughter, Ilocos Governor Imee Marcos, described the ceremony as "simple, private, and solemn." For the Marcos family's critics, the burial was sneaky. The Supreme Court's decision was not yet final and executory, and so petitioners appealed to the court to reconsider its decision. This appeal, it seems, fell on deaf ears. The Marcos family, with the cooperation of the Armed Forces of the Philippines, held the interment. Hours after the funeral, there was an eruption of indignation protests across the nation. Students—those who were not yet born during the dictatorial regime—took to the streets to express disgust over what they called a "blitzkrieg burial" and showed the world how to protest—millennial-style. Their placards carried indignant yet Instagram-ready messages. One sign, for example—"Imee's face is a national treasure. We paid for it."—establishes the link between the Governor's glamorous lifestyle and the family's stolen wealth. Another sign read "Sandro, you can't sit with us," appropriating the line from the cult film *Mean Girls* to stigmatize the dictator's grandson who has gained celebrity status in the upscale social scene. A week later, a major rally at the Rizal Park in Manila attracted almost 20,000 participants. Martial law survivors testified in front of thousands of youth to keep the memory of the Marcos atrocities alive. Many more expressed their rage on social media with the hashtag #MarcosNOTaHero trending the whole day.

The Marcos burial and the wave of protests that emerged from it started with a campaign promise. In 2016, then presidential candidate Rodrigo Duterte categorically said he would allow the burial because it is legal. "I was just being legalistic about it," the president said. Marcos "was president for so long, and he was a soldier. . . . Whether or not he performed worse or better, there is no study, there is no movie about it," he adds. The president then called for national unity and appealed to the protesters to find a space in their hearts for forgiveness.

These insidious denials and appeals for national unity constitute what I will refer to in this chapter as Rodrigo Duterte's other war: the battle for EDSA People Power's memory. While Duterte is often associated with the bloody war on drugs, this chapter argues that this war is nestled in a broader war against the legacy of the EDSA regime. For the past three decades, the narrative of Philippine democracy has pivoted around the idealized narrative of the 1986 People Power Revolution. Weeklong commemoration of the revolution happens in February every year, from programs in the EDSA shrine to the routine screening of martial law documentaries on government-run television stations and schools. These rituals of remembering establish the importance the nation accords to the restoration of democracy.

This has changed in the time of Duterte. Instead of following the lead of all his predecessors in dutifully commemorating the revolution, he is practicing the converse by disrupting, devaluing, and delegitimizing the rituals of EDSA. He is, I argue, promoting public amnesia over collective remembering.

How exactly does Duterte's regime perpetuate the politics of forgetting? Which segment of the public supports this counter-narrative? I answer these questions in two parts. In the first part of this chapter, I characterize the changes in the rituals of commemoration under the Duterte regime, and examine the meanings of his claim that the nation needs to move on from the past. In the second part, I examine the relationship between the call to move on to the triumphant return of the Marcoses to the national stage. These two related themes on the politics of forgetting are closely intertwined with the story of Duterte's political victory.

"It's Time to Move On":
Commemoration in the Time of Duterte

Over the years, the memory of EDSA People Power has assumed the status of a "civil religion" (Bernhard and Kubik 2014). Its narrative was simple: In February 1986, the nation came together at the stretch of the Epifanio de los Santos Avenue (EDSA) to oust the repressive regime of Ferdinand Marcos. Ordinary citizens faced soldiers riding in tanks and carrying big guns, and installed Corazon Aquino—the widow of a martyred senator—as president of the Philippines. Not a single shot was fired. This triumph of democracy is a significant achievement. It has inspired many democracy movements around the world. The revolution has earned its place in the national memory, marked by rituals of commemoration. This was most pronounced on its 30th year, as Benigno S. Aquino III, the son of democracy icons Corazon and Benigno, made sure that his last celebration of EDSA as the president of the country was used to warn the nation about the creeping return of authoritarian leaders.

New ways of remembering and forgetting

On the revolution's 31st year, the celebrations took a different turn. "Sober, simple with no fanfare" was how Malacañang officially put it. This stands in contrast to the extravagant and self-congratulatory ethos that defined previous celebrations. Yet there is more to this statement than meets the eye. Three of these changes were both consequential and symbolic.

First, foregoing the traditional Salubungan (Encounter) rites reflected Duterte's disregard for the key symbols of the EDSA uprising. Secondly, changing the location of the official national celebration from the streets to the military camp showed Duterte's attempt to redefine the victors of EDSA People Power. And lastly, the absence of the president in the commemoration activity unlike previous presidents who associated themselves closely to EDSA revealed Duterte's distant and sometimes even conflicting relationship with its memory.

Since 1987, the 31st anniversary was the first time that the government chose to forego the traditional Salubungan as one of the highlights of the official commemoration. The Salubungan is a reenactment of one of the defining moments of the revolution. It refers to the symbolic meeting (*salubong*, or encounter) of the police and the military force leading to the People Power Revolution.

In Aquino III's final commemoration rites, the celebration at the People Power Monument began with a spectacular high-speed opener pass of two military fighter jets. Thousands of students, government employees, police, and military witnessed this extravaganza as they marched along EDSA. Former President Fidel Ramos and Senator Juan Ponce Enrile, who served and defected as Marcos's police chief and defense minister, respectively, led the Salubungan rites. Top government officials, including foreign dignitaries, were invited to witness the commemoration. The jubilant atmosphere was made more festive by the tanks decked in flowers, advancing with the marching crowd. Helicopters then dropped yellow confetti on EDSA. President Duterte's first commemoration appears muted compared to Aquino's. Breaking the tradition of holding a reenactment of the union of forces was one of the substantial changes made in his first EDSA uprising anniversary. No other previous government has dared to disregard a symbolic moment like the Salubungan.

The shift in the date and location of the official commemoration was another significant change that Duterte introduced. Traditionally held on the 25th of February, the main remembrance program was re-scheduled a day earlier. It was also transferred from the People Power Monument to the military headquarters in Camp Aguinaldo. This was only the second time that the government's commemoration was held elsewhere. Aquino III relocated the 24th anniversary commemoration activity in Cebu City where in 1986 former president Corazon Aquino, his mother, made the historic appeal to Filipino civilians to defend military defectors from being attacked by Marcos's forces. Symbolically, Aquino III pulled the direction of the memory toward a more civilian route. This extends the practice of EDSA remembrance programs being held in the People Power Monument to reflect the privileging of the role of the ordinary Filipinos in the success of the peaceful uprising.

Duterte did the exact opposite. He held the celebration in a military headquarters because, according to him, this is where the revolution "actually all began." This deviates from the narrative of the revolution. Duterte provides less emphasis on its civilian nature and instead redefines the military as the true heroes of the EDSA revolt.

Lastly, the controversial changes to the conduct, date, and location of the celebration were matched by an equally symbolic move by Duterte to skip the commemoration altogether. He chose to stay in his hometown Davao City and, just like any other ordinary day, Duterte attended to his routines as president. He also skipped the traditional wreath laying ceremony at the People Power Monument. The celebration was not just low-key but also without the symbolic presence of the head of state and government and commander-in-chief. In his stead, he sent his Executive Secretary Salvador Medialdea. Preempting questions on the president's absence, Medialdea was quick to mention that the absence of the chief executive in the celebration should not be taken to mean that the Duterte government was giving less significance to the historic protests that ended the Marcos dictatorship (Romero 2017). Yet his symbolic absence speaks volumes on how differently he approaches the memory of the EDSA People Power compared to his predecessors. Whereas in post-EDSA governments the revolution was a cause for triumphalist recollection, particularly for his immediate predecessor, Aquino III, Duterte displayed less eagerness and willingness to commemorate it.

Duterte's mnemonic regime

These changes in the government's practice of remembering the EDSA uprising is revealing of Duterte's mnemonic regime. A mnemonic regime refers to the dominant pattern of memory politics in a particular society in a particular time (Bernhard and Kubik 2014). The state strategically uses these activities to socialize the members of a nation to remember or forget a historical event to serve their political ends. The state of the mnemonic regime is best reflected in public commemoration over which state authorities and other major political actors have direct control. How the sitting government chooses to officially remember the EDSA uprising is explicitly telling of what specific use is its memory being deployed. Duterte's mnemonic regime markedly deviates from how previous regimes deployed the memory of the People Power Revolution.

The changes in the way the Duterte regime commemorates EDSA were deeply meaningful. These moves reflect the role of Duterte as a mnemonic political actor who is keen on a specific interpretation of the past. While previous administrations used the occasion to demonstrate their connection to EDSA to legitimize their governments, Duterte does the exact opposite. He draws legitimacy from his unique mnemonic position that minimizes, if not rejects, the centrality of the revolution in the story of the nation. The simple commemorative activity was not accidental. By keeping the celebration quiet, they provided a signal to the public that, as Malacañang puts it, "[that] it's time to move on from just celebrating the past." He was not only absent in the main commemoration activity but he even acted in such a way that nothing needs to be especially remembered on that day. He remained in Davao City, the farthest possible place that he can be from the center of celebrations in the country's capital. In changing the date and location of the commemoration program, he was nudging the public to remember the EDSA uprising differently. All these spatial, temporal, and symbolic dimensions of the Duterte government's commemoration activities of the EDSA People Power Revolution contests, challenges, and even rivals the prevailing mnemonic regime.

Yet none of this was unexpected. Duterte's political debt to the family of the deposed dictator is publicly known. Prior to his assumption of the presidency, his presidential campaign rhetoric centered on narratives contesting the legacies of the EDSA People Power Revolution. For Duterte, the 1986 peaceful uprising in EDSA restored democratic institutions but "the economic and social structure remains a lopsided equation in favor of the few, and the many are poor and neglected." The revolution "restored democracy" but "it is only for the elite." Duterte took the occasion of the 31st anniversary to tame the triumphalist memory of the revolution. In memory politics, these kinds of muted celebrations or silences are as important as changes in the official practices of remembering.

What has been done so far is an attempt to downplay the narrative
of EDSA uprising as a "civil religion" that political actors depend on
for legitimation of their power.

Who will reclaim the streets?

Large protests organized by opposing political forces
out-staged the uneventful commemoration of the revolution's 31st
anniversary. The remembrance of a historical event that symbolically united Filipinos against Marcos in 1986 has now become a
cause for division in the time of Duterte.

One group found it the most appropriate way to celebrate the
anniversary by organizing a protest demanding that Duterte reverse
his order to bury the remains of the dictator Marcos in Libingan ng
mga Bayani. Another group in which Aquino III himself was present
commemorated the revolution in a separate, "unofficial" venue. The
Catholic Church, which played a key role in the 1986 EDSA uprising,
called on its parishes to organize processions and prayer rallies to
remember the historic event.

Yet the most striking deviation from these commemorative
protests was a rally organized by political forces identified with
Duterte. As if taunting those who wish to keep the liberal memory
of EDSA alive, Duterte's supporters, including some of his cabinet
members, attended a "Freedom Rally Against Crime, Corruption
and Drugs." The event was staged to showcase public support
for Duterte's illiberal drug war, but, symbolically, it also contests
EDSA's memory by offering a counter-narrative of freedom. This,
arguably, was a space previously unavailable when the EDSA regime
has claimed the discourses of freedom and democracy. Strategies of
forgetting also gained traction in social media where counter-mem-
ories of the revolution have emerged. Claims that the Martial Law
was the golden age of the Philippines and stories about the Aquino
family's abusive record with farmers both serve to challenge what is
demonized and idealized.

The changes in the official mnemonic regime initiated by
the Duterte government has spilled over and interplayed with
the wider sphere of public memory. Although the government

does not directly control public memory, its dynamic relationship with official memory makes it open to influence by state authorities (Olick, Vinitzky-Seroussi, and Levy 2011). The pro-Duterte, anti-EDSA protests revealed how serious Duterte was in changing the mnemonic regime. To organize a major non-commemorative protest on the remembrance days of the EDSA uprising was one thing. But to hold a protest—both online and offline—to evoke an anti-EDSA spirit was another thing. The attempt was not only to tone down the celebratory memory of EDSA but also to directly challenge it, even to replace it.

For Duterte, the nation must already move on from the memories of the EDSA People Power Revolution. But to move forward requires knowing where to go. How his government celebrated its 31st anniversary answers these questions. Under the Duterte presidency, the commemoration activities of the EDSA uprising were not acts of celebration but of political recrimination. This is the first theme on Duterte's performance of public amnesia. In the next section, I discuss what comes after the appeal to move on: a call for the nation to forgive.

"A Space in the Heart for Forgiveness": The Resurrection of the Marcoses

Until the 2016 Philippine national elections, the return of the Marcos family in the political arena had never been so undeniably explicit. Three decades after EDSA ended his father's dictatorship, Senator Ferdinand "Bongbong" Marcos Jr. gunned for the vice presidential post. While he lost in his bid, the resulting extremely tight race was already very telling. It was symbolic of the extent to which the Marcos family has regained their political capital as well as their status as legitimate political actors in the post-authoritarian order. Consequently, this also revealed how far the memory of the legacies of the Marcosian years and the People Power revolt has been successfully refashioned in the public imagination.

The return of the Marcoses in the political scene is indeed a puzzle. But have the Marcoses really left? I argue otherwise (Arguelles 2016a). Since the overthrow of their rule by the EDSA uprising, the Marcos family has used to their advantage the spaces that we have maintained for a fragmented memory of the martial law rule. While it takes a whole nation to remember, it takes the same whole nation to forget. This public forgetting is best seen in two expressions: the gradual successive electoral triumph of the Marcoses since the end of their dictatorship and the burial of the dictator patriarch in the Libingan ng mga Bayani. In both cases, Duterte's fingerprints are all over.

Bongbong's presence in the Senate was the first national post that the family won since returning from exile. In their home province of Ilocos Norte, a stronghold of their family for many decades, his sister Imee sits as governor. The matriarch, Imelda Marcos, is a district representative at the lower house of the Philippine Congress. Yet the re-consolidation of the Marcos political dynasty was foreseeable. After fleeing the country in disgrace with crates of gold, dollars, and jewelry, they were embraced by their political allies upon their return from exile in 1991.

Despite facing numerous court charges of plunder, Imelda arrived in Manila to the cheers of a crowd of the family's supporters holding signs that declared the family's innocence of the charges against them (Mydans 1991). They are called "loyalists", a collection of organized groups and unorganized individuals professing loyalty to the Marcos family and their vision of a Bagong Lipunan/New Society. Since the time of the end of their rule and until now, loyalist groups have been awaiting the return of the family in Malacañang. During my fieldwork[1] in three urban poor communities in Quezon City during the 2016 national elections, it was not unusual to hear wishes of victory for Bongbong. As Leo, sixty-six years old and long-time resident in a poor barangay, said, his "only wish before his death is to see a Marcos back in the presidential palace" (personal interview 2016). He claimed to have suffered so much under the post-EDSA administrations and fervently believes that the younger generation of Filipinos will experience a better life under another Marcos rule. These loyalist groups served as a social base for the second political rise of the Marcos family.

In 1992, the first presidential elections after the People Power Revolution, Imelda lost her bid for the presidency under the platform of making the Philippine nation "great again." But Bongbong then was elected as representative of his home province. That Imelda ran for president and Bongbong easily regained his family's political bailiwick just a few years after the family was ousted speaks of the speed with which they have been welcomed back into the fold. In 1995, Imelda unsurprisingly successfully won the election for a congressional seat representing her home province of Leyte. By 1998, they fully regained control of Ilocos Norte. While Imelda withdrew from the presidential race, Bongbong was elected provincial governor and Imee took over as congressional representative. In 2010, with the family secured in its provincial control and comfortable with their renewed political power, Bongbong rose to the senate while Imee succeeded him as governor. Imelda, on the other hand, was back in congress as representative of Ilocos Norte. Both Imee and Imelda were re-elected for another three years by 2013. The story of the political careers of the Marcoses quickly shifted from that of a humiliating defeat to a triumphalist return. While the country slowly rebuilds its democratic institutions and culture from 1986 onwards, the Marcoses were working in the background to re-root themselves back into the political scene.

Bongbong's candidacy for the vice presidency in the 2016 elections was a crucial moment for the family's political project. This put them a step closer toward fulfilling their goal of, in the words of the matriarch Imelda, "reclaiming the Philippine presidency." His candidacy expectedly evoked a public discussion on the legacies of authoritarianism in the country. Many civil society groups, including prominent victims of martial law, formed a movement called the Campaign Against the Return of the Marcoses in Malacañang (CARMMA) to counter Bongbong's candidacy. Expectedly, his campaign was haunted by questions on the ill-gotten wealth and human rights abuses perpetrated by the family during martial law. More importantly, for some groups, his lack of willingness to recognize and atone for his family's sins made him an illegitimate political actor in post-EDSA time (Cornelio 2016). Yet public support for his candidacy remained high. While Bongbong's candidacy alarmed many, it was not the only significant event in 2016 for the family's political project.

The burial of Ferdinand Marcos represented the peak of the political resurrection of the Marcoses. No less than president Duterte made this order in public. Twenty-seven years after Ferdinand died while he was in exile in Hawaii, the remains of the dictator were finally buried. Since Ferdinand's death, the family has always insisted on burying him at the Libingan ng mga Bayani with a funeral ceremony that would befit a former president. Since the first post-EDSA government, this request has been denied, recognizing its symbolic consequences. In fact, the dead body of Marcos was banned from returning to the Philippines until 1992. Awaiting a presidential funeral and burial, the Marcos family kept Ferdinand's body in a refrigerated coffin inside one of the closets at their residence in Hawaii. His body was treated as though he was alive. For example, in 1990, Imelda even wheeled him into their living room where friends and neighbors gathered around to sing "Happy Birthday" to the corpse (Brauchli 1997). His body was only eventually allowed to return to the Philippines after a compromise agreement was made between the family and the Ramos administration. He was only to be buried in his hometown of Batac and without any military honors. Yet while the family brought his corpse back to Ilocos Norte, he was not buried. The body of the dictator was preserved and placed in a glass casket below the seal of the presidency at a mausoleum in their home province. The former president was dressed in Barong Tagalog and a chest sash bearing fake World War II military medals.

The politics of dead bodies

This state of perpetual embalming had been the proof of the family's narrative of state cruelty against them: for disallowing a proper burial for Ferdinand, for the desecration of the dead. On 18 November 2016, while Duterte was outside the country, Ferdinand was buried at the Libingan ng mga Bayani with full military honors. For the Marcoses and their supporters, the private ceremony marked the end of their long journey to the state recognition of their patriarch's contributions to the nation. For others, it reopened past wounds inflicted by the family's cruel rule. At the end of the ceremony, a military general presented the Philippine flag to Imelda with a note on behalf of the nation: "on behalf of the president of the Philippines and the people of a grateful nation, may I present this flag as a token of appreciation for the honorable and faithful service your loved one has rendered this nation."

Dead bodies assume political life even in other places. Corpses are material representations of memories. They enjoy a significant position in shaping a mnemonic regime. From ancient times to today, cadavers have been transported to and from sites across continents, countries, and cities, depending on their significance to the memory project of dominant political actors. Ferdinand's body travelled from Hawaii to Ilocos Norte to Metro Manila, depending on the shifting political fortunes of the Marcos family.

Reburials are also done to symbolize changes in the way states remember an important historical event. Beginning in 1989, former communist states ordered reburials of many leaders to mark their break from communist heritage and resuscitate democratic roots (Verdery 1999). Corpses of communist leaders were removed from grand mausoleums and reburied in ordinary gravesites while bodies of democratic leaders that were killed during the communist era were dug and given grand reburial ceremonies as they were transferred to national pantheons of heroes. By contrast, the burial of Marcos resuscitates authoritarian fantasies of the Philippine nation while de-legitimizing democratic legacies of the EDSA People Power. Furthermore, while re/burial ceremonies in the case of former communist states were grand public affairs, Marcos's was done in secret. This may be interpreted as a sign of the incompleteness of Duterte's project to replace the dominant memory of the martial law years and the eventual peaceful revolt. In Latin America, the transition to democracy has also been accompanied by a great deal of movement of dead bodies of former dictators (Verdery 1999). Bodies of former dictators were moved largely as a consequence of the success of their own democratization projects. In comparison, the burial of the corpse of the Philippine dictator has been used to restore its honor and the authoritarian political project it represents.

Duterte's decision to bury Ferdinand's body in the Libingan

ng mga Bayani restored the honor of the disgraced arch-nemesis of the 1986 EDSA People Power Revolution. By doing this, Duterte provided himself ample opportunities to complete his memory project. It provided materiality to his claims of Marcos being the country's "best president." While Duterte claimed that the burial was only a legal and not a political question (Cepeda 2016), this seemed to be less convincing when situated in the bigger picture of his challenges against the prevailing memory of the legacies of the EDSA uprising. Even without the honor of being buried at the Libingan ng mga Bayani, the Marcoses have always maintained that none of them were convicted and claimed innocence of the crimes committed during their rule.

Now, with a visual and visceral proof to their claims, the memory of EDSA has become more vulnerable. Its long-term effects on how the nation remembers the peaceful revolt is captured by the Philippine Supreme Court Chief Justice Maria Lourdes Sereno in her dissenting opinion on the issue of the burial:

> [Duterte officials] may deny the implications of their actions today, but the symbolism of the burial will outlive even their most emphatic refutations. Long after the clarifications made by this administration have been forgotten, the gravesite at the LNMB [Libingan ng mga Bayani] will remain. That is the peculiar power of symbols in the public landscape—they are not only carriers of meaning but are repositories of public memory and ultimately, history. (Supreme Court of the Philippines 2016, 71–72)

By repositioning dead bodies, reinstating their glory, or just merely pulling public consideration toward them, the departure of corpses from one grave and arrival into another symbolizes significant changes in a nation's universe of memories and meanings, as constitutive of the wider processes of political metamorphosis. Cemeteries are memorial spaces that serve as a space for a symbolic encounter between the memories of the dead and the lives of the living (Foote and Azaryahu 2007).

Yet the Libingan ng mga Bayani is not just another ordinary cemetery where this meaningful ritual of encounter among the living and the dead can come about. Instead, national cemeteries are significant spaces that embody the stories of the nation. The bodies buried in these national cemeteries occupy a privileged position in the national memory. And so, Duterte knew that in burying Marcos there was an effective move to aid the institution of his divergent mnemonic regime. How the body of the former dictator is treated by the state is central to how and to what extent the prevailing interpretation of the EDSA revolt can be contested, if not replaced. Duterte, through the dead body of Marcos, uses the specific biography, memory, and myth of the dead dictator to persuade the public to reexamine their memories of the national past.

By resurrecting a dead body and reburying the imagined suffering corpse of Ferdinand, political time is reconfigured. The time between the death and the final burial is put into brackets and a different chronology is constructed by the "immediatization of the remote" (Rév 2005, 43). The past is made present and the dead given life. Duterte harnesses the posthumous political life of Ferdinand Marcos in creating a new mnemonic regime that can legitimate his rule. The public forgetting of the EDSA uprising, seen in Duterte's disregard for its commemoration and his role in the resurrection of the Marcoses, is interwoven with the story of Duterte's electoral triumph and continuing political success.

"What Have We Achieved After EDSA?": The Rise of Duterte and the EDSA Revolt

Symbolically, the rise of Duterte is a break from the post-EDSA order (Arguelles 2016b). The EDSA uprising tells the story of a public rejecting the sacrifice of liberties in the name of a national project to defend the republic. The message was that the detentions, tortures, and killings of communists and government critics that defined the Marcos regime could no longer be used to restore public order. Three decades later, this seems to be where Duterte is returning: a suspension of liberal democracy to save the nation from further decay. The use of state-sanctioned incarcerations and killings to purge the country of its enemies serves as the pillar of Duterte's government. While the communist insurgency was the source of threat for Marcos, it is the illegal drug industry for Duterte. The traditional notion of democracy founded on robust human rights has to be tamed. For both presidents, their departure from this traditional rule is justified by a nation that is under a perpetual state of emergency. While Duterte and Marcos both heavily relied on the rhetoric of crisis, post-EDSA governments mostly used the language of growth and progress to legitimize their rules. Duterte's challenge to the prevailing mnemonic regime is geared toward legitimating his different type of politics. Regime change is about the reconstruction of legitimizing meanings, identities, and myths as much as it is about the restructuring of economic and political relations. These twin components of regime changes cannot be realized without a congruent national memory (Müller 2002). Duterte's controversial war on drugs is accompanied by a war on memory. They feed on each other for legitimacy. Duterte's war on memory is focused on the changing modes of practices in remembering the EDSA People Power. From the muted commemoration of the 31st anniversary of the EDSA revolt to the repositioning of Marcos's dead body in the Libingan ng mga Bayani, these two significant moments in the first year of Duterte's presidency have engendered a remarkable shift away from the idealized narratives and practices of remembering of the EDSA uprising. But this was not solely Duterte's doing. To isolate Duterte's challenges to the prevailing mnemonic regime from the post-EDSA realities is to miss how fragmented and eroded the EDSA revolution memory had already been.

Public memories, even in the hands of an empowered mnemonic interventionist like Duterte, are not fully malleable. While instrumentalist mnemonic actors reconstruct memories and deploy them for various political reasons, the manipulation of memory is limited by historically, socially, and culturally constructed credibility (Kubik 1994). Mnemonic actors frequently attempt to instrumentalize memories, creating narratives that they think will result in the most potent legitimation for their rule. Yet their reconstruction of memories is not limitless as they are constrained by the need to be credible and persuasive.

In short, the memory of the EDSA uprising is only malleable to the extent that it can still resonate with the public. Attempts to challenge a mnemonic regime must effectively navigate the thin line between what is believable and what is not. For Duterte, the failed promises of the People Power revolt provided the foundation of the credibility of his war on memory. Duterte does not need to complicate things to gain credibility for his new mnemonic regime. He only has to ask this simple question: "Thirty-one years have passed since the EDSA People Power Revolution . . . what have we achieved after EDSA?"

This story of unfulfilled promises casts a pall on EDSA's memory. While others do not necessarily contest the triumphalist narrative of the EDSA revolt, what is projected onto its memory is a painful realization among many Filipinos that the story of EDSA has now become just a narrative of transfer of power from an abusive family to a new political elite.

Duterte did not singularly pave the long road to a newly emerging mnemonic regime. The post-EDSA elites were as crucial as Duterte in making the war on memory possible. In transition periods like the shift from martial law to the return of democracy in the Philippines, institutionalized modes of remembering are significant in shaping the political culture that emerges after it. State commemoration projects do not necessarily mean fully controlling the public's mind. Rather they rely on their ability to influence the nation's "will to remember" (Olick, Vinitzky-Seroussi, and Levy 2011) through the use of school, media and other similar cultural institutions that are consequential in shaping a mnemonic regime.

Prior to Duterte, institutions on which people supposedly relied as repositories of public memories have been weakly utilized. History textbooks long used in public and private schools have been found to be silent on the history of abuses, greed, and violence perpetrated by the Marcos government. In issues of collective memory, silence is as crucial as remembering. But media institutions have not been silent. Yet the annual regular commemoration programs often portray the overthrow of the dictatorship as an uprising that emerged and centered only in the capital. National memories are prone to exclude local memories of the EDSA uprising, disallowing areas from the margins of the metropolis to have a stake in the mnemonic regime. Even public monuments that are constructed to remember the historic revolt illustrate the same problem. Most of the names in the Wall of Remembrance that was set up to honor the martyrs and heroes who fought against the Marcos dictatorship are urban and professional-centric. Many poor workers and farmers from far-flung areas still await recognition of their contribution to the anti-dictatorship struggle.

The most crucial weakness on the part of the post-EDSA mnemonic institutions is the failure to institute an inclusive, public, and national process of trials to confront and settle authoritarian legacies. For example, the absence of a truth commission to set historical memories straight presented the Marcoses and now Duterte with an opportunity to pull the nation's memory in different directions. No post-EDSA administration has formally attempted to keep the memory of injustices, human rights violations, and corruption alive. Historical truths were easily made fictional in the absence of complete prosecution of the actors: then and now the Marcoses have used to their advantage the fact they have never faced imprisonment for their actions. Official truth commissions are a nation's weapon against memory extinction, fighting social amnesia, denials, evasions, and other nefarious modes of revi-sionism whereby past atrocities are either legitimized or forgotten. On the other hand, trials may serve as a public theater that provides collective lessons in justice. Thus, the truth commissions, trials, and other ways of institutionalized remembering are moments for public memory making that may unite a community, as well as serve as a venue to collectively discuss and confront the past in relation to the present and the future. While the assumption of the presidency by Duterte meant the mobilization of state resources to the perfor-mance of public amnesia, the years before that are critical junctures that resulted in a path of unconscious complicity in the erosion of the national memory of EDSA People Power.

The rise and rule of Duterte must be studied and understood beyond the politics of elections, policies, and mobilization. It must also be situated in the politics of memory. Nations are products of memories as much as they are imagined. Memories constrain polit-ical actions, reshape realities, and legitimize distributions of power. Collective activities of remembering and forgetting are instruments of justifying discourses as well as generating political obligations and loyalties. Control over what public memories contain and how it is transmitted is control over the construction of narratives for an imagined future. Mnemonic regimes reflect the struggle for power over a society's future. What and how nations choose to remember and forget narrows the future path of a society.

How Duterte deals with the nation's memory of the past provides a glimpse of what legacies he will leave behind. The results of Duterte's war on the memory of the EDSA People Power revolution will ultimately reveal the prospects of the country's ongoing democratization project. Indeed, the past is never dead. It's not even past.

Endnote

[1]   The fieldwork was done as part of two research projects where I was research assistant: The "Vote of the Poor 2016" study funded by the Institute of Philippine Culture at the Ateneo De Manila University and the research on "Money Politics in Southeast Asia" financed by the Australian National University and the De La Salle University. In both research projects, grounded perspectives on the electoral process were surfaced.

References

Almario, Anjo. 2017. "Duterte Supporters Gather at Luneta." *CNN Philippines*, 25 February http://cnnphilippines.com/news/2017/02/25/president-duterte-support-luneta-davao-cebu.html.

Arguelles, Cleve Kevin Robert. 2016a. "It Takes a Nation to Raise a Dictator's Son." *New Mandala*. http://www.newmandala.org/it-takes-a-nation-to-raise-a-dictators-son/.

———. 2016b. "How a Failed Peaceful Revolution Led to Rodrigo Duterte." *TIME*. http://time.com/4608306/rodrigo-duterte-power-revolution/.

Bernhard, Michael, and Jan Kubik, eds. 2014. *Twenty Years After Communism: The Politics of Memory and Commemoration*. Oxford: Oxford University Press.

Brauchli, Christopher. 1997. "The Chilling Adventures of Marcos' Corpse." *Baltimore Sun*, 28 Mary. http://articles.baltimoresun.com/1997-05-28/news/1997148078_1_imelda-corpse-philippines.

Cepeda, Mara. 2016. "SC Orals Day 2: How Justices Pursued Issues on Marcos Burial." *Rappler*, 8 September http://www.rappler.com/nation/145629-sc-orals-day-2-how-justices-pursued-issues-marcos-burial.

Cornelio, Jayeel. 2016. "Why is it Difficult for Bongbong Marcos to Apologize?" *Rappler*, 14 April. http://www.rappler.com/thought-leaders/129457-bongbong-marcos-difficulty-apology.

Foote, Kenneth, and Maoz Azaryahu. 2007. "Toward a Geography of Memory: Geographical Dimensions of Public Memory." *Journal of Political and Military Sociology* 35 (1):125–44.

Jonathan. 2016. Personal interview.

Kubik, Jan. 1994. *The Power of Symbols Against the Symbols of Power: The Rise of Solidarity and the Fall of State Socialism in Poland.* University Park: Penn State University Press.

Leo. 2016. Personal interview.

Müller, Jan-Werner. 2002. *Memory and Power in Post-war Europe: Studies in the Presence of the Past.* Cambridge: Cambridge University Press.

Mydans, Seth. 1991. "Imelda Marcos Returns to Philippines." *New York Times*, 4 November. http://www.nytimes.com/1991/11/04/world/imelda-marcos-returns-to-philippines.html.

Nelson, Robert, and Margaret Olin. 2003. *Monuments and Memory, Made and Unmade.* Chicago: University of Chicago Press.

Official Gazette. 2016. "President Aquino Speaks at the 30th Anniversary of the EDSA Revolution." http://www.officialgazette.gov.ph/2016/02/25/aquino-speech-english-edsa-30/.

Olick, Jeffrey, Vered Vinitzky-Seroussi, and Daniel Levy. 2011. *The Collective Memory Reader.* Oxford: Oxford University Press.

Rév, István. 2005. *Retroactive Justice: Prehistory of Post-communism.* Stanford, California: Stanford University Press.

Romero, Alexis. 2017. "EDSA Anniversary to be 'Simple, Quiet,' says Palace." *Philippine Star.* http://www.philstar.com/headlines/2017/02/16/1672849/edsa-anniversary-be-simple-quiet-says-palace.

Rosario. 2016. Personal interview.

Verdery, Katherine. 1999. *The Political Lives of Dead Bodies: Reburial and Post-socialist Change.* New York: Columbia University Press.

WHO WILL BURN DUTERTE'S EFFIGY?

Emerson M. Sanchez

Every year, the Philippines bears witness to two versions of the State of the Nation Address (SONA). There is the official version, one where the president of the republic delivers a speech addressed to the joint session of Congress to outline the administration's agenda and report its accomplishments. Then there is the street version—The People's SONA—where a contingent of peasants, workers, disaster survivors, indigenous peoples, urban poor, and students march to the Batasang Pambansa (National Legislature) Complex to provide a counter-narrative to the president's rosy claims. SONA is a prime occasion for progressive movements to register their dissent against incumbent regimes' policies, whether it is on the issue of land reform, transportation, privatization, wages, or foreign relations. Effigy burning is a staple of this protest, symbolizing the progressive movement and their mass supporters' utter discontent with government failures.

Year 2016, however, was a different time. As far as the official SONA is concerned, President Rodrigo Duterte, perhaps unexpectedly, deviated from reading his prepared speech, and went on his usual off-the-cuff remarks. His promise of a simple SONA materialized as well. There was no "fashion show" of flashy Filipiniana outfits among female politicians and congressional spouses on the red carpet. Only four lawmakers welcomed the president, a departure from the image of an entourage of lawmakers hustling to escort the president. The menu was also a point of interest among observers: the merienda featured simple local fares meant to reflect the president's humble approach to traditionally ostentatious events.

Outside the halls of Congress, the SONA in the streets was equally historic. Unlike the previous SONAs marked by blockades and skirmishes between protesters and the police, Duterte's first SONA was defined by the state's hospitality to activists. Police Chief Ronald Dela Rosa went on stage and assured the protesters that the police are there to protect, not to hurt them. I was present at this rally. I personally witnessed a police officer instructing motorists at an intersection to give way to protesters. In terms of headcount, the 2016 rally was considered to have one of the largest contingents, including a delegation from Mindanao, Duterte's regional turf. There were the usual placards and chants, but the mood was peaceful, if not jubilant. Protesters were able to get as close as 500 meters from the Batasan—an unprecedented proximity.

Conspicuously absent in this SONA rally was the burning of the president's effigy. In fact, there was no effigy of the president—a first in sixteen years. Instead, the rally featured a six-piece mural called *Portraits of Peace*. The mural featured six themes: national industrialization, land reform and agricultural development, progressive social policy, sovereignty, human rights and peace, and people's governance. The mural is the creation of artists associated with the progressive alliance Bagong Alyansang Makabayan (Bayan), or New Patriotic Alliance. *Portraits of Peace* aims to convey "a positive message" by visualizing "the people's aspiration for a better society" (Bayan 2016b).

Indeed, the mass mobilization during Duterte's first SONA was not a protest, but a "show of support" to the newly elected president. The "sharp line" came in the form of a challenge, where activists asked Duterte to address poverty, unemployment, landlessness, and lack of social justice. The President reciprocated the protesters' support by doing what is perhaps the warmest reception any head of state has extended to progressive movements. He invited their representatives inside the House of Representatives' lounge for a conversation about peace, indigenous peoples, and social services. This unique moment of people meeting power will be perhaps a point of discussion in years to come, for it is a rare episode in the history of SONAs where the president himself reaches out to oppositional publics.

The Militant Left-Duterte Alliance

The cordial turn of a militant organization is not surprising considering Duterte's (1) policy pronouncements; (2) gestures toward the left; and (3) historical relationship with the movement.

As far as policy pronouncements go, Duterte has made clear that his positions are consistent with Bayan's agenda. In his campaign speeches, Duterte did not hesitate to call himself a socialist. He has been critical of contractual labor and irresponsible mining. His anti-American rhetoric and pursuit of an "independent foreign policy" also sat well with nationalistic activists. Duterte declared that he would pursue the country's industrialization starting with the revival of the steel industry. He reasoned that industrialization is the key to economic growth, particularly in generating jobs. This is consistent with Bayan's proposal for prioritizing national industrialization as a key driver of development. "We support Duterte's pro-people pronouncements and programs, even as we offer alternatives to many of the government's program," said Bayan secretary general Renato M. Reyes Jr. (Bayan 2016c).

Duterte's gestures also provided indications of the president's seriousness in building an alliance with the militant left, even though they officially supported another candidate during the campaign. Just days after Duterte won the presidency, he offered cabinet positions to nominees of the Communist Party of the Philippines (CPP). The CPP, through its armed group, the New Peoples' Army (NPA), has been waging one of the world's longest Maoist insurgencies since 1968 (So 2016; Viray 2016). CPP's founding chairman Jose Maria

Sison describes Duterte's gesture as a "magnanimous offer." Rafael Mariano, the chairman of the farmers' group Kilusang Mambubukid ng Pilipinas, was appointed Secretary of the Department of Agrarian Reform. Judy Taguiwalo, a social worker and feminist professor from the University of the Philippines, became the Secretary of the Department of Social Work and Development. Former Gabriela Party List Representative Liza Maza was appointed Lead Convener of the National Anti-Poverty Commission. Joel Maglungsod, former labor partylist solon, became Undersecretary of the Department of Labor and Employment. Former youth leader Terry Ridon was appointed Chair of the Presidential Commission on the Urban Poor. Personalities known to be allies of the mass movement were also appointed in key government posts. Silvestre Bello III became Secretary of the Department of Labor and Employment—a key position to push the agenda against unfair labor practices. Leonor Briones, the former national treasurer who took an active role in monitoring pork barrel allocations in the national budget, was given the role of Secretary of the Department of Education. These appointments support Duterte's pro-people, socialist image. These cabinet appointees, as his alter-ego, are expected to pursue the agenda of progressive governance.

Aside from appointing progressive allies in key cabinet posts, Duterte also announced the beginning of peace talks, a fundamental agenda for the militant left since the downfall of Ferdinand Marcos's dictatorship. The peace talks aim to end the nearly five-decade struggle between government troops and communist rebels that is affecting the countryside. The substantive peace agenda includes social, political, and economic reforms, which the National Democratic Front (NDF) of the Philippines, the CPP's political wing at the frontline of the talks with the government, maintains are essential to achieving lasting and just peace.

Part of the president's confidence-building measures for the peace talks are the release of political prisoners. According to human rights group Karapatan, there are at least 543 political prisoners as of May 2016. A number of these prisoners are sick and aging. A few weeks into Duterte's term, CPP leaders Benito and Wilma Tiamzon, among others, were released on bail. This gesture is significant because the release of political prisoners has been an important demand by the NDF. In the previous Aquino administration, the NDF's demand for the release of political prisoners resulted in the peace talks' deadlock.

One may ask why Duterte is in a unique position to engage with the militant left. Is there not a disconnect between the tough-talking leader's heavy-handed approach to politics and the progressive left's people-centered agenda?

Part of the reason, as some observers suggest, has to do with Duterte's long history with the movement and their members. On the level of personal relationships, Duterte is known to be a close political ally of Leoncio "Jun" Evasco Jr., a priest turned NPA rebel in the 1970s. Upon his release from captivity, Evasco served as Duterte's staff in the city hall. Today, Evasco is in charge of Kilusang Pagbabago (KP), a nationwide mass movement of Duterte supporters. Evasco intends to create a KP unit in each village, reminiscent of the CPP's grassroots organizing. Duterte's links to the mass movement also go back to his student days, as Sison was his teacher in Lyceum in the 1960s. Sison claims that Duterte was once a member of Kabataang Makabayan, a youth group allied with the NDF, and Bayan, and vouched for his "track record and good qualities." For Sison, Duterte has been "very cooperative with the revolutionary movement in ways beneficial to the people" (Alberto-Masakayan 2016). Duterte's "cooperation" with the movement took many forms while he was still Davao City mayor. In 2015, he allowed a hero's burial for NPA leader Leoncio Pitao (aka Commander Parago) in Davao City. Over 10,000 NPA supporters clad in red marched in the streets of Davao City, waving communist banners, parading the coffin of the slain commander with a hammer and sickle flag. Duterte received criticism for this decision, which he defended as his way of preserving lines of communication with the movement. Duterte was also able to openly talk about the payment of revolutionary taxes to the NPA, even though this has been condemned by the national government.

Duterte has been consistent in defending his sympathies with the left. "I am not against you. I will not fight against you. We have the same view of the government and politics," he said in one interview (Santos 2015). Where Duterte drew the line was the movement's belief in armed struggle.

The Struggle Amidst the Unity

The engagement between militant groups and the Duterte administration holds the promise of delivering lasting peace in a protracted war. This, however, may come at a high cost for the country's oppositional public sphere. Such close ties between the state and militant left may create a void in critical discourse formation and cripple a militant vocabulary necessary in a controversial regime. Critics have already raised concerns over the left's muffled voice on controversial issues, like the war on drugs, where they may have been expected to be utterly critical.

One way of examining the relationship of the militant left and the Duterte regime is to evaluate how the former engages the latter when it comes to the most controversial positions of the regime to date: the bloody war on drugs, economic policies, and the Marcos burial. A careful review of their statements, interviews, and press coverage suggests that critique is very much present in their discourse. These movements, I argue, have not abandoned their oppositional role in the public sphere, although the intensity of critique and the adversarial character of their repertoire have changed.

Human rights and war on drugs

There is high expectation of Bayan and its allies to take action against human rights violations in Duterte's drug war. After all, it is these groups that have the experience of defending, investigating, and demanding justice for human rights victims from their ranks since the rule of Ferdinand Marcos. Human rights scholar Jayson Lamchek (2016) noted that human rights workers from progressive groups have "systematically and painstakingly" investigated the extra-judicial killings of activists, and urged them to do the same for drug-related killings.

For some observers, the concessions the left has received from the Duterte regime have effectively curbed their appetite for critique. Political scientists Ronald Holmes and Mark Thompson (2016) argue that having received key cabinet positions and because of their eagerness for the peace deal, the left's critique of the drug war "has been muted." This interpretation is akin to corporatism wherein states accommodate representatives of interest groups in policy- or decision-making; the relationship accords the former legitimacy while the latter gains some of their demands that are often moderated by the corporatist relationship (Williamson 1989). Similar interpretations of Philippine politics were argued during the administrations of Ramon Magsaysay and Fidel Ramos (Clarke 1998, 212–14), and Corazon Aquino (Grodsky 2009, 903; Clarke 1998, 213). A more recent example of a similar engagement between a ruling party and a progressive group is the formal coalition between the Liberal Party and Akbayan Partylist since 2010. Some Akbayan members admitted that the coalition resulted not only in legislative gains but also in compromises on their stand on some issues (Cay and Nonato 2014).

Are these critiques of the left warranted? A cursory inventory of the militant left's responses to Duterte's bloody war illustrates that the movement continues to take a critical stance against what they consider to be unacceptable practices of the regime. Here are some examples:

1. Call for due process. On 1 July 2016, a day after Duterte's inauguration, Duterte enjoined the CPP's revolutionary forces to help in curtailing drug trafficking. CPP accepted this call and ordered the NPA to "carry out operations to disarm and arrest the chieftains of the biggest drug syndicates, as well as other criminal syndicates involved in human rights violations and destruction of environment" (CPP 2016). The Party, however, emphasized due process when conducting these arrests.

2. Speaking up against the killings. On 7 July 2016, Bayan (2016d) expressed concern "over the spate of extra-judicial

killings of alleged drug dealers over the past few weeks."
Even during the SONA rally—a supposedly cooperative
moment between the state and the movement—Bayan
called on the administration to uphold due process and
respect human rights amid the spate of drug-related vigilante killings. Former solons associated with progressive
groups Saturnino "Satur" Ocampo and Teodoro "Teddy"
Casiño urged the president to address the issue of extra-judicial killings (Sabillo 2016).

3. Unequivocal condemnation. On 4 August, Bayan (2016e)
denounced "in the strongest terms the unabated killings in
relation to the war on drugs." They urged government to
take up social and rehabilitative approaches to solving drug
dependency and to address the socio-economic roots of the
problem (Bayan 2016e). Eight days later, the CPP denounced
Duterte's attack on human rights defenders and called the
war on drugs "anti-people, undemocratic" (Bueza 2016).
On 23 August, human rights group Karapatan (2016a) urged
Duterte to publicly express and act on the stopping of the
drug-related killings. Karapatan is associated with Bayan.

Based on these select statements, interviews, and press
coverage of the militant groups, it is fair to say that they have been
steadfast in calling out the excesses of Duterte's war on drugs.
Even in the early days of the war on drugs, the CPP and Bayan
have emphasized their call for due process amid the escalation
of drug-related killings. In just a few weeks, they expressed their
opposition to the war on drugs using strong language, even calling
on the administration to end the drug-related killings. Contrary to
what their critics say, the left's voice has not been muffled but has
always been critical of the war on drugs. What is apparent is their
reluctance to publicly protest in the streets on this issue as they
may have been expected. However, this reluctance will change later
on, amid a crucial issue (Marcos burial) that will test the alliance
between the left and the Duterte administration.

Economic policies

Aside from the war on drugs, another issue about which Bayan has been vocal in their opposition is the economic agenda. Days after his victory, Duterte's transition team released an early version of the administration's economic policy. The first point is to "continue and maintain the current macroeconomic policies." Other points were on infrastructure spending, foreign direct investment, agricultural development, land management, basic administration, income tax, and the conditional cash transfer program (Cepeda 2016). Bayan criticized the agenda, which they consider to be a continuation of the Aquino administration's neoliberal policies. Instead, they proposed a progressive agenda that rejects "'business as usual' politics" (Bayan 2016a).

Even before Duterte took office, political analyst Bobby Tuazon (2016) predicted this predicament: "how will Duterte be able to balance and rein in a government of incongruent political forces—the left armed with a progressive ideology and rightist groups representing neoliberal and pro-elite interests?" Among Duterte's economic team are Finance Secretary Carlos Dominguez, Budget Secretary Benjamin Diokno, and Economic Development and Planning Director-General Ernesto Pernia. Dominquez is Duterte's fellow Mindanaoan and served as Duterte's fundraising and campaign finance manager. Aside from a few years of government service under Corazon Aquino, Dominguez has had a long business career as a top executive in various industries like mining, tobacco, retail, and energy. Diokno is also no rookie in government service, having held the same position under the Estrada administration. Pernia served as consultant or adviser for various international organizations but served longest at the Asian Development Bank in different posts, including lead economist. Both Diokno and Pernia have professional experience as academics at the University of the Philippines (UP) School of Economics. Diokno is Professor Emeritus at the UP.

A hundred days into Duterte's term, nationalist socio-economic think tank IBON Foundation's answer to Tuazon is that, although there are some gains for the people, the rightist groups are ruling over the economic agenda. IBON praised government efforts to pursue the peace talks and an independent foreign policy. Both agenda open the possibility for a nationalist economic agenda. But they criticized the government's neoliberal policies that are inconsistent with Duterte's pro-people pronouncements and appointment of progressive Cabinet members (IBON 2016). IBON Foundation shares the progressive agenda of Bayan and its allies.

IBON noted the disregard for national industrialization by Duterte's economic team whose policies do not truly propel production by Filipino industrial firms. At best, the industrial policy privileges foreign firms and their subcontractors to set up their production in the Philippines. IBON also criticized the government for the following: its openness to entering into unfair agreements with other states and regions; its neglect of wage increase and ending labor contractualization that favor the elites; subsidizing private firms through public-private partnerships; its pro-rich moves to lower taxes on wages, estate, land, and capital income; and anti-poor moves to impose value-added tax and increase excise tax on some items. To counter these, IBON proposed the following: a new, progressive, and long-term national industrialization policy; government procurement of Filipino products and removal of unfair incentives for foreign manufacturers; the creation of a national industrialization council, among others; the renegotiation or withdrawal from unfair trade agreements; the expansion of economic relations outside of traditional trading partners; the withdrawal from the Partnership for Growth with the United States that is not beneficial to the Philippines; and joining alliances with other states taking action against large and aggressive capitalist states (IBON 2016).

Marcos burial

The burial of former President Marcos at the Libingan ng mga Bayani (Heroes' Cemetery) is the most glaring disagreement between the left and the Duterte regime.

Since the campaign period, Duterte has been clear in his support for the burial of the former dictator in the Heroes' Cemetery, saying this will "erase from our people one hatred" (Ranada 2016). On 7

August, Duterte authorized the interment of Marcos at the Libingan ng mga Bayani. Bayan (2016f) reacted by saying they "oppose any official honors for the dictator Marcos, whether as a hero, soldier or former president." Duterte's decision to allow the Marcos burial "opened up old wounds," political scientist Ramon Casiple said (Gomez 2016). The left was a major opposition to the Marcos dictatorship, as several of their colleagues suffered human rights violations at the hands of his government forces.

Six petitions were filed at the Supreme Court to stop this move. Some of the petitioners are members or allies of Bayan. Among them are Bayan Chair Maria Carolina Araullo and former Bayan Muna solon Satur Ocampo. The interment was postponed three times until 8 November, when the Supreme Court ruled that the Marcos burial could proceed, with nine voting in favor, five against, and one abstention.

Petitioners sought to challenge this decision by filing a manifestation that they have not received copies of the decision and urged the court to once again postpone the interment. However, on 18 November, the Marcoses, with the support of the Armed Forces of the Philippines, swiftly buried the former dictator. The public found out only on the day itself through news sources that posted reports and onsite videos of the burial.

That afternoon, protests were organized against the surprise burial. Militant groups, students, and civil society organizations converged in different parts of Metro Manila. Bayan and its allies scheduled noise barrages in Monumento, Philcoa, Marikina, Alabang, E. Rodriguez, Taft Ave., Intramuros, and Morayta. Ateneo de Manila University shrouded its walls in black; Katipunan Avenue was filled with Ateneo students who walked out of their classes. At the University of the Philippines-Diliman campus—the hotbed of militancy during the Marcos era—students staged a protest rally, with the veterans of First Quarter Storm speaking to millennials about the dark days of the dictatorial regime.

Bayan took an active part in these mobilizations. They supported the Campaign Against the Return of the Marcoses to Malacañang (CARMMA), a campaign network composed of martial law victims, civil libertarians, peace and freedom advocates, and militant groups with roots in the anti-Marcos movement since the 1970s. "It is a wakeup call. Years of political accommodation and the failure to achieve true justice have brought us here. When we say 'never again,' we say it with a greater sense of urgency because a Marcos restoration has just become very real," read the Bayan (2016i) statement.

On 25 November, Bayan held its first major protest directed against Duterte, dubbed #BlackFriday. Bayan condemned the "Duterte-Marcos alliance" and called the people to hold Duterte accountable for the burial. Days later, Bayan and its allies took to the streets again to protest in time for International Human Rights Day on 10 December (Bayan 2016j). The call for protest coincided with the growing tension between government and CPP-NDF peace panels. At that point, Duterte refused to release 130 political prisoners unless the communist rebels signed a bilateral ceasefire agreement (Merez 2017). Karapatan (2016b) said that "these rallies are meant to sustain protest actions against the hero's burial of dictator Ferdinand Marcos and press the call for justice for and indemnification of martial law victims." Bayan (2016j) outlined four demands:

1. We demand justice for all Marcos human rights victims and all victims of continuing human rights violations and state fascism. The Marcos burial and restoration threatens efforts for meaningful indemnification of Marcos human rights victims.
2. We call for the immediate release of more than 400 political prisoners who have been unjustly detained. They should not be made bargaining chips by the government panel in peace negotiations.
3. We call for a stop to the militarization of the countryside. Hundreds of farmers from the Visayas, affected by militarization, are in Manila now to join the protest actions.
4. We call for an end to impunity in the war on drugs, as the death toll rises and as state agents are emboldened by presidential pronouncements.

The centerpiece of this protest is an effigy, a first since Duterte took office. This development is very telling of the growing tension between the left and the Duterte regime. The effigy features the head of the late dictator Marcos, with a bloody ironclad hand and corpses. "The effigy depicts the political rehabilitation of the Marcoses and continuing state fascism, including extrajudicial killings, the non-release of political prisoners, and continuing military operations," said Karapatan (Tupaz 2016). On the day of the rally, protesters burned the monstrous effigy symbolizing the authoritarian tendencies of Duterte. The move clearly attacked Duterte. The effigy may have featured Marcos's head, not Duterte's, but the other images refer to human rights issues in the Duterte administration.

Conclusion

In the lead-up to their rally timed for Duterte's 100th day in office, Bayan released a statement that encapsulates the kind of relationship they have with the Duterte regime. They "remain conscious of differences with the Duterte administration on other issues, particularly the war on drugs." They will, however, continue "to engage in principled 'unity and struggle' with the administration" (Bayan 2016g). On the day of the rally, they "lauded the resumption of the peace negotiations with the National Democratic Front of the Philippines and the acceleration of negotiations on substantive issues" but they also "lamented the government's failure to release more than 400 political prisoners as part of a supposed amnesty proclamation that aims to correct a gross injustice committed by previous regimes" (Bayan 2016h). In this regard, the left's relationship with the Duterte administration is one of critical engagement.

The first year of Duterte's presidency illustrated the changing character of the militant left movement in the country. The informal alliance started on an optimistic note. Rallies were organized to show support for the Duterte administration. Using a classic corporatist lens, Duterte has been able to use the progressives in his Cabinet in order to maintain his socialist and pro-people persona. For the militant left, having allies inside the administration enables them to pursue progressive endeavors favoring their mass base, most importantly in the resumption of the peace talks and promotion of socio-economic reforms. In the early days of the Duterte administration, the militant left's critical appetite became moderated as shown in their reluctance to protest against Duterte. Even on sticking points, such as the war on drugs, they have maintained their position through statements, but not through their usual public demonstrations.

However, nearing Duterte's sixth month in office, the militant left broke out of classic corporatism, and went out again to the streets to protest the Marcos burial and human rights issues. While the left never relinquished their role in criticizing the excesses of the Duterte regime, particularly in the war on drugs, it was the Marcos burial that tipped the scales to more confrontational forms of political action. For the first time in Duterte's administration, the left organized a massive protest to show indignation and demand accountability from Duterte. The tense situation in the peace talks must have also contributed to subsequent protests on International Human Rights Day, which featured an effigy—another first in this administration. It was also the first time that they protested to demand an end to impunity in the drug war, which has already escalated and become controversial by Duterte's sixth month in office.

Looking at Philippine civil society in general, one could argue that the militant left's lack of street protest against the drug war during the Duterte administration's early days may not be that crucial. Other progressive groups have been organizing protests early on, albeit on a smaller scale. However, as Duterte's allies, the militant left has the opportunity to be the decisive voice that could sway Duterte toward a more human rights-respecting approach. But this opportunity depends on Duterte's commitment to progressive ideals. It remains to be seen how much the left could influence Duterte to fulfill his progressive pronouncements, such as pursuing the peace process. It is apparent that the peace talks are important for Bayan and its allies because of the talks' substantive social and economic agenda. If Duterte truly commits to the peace process, the left could take on the drug war as an agenda in the talks, making their pursuit of lasting and just peace more meaningful for our times.

Epilogue

The left planned to burn Duterte's effigy in his second State of the Nation Address last 24 July 2017 to protest the stalled peace talks. Due to rains, however, they smashed the effigy instead.

References

Alberto-Masakayan, Thea. 2016. "Joma Sison Eyes Ceasefire, Return to PH If Duterte Wins." ABS-CBN News. 27 April. http://news.abs-cbn.com/halalan2016/nation/04/27/16/joma-sison-eyes-ceasefire-return-to-ph-if-duterte-wins.

Bayan. N.d. "Member Organizations." Bagong Alyansang Makabayan. http://www.bayan.ph/what-is-bayan/member-organization/.

———. 2016a. "On Duterte's 8-Point Economic Agenda." Bagong Alyansang Makabayan. 13 May. http://www.bayan.ph/2016/05/13/on-dutertes-8-point-economic-agenda/.

———. 2016b. "Groups Gearing for People's Summit on Eve of Duterte Inauguration." Bagong Alyansang Makabayan. 17 June. http://www.bayan.ph/2016/06/17/groups-gearing-for-peoples-summit-on-eve-of-duterte-inauguration/.

———. 2016c. "'Genuine Change and a Just Peace!'—National People's Summit." Bagong Alyansang Makabayan. 29 June. http://www.bayan.ph/2016/06/29/genuine-change-and-a-just-peace-national-peoples-summit/.

———. 2016d. "On Duterte Administration's Campaign against Illegal Drugs." Bagong Alyansang Makabayan. 7 July. http://www.bayan.ph/2016/07/07/against-illegal-drugs/.

———. 2016e. "BAYAN Statement on the Killings in Relation to War on Drugs." Corporate site. Bagong Alyansang Makabayan. 4 August. http://www.bayan.ph/2016/08/04/bayan-statement-on-war-on-drugs/.

———. 2016f. "BAYAN Statement on the Marcos Burial." Corporate site. Bagong Alyansang Makabayan. 8 August. http://www.bayan.ph/2016/08/08/bayan-statement-on-the-marcos-burial/.

———. 2016g. "Rally to Mark Duterte's 100 Days in Office Set on October 8 as Groups Support Assertion of Sovereignty, Peace Talks." Bagong Alyansang Makabayan. 28 September. http://www.bayan.ph/2016/09/28/rally-to-mark-dutertes-100-days-in-office

-set-on-october-8-as-groups-support-assertion-of-sovereignty-peace-talks/.

———. 2016h. "#Duterte100Days Struggle for Change Continues, Expect Intensifying Contradictions." Corporate site. Bagong Alyansang Makabayan. 8 October. http://www.bayan.ph/2016/10/07/dutert e100days-struggle-for-change/.

———. 2016i. "National Day of Unity and Rage- November 25." Bagong Alyansang Makabayan. 23 November. http://www.bayan. ph/2016/11/23/national-day-of-unity-and-rage-november-25/.

———. 2016j. "President Must Resolve Four Urgent Human Rights Issues." Bagong Alyansang Makabayan. 7 December. http://www. bayan.ph/2016/12/07/president-must-resolve/.

Bueza, Michael. 2016. "CPP: Duterte's War on Drugs 'Anti-People, Undemocratic.'" *Rappler*, 13 August. http://www.rappler.com/ nation/142967-cpp-duterte-war-drugs-anti-people-undemocratic.

Cay, Darlene, and Vince Nonato. 2014. "Akbayan Gives in to LP Framework." *Inquirer.net*, 13 July. http://opinion.inquirer.net/76488/ akbayan-gives-in-to-lp-framework.

Cepeda, Mara. 2016. "Transition Team Bares Duterte's 8-Point Economic Agenda." *Rappler*, 12 May. http://www.rappler.com/nation/politics/ elections/2016/132850-duterte-8-point-economic-agenda.

Clarke, Gerard. 1998. *The Politics of NGOs in South-East Asia: Participation and Protest in the Philippines*. Routledge.

CPP. 2016. "Response to President Duterte's Call for Anti-Drug Cooperation." National Democratic Front of the Philippines, International Information Office. 2 July. https://www.ndfp.org/ response-president-dutertes-call-anti-drug-cooperation/.

Gomez, Jim. 2016. "Anti-Marcos Burial Protesters Unite at 'Black Friday' Rally." *Philstar.com*, 26 November. http://www.philstar. com/headlines/2016/11/26/1647626/anti-marcos-burial-protesters -unite-black-friday-rally.

Grodsky, Brian. 2009. "From Neo-Corporatism to Delegative Corporatism? Empowerment of NGOs during Early Democratization." Democratization 16 (5):898–921. doi:10.1080/13510340903162093.

Holmes, Ronald D., and Mark R. Thompson. 2016. "Duterte's Anti-Drug Crackdown Poses Risks to Rule of Law." East Asia Forum. 21 August. http://www.eastasiaforum.org/2016/08/21/dutertes-anti-drug -crackdown-poses-risks-to-rule-of-law/.

IBON. 2016. "On the Duterte Administration's Economic Direction in

Its First 100 Days: Neoliberal Economics Continues, but Nationalist Change Still Possible." IBON Foundation. 5 October. http://ibon. org/2016/10/on-the-duterte-administrations-economic-direction-in-its-first-100-days-neoliberal-economics-continues-but-nationalist-change-still-possible/.

Karapatan. 2016a. "Drugs Can Be Eliminated without Curtailing Rights | Karapatan." Karapatan: Alliance for the Advancement of People's Rights. 23 August. http://www.karapatan.org/ Drugs+can+be+eliminated+without+curtailing+rights.

———. 2016b. "Karapatan to Jointly Lead Nationwide Rallies on Int'l Human Rights Day | Karapatan." Karapatan: Alliance for the Advancement of People's Rights. 9 December. http://www.karapatan.org/.

Lamchek, Jayson. 2016. "A Storm of Bullets, a Wave of Apathy." Academic site. New Mandala. 16 August. http://www.newmandala. org/storm-bullets-wave-apathy/.

Makabayan. N. d. "The Makabayan Coalition | Makabayan." Corporate site. Makabayan. http://www.makabayan.net/node/5.

Merez, Arianne. 2017. "TIMELINE: Gov't, CPP-NPA Ceasefire Breakdown." *ABS-CBN News*, 4 February. http://news.abs-cbn.com/ focus/02/03/17/timeline-govt-cpp-npa-ceasefire-breakdown.

Molina, Oscar, and Martin Rhodes. 2002. "CORPORATISM: The Past, Present, and Future of a Concept." Annual Review of Political Science 5 (1):305–31. doi:10.1146/annurev.polisci.5.112701.184858.

Ranada, Pia. 2016. "Duterte: Marcos Burial 'Can Be Arranged Immediately.'" *Rappler*, 23 May. http://www.rappler.com/nation/13 4025-duterte-marcos-burial-heroes-cemetery.

Sabillo, Kristine Angeli. 2016. "Former Solons Happy with Sona but Ask Duterte to Address Killings." *Inquirer.net*, 26 July. http://newsinfo. inquirer.net/799690/former-solons-happy-with-sona-but-ask-duterte-to-address-killings.

Santos, Dennis Jay. 2015. "Duterte Defends Allowing Hero's Burial for Slain NPA Leader." *Inquirer.net*, 11 July. http://newsinfo.inquirer. net/704460/duterte-defends-allowing-heros-burial-for-slain-npa-leader.

So, Levi A. 2016. "Joma Sison Welcomes Duterte's Offer of Peace, but Declines Cabinet Position." *Philstar.com*, 16 May. http://www.philsta r.com/headlines/2016/05/16/1584010/joma-sison-welcomes-dutertes-offer-peace-declines-cabinet-position.

Tuazon, Bobby M. 2016. "Duterte's Socialist Experiment." *Inquirer. net*, 21 May. http://opinion.inquirer.net/94843/dutertes-socialist -experiment.

Tupaz, Voltaire. 2016. "WATCH: Left's 1st Effigy under Duterte Depicts Fascist Monster." *Rappler*, 10 December. http://www.rappler.com/ move-ph/155140-left-burn-effigy-duterte-authoritarian-tenden- cies.

Viray, Patricia Lourdes. 2016. "Duterte Offers Top Gov't Posts to CPP." *Philstar.com*, 27 May. http://www.philstar.com/headlines/2016/05/1 6/1583797/duterte-offers-top-govt-posts-cpp.

Williamson, Peter J. 1989. *Corporatism in Perspective: An Introductory Guide to Corporatist Theory*. London; Newbury Park: Sage Publications.

ENGAGING DUTERTE
THAT SPACE IN BETWEEN POPULISM AND PLURALISM

Carmel Veloso Abao

Very early into the Duterte presidency, I claimed that change under Duterte was likely to be "from above" rather than "from below" (see Abao 2016). Now that the president has been in office for almost a year and there is more data from which to draw one's reflections, I revisit this claim using the lens of "populism."

I use populism to re-examine the nature and dynamics of change under Duterte because the term has become a sort of buzzword lately. President Duterte is also often characterized as a populist leader. Is such characterization accurate? If it is and Duterte is populist, how should we citizens engage him? What kind of opposition is needed?

Populism Versus Pluralism

According to the American journalist John B. Judis, there is now a "populist explosion" and "populist parties and candidates are on the move in the United States and Europe" (Judis 2016, 55–56). Judis's list of those to be considered "populist" is quite long. Interestingly, it includes individuals and groups from both the "left" and the "right"—all of which, he argues, emerged "in the wake of the Great Recession." Judis mentions Donald Trump, Bernie Sanders, the Tea Party, the Occupy Wall Street Movements in the United States, Marie Le Pen and the National Front (FN) in France, the People's Party (DF) in Denmark, the Swiss People's Party in Switzerland, the Progress Party (FrP) in Norway, Geert Wilder's Freedom Party (PVV) in Netherlands, the United Kingdom Independence Party (UKIP) of Britain, comedian Beppe Grillo's Five Star Movement in Italy, the Podemos Party in Spain, and the Syriza Party in Greece (Ibid.).

Populism has no singular definition. Judis draws from the historian Michael Kazin, who defines populism as

> a language whose speakers conceive of ordinary people as a noble assemblage not bounded narrowly by class; view their elite opponents as self-serving and undemocratic; and seek to mobilize the former against the latter. (Judis 2016, 87)

While agreeing with Kazin's definition, Judis claims that the rise of populists from all sides is a signal of the rise of a different kind of Left and a different kind of Right. Leftist populists, according to him, are not necessarily for the abolition of capitalism but "assumes a basic antagonism between the people and the elite" (Ibid.). Rightist populists, meanwhile, are different from the usual conservatives because they may or may not identify with the "business classes" and may or may not operate within a democratic set-up.

According to political theorist Paulina Ochoa Espejo, among the many definitions of populism, Cas Mudde's is the most useful: "populism is a thin-centered ideology that considers society to be ultimately separated into two homogenous and antagonistic groups, the 'pure people' and 'the corrupt elite' and which argues that politics should be an expression of the *volonte generale* (general will) of the people" (Espejo 2015, 62).

For Espejo, Mudde's definition captures the idea of populists that "politics should be an expression of the general will" and elucidates "five widely held intuitions about populism," namely:

1.   Populist leaders and movements often seek legitimacy by

going directly to the people instead of utilizing institutional, representative mechanisms.

2. Populism presents a demoralized "us (the people)" against "them (the elite, the foreigners or the other).

3. In populism, "the people" is a "symbolic or normative construct" and not the usual democratic notion of the people as "a collection of individuals or a type of government"; thus, while democracy is a "regime," populism is an "ideology."

4. Populism as "thin-centered" points to its "malleability" and thereby its applicability to many variations (i.e., Left and Right).

5. Populism draws the line between "the people and the elite" and is therefore incompatible with liberal democracy that considers "both masses and the elite as part of the people."

Political sociologist Robert S. Jansen, meanwhile, posits that populism must be viewed from the perspective of "political practice" and not from the perspective of some coherent worldview. For Jansen, what must be examined is "populist mobilization" that is a "political *means*" that can be employed by (any kind of) political players, challengers or otherwise—for any agenda (Jansen 2015, 161). According to this view, populism is best viewed as a "sustained, large scale political project that combines *popular mobilization* with populist *rhetoric*" (2015, 161; italics mine).

Populism is, thus, a highly contested political concept because it can refer to a number of things: a movement, a party, an ideology, a political strategy, a leader. Indeed, there is no one valid definition of what constitutes a "populist." What cuts across the various definitions, however, is the presentation of "the people" as fighting back against some enemy.

Given all this, it can be deduced that there are stark differences between populism and the current liberal democratic notion of "pluralism." Pluralism is the opposite of populism because it places importance on the "rule of law" that structures the "rule of the people." People, in this case, are "represented" by elected leaders that in turn follow certain rules and procedures. Populist leaders, on the other hand, "embody" rather than represent the people. Populists also tend to conceive of a homogenous "people" unified against some notion of an "other." Pluralists, in contrast, conceive of "the people" as heterogeneous.

This rejection of the pluralist conception of the heterogeneity of "voices," "political equality," and "rule of law" tends to lead populist leaders to think that their mandates are incompatible with human rights. This means that populist leaders are more likely to resort to authoritarian or even fascist strategies to push their (people's) agenda. It should be noted, however, that populism is not necessarily the same as fascism. Unlike fascism, where all state apparatuses are utilized to maintain a very high level of social control, populism can thrive even within democracies. Populist leaders are, in fact, often products of overwhelming electoral victories and, once elected, are often backed by majority parliamentary support.

In his study of populist leaders Hugo Chavez of Venezuela and Alberto Fujimori of Peru, Braun also concluded that populists are indeed repressive. Braun observed, however, that while human rights abuses were visible in both Latin American cases, Peru's Fujimori was, in fact, more repressive because of his regime's decreasing capacity to finance the social programs that it had promised the masses (Braun 2011, 9). Chavez, meanwhile, faced no such problem because his populist rhetoric was well supported by the Venezuelan oil-rich economy. The populism of Chavez has been touted to be a redemptive force rather than a destructive one because it has been seen as taking wealth away from the traditional elite and giving it back to the people—without having to resort to full-scale fascism.

Both populism and pluralism, therefore, can be presented as having positive values because both are preoccupied with popular sovereignty or "giving power (back) to the people." However, both also hold negative values and therefore should not be accepted uncritically. *I posit that populism overvalues power and ends up producing authoritarianism while pluralism undervalues power and ends up producing elitism.*

Because both populism and pluralism have no real or tangible mechanisms by which to link people to government and channel people's participation in politics, both end up relegating the concept of giving "power to the people" to the realm of mere rhetoric. In actual governance within both regimes, power is concentrated and embedded in actors or institutions other than "the people." In populism, power is often lodged in a "strongman" while in pluralism, power is often lodged in an "elite."

Duterte's Populism

Based on the discussion above, President Duterte can be characterized as a populist leader and his administration as a populist regime.

As early as the electoral campaign leading to the May 2016 elections, the presentation of "the people versus others" and the "combination of popular mobilization and populist rhetoric" were already discernible. In September 2015, the drumbeating for Duterte's candidacy achieved its first milestone when Duterte was presented as "the People's Call for Change" (Agoncillo 2015). At the time, Duterte had not made a decision to run for President and had, in fact, made a pronouncement that he did *not* want to run for President.

The entire episode of the back-and-forth between the candidate Duterte and the clamoring supporters galvanized a faithful following and established the message that he was "of the people" and "for the people," choosing to run "for the good of the country" despite his reluctance to seek higher office. While there is no hard evidence that the tug-pull, against-all-odds episode was merely a concocted political strategy of the Duterte campaign team, it did prove to be an effective method to generate enthusiastic and loyal support for Duterte.

The campaign slogan "change is coming" resonated well with voters because it had visible basis: Duterte was indeed new to the national scene but was not a political neophyte. He was a reluctant leader (and therefore not power-hungry) but was a capable contender—the ideal challenge to entrenched national forces. Duterte was fresh change, a much-needed break from the corrupt, unchanged environment of national politics.

The roots of Duterte's populism, in fact, can be traced to the context of a "perfect political storm." A ruling elite was perceived to have failed to meet its own high bar of "daang matuwid" and had committed a series of political blunders in its six years in office (i.e., inadequate response to the Haiyan disaster and reconstruction, Mamasapano encounter, rampant killings of indigenous peoples, the Kidapawan conflict, and the implementation of the controversial Disbursement Acceleration Program). The ruling administration's standard bearer was perceived to be unapologetic of the ruling elite's failures and therefore not worthy of the people's vote. The mainstream political contenders were perceived to be just as elitist and corrupt as the ruling elite. There were no political parties or movements to structure or temper the political intramurals among factions of the elite. A large section of the population could not feel the effects of the "high economic growth" touted in broadsheets as record-breaking percentages. Instead, many felt that their everyday problems like heavy traffic, unemployment/underemployment, health risks, crime, drought, hunger remained unaddressed. An even larger section of society had embraced a political and social culture that was deeply embedded in compliance-seeking, undemocratic, patriarchal social institutions (i.e., families, schools, workplaces, churches).

All these structural and conjunctural factors produced fertile ground for the rise of a populist leader. Consequently, the message of Duterte as "the man/solution/savior" proved to be effective: Duterte was the perfect candidate that could ride out and take advantage of the perfect storm. Duterte would not only represent the people—he was to be the embodiment of the people. Duterte *was* the people ready to take back power from them elites.

Duterte's embodiment of the people was sustained in the post-campaign period and all throughout the first year of his administration. As president, Duterte demonstrated that "the people" was indeed different from "the elite": crass and rough but sincere and not superficially polite, action-oriented and not all talk, practical and not aloof nor too intellectual, macho and not *bayot* (a Visayan term meaning homosexual that Duterte has repeatedly used derogatorily in public) homegrown and not imperialist, proud nationalist and not anyone's puppet.

The "elite" as "the other" is not to be taken literally as the oligarchy or the economic elite but simply as an abstraction of the powerful few perceived to have marginalized (cheated!) the masses throughout the past decades. While Duterte has claimed to be Socialist and Leftist, his populism does not seem to be ideological—he does think in terms of class struggle.

At the start of his administration, Duterte exhibited some class bias with his pronouncements against labor contractualization and against big mining interests. This bias, however, has been cancelled out by other actions and pronouncements that point to either a friendly attitude toward oligarchs (e.g., dinner with tycoons; "win-win" solution to contractualization problem) or a disdain for the poor (e.g., "I have not seen a son of a tycoon peddling drugs"). Despite this, his pro-poor rhetoric has been maintained—not by actual pro-poor policies, but by sustained public messaging that he is as an "ordinary man" on a mission to fight the enemies of the people.

Instead of lodging his populism on a particular ideology, Duterte has chosen the "war on drugs" as the anchor of his administration. As a strategy to maintain his popularity, this choice has been effective. In this war, Duterte has identified drug criminals, specifically those peddling and using *shabu* (methamphetamine), as the "other." This choice of "enemy" seems to be a logical choice, if one considers the president's background: he had maintained power as mayor of Davao City—for more than two decades—primarily by being tough on criminals, especially those involved in drug trafficking and abuse. Davao City is his showcase for how the war on drugs using his method (i.e., no limits) is necessary and feasible. Only the outcome and not the process of solving the drugs problem mattered: the citizens of Davao were/are safe. Duterte's election to the presidency has, in fact, been presented as an opportunity to replicate the results of his mayoralty in Davao throughout the rest of the country.

Unlike Davao, however, Duterte's national governance has not yielded clear-cut outcomes. On the contrary, the endgames of his initiatives are becoming vaguer. The spaces that he had opened are increasingly eroding or becoming dim. The anti-contractualization agenda, which initially promised an end to contractualization that "was not open to compromises," has been watered down through a "win-win solution" that has been rejected by trade unions, the representatives of the labor sector that this agenda was supposed to benefit. The peace process with the Communist Left seems to hang in the balance after an abrupt end, and now a possible return, to a ceasefire (CNN Philippines 2017). The anti-mining agenda has been reduced to a fight over the appointment of an environmental advocate as Secretary of the Department of Environment and Natural Resources. The federalism-parliamentary agenda has been limited to negotiations in Congress over ways to change the Charter. This has not led to widespread public discourse on local-national relations or executive-legislative relations. The foreign policy agenda initially appeared to be anti-US and was veering toward a diversification of allies to include non-traditional allies like China and Russia. Duterte's openness toward US President Donald Trump, however, raises questions about this anti-US position. Of late, it seems that Duterte may not actually be anti-US but merely against Obama or any other government or foreign entity critical of his war on drugs—including and perhaps most especially the European Union. Duterte's Cabinet has had to downplay the president's public tirades against the EU's health-based approach to the drug problem (ABS-CBN News 2017).

Duterte's populism has been so effective that his supporters have focused not on outcomes but on the radicalness of his ways. It seems that to many, that radicalness already approximates the change that they had envisioned even if the actual policy changes are yet to be seen. Even the spate of extra-judicial killings has not been deemed by Duterte supporters alarming. To them, those killings are a necessary and straightforward effect of the anti-drug campaign Duterte-style and is central to Duterte's promise to return peace and order throughout the country.

That Duterte can do no wrong is a message that has been developed not only by the president himself but also by an entire machinery behind him. Duterte's Cabinet members, for example, take the cudgels for him when he makes controversial statements. He also has a media team that is active in both mainstream and social media. This media team has been quite successful in framing the challenges to Duterte's governance as a fight between two groups that have deemed each other as being too fanatical: the *Dutertards* (usually proclaimed by the administration as being the people or the masses) and *Yellowtards* (conceived by the administration and their supporters as the elites). This framing has greatly enhanced the president's rhetoric of the elites as being the enemies of the people.

Duterte's team has also gone beyond media work to mobilizing warm bodies through the Kilusang Pagbabago, a political party formed by a Cabinet Secretary that specifically aims to protect the president and his agenda against his detractors (Fonbuena 2016).

Thus far, however, the most consequential source of support for Duterte has come from the arena of mainstream political institutions. This support has been essential in legitimizing and institutionalizing Duterte's populist strategies and authoritarian tendencies. In the Judiciary, Duterte obviously has support in the Supreme Court—as evidenced by the High Court's approval of the late dictator Marcos's burial at the Heroes' Cemetery, which was a Duterte agenda. This judicial support is expected to strengthen in the next five years as Duterte appoints eleven of the fifteen justices of the Supreme Court. In the legislature, Duterte enjoys a "super-majority" where more than 200 out of 297 Congressional repre-sentatives are members of the ruling coalition while key allies in the Senate hold the Senate leadership (Romero 2017). In the House of Representatives, this high level of support was revealed most dramatically by the passage of the Death Penalty Bill and the subse-quent purging of dissenting members from important posts within the House, even those who were thought to be allies to the president for their dissenting vote on the issue (Cruz 2017).

In the Senate, this was made manifest in the successful move to oust anti-Duterte Senators from the majority bloc. This means that there is minimal dissent in the arena of institutional politics especially in the legislative branch that, theoretically, is supposed to serve as a check on the executive. This is due in large part to the reality that there are no real political parties and therefore it was not very difficult for the Duterte camp to gain a supermajority in Congress.

Moreover, as shown in the case of Senator de Lima, dissent has a very high price. The senator is now in jail for allegedly coddling drug syndicates during her stint as Secretary of Justice in the previous Aquino administration. It is not a coincidence that the case against Senator de Lima was filed after she headed a Senate investigation on the extra-judicial killings and brought in a supposed former member of Duterte's "Davao Death Squad" (DDS) as witness and resource person. During said investigation, the tables were quickly turned and it was de Lima who found herself answering accusations. Government not only accused Senator de Lima of having links with drug lords, it also publicly shamed the senator for having an extramarital relationship with a former driver-bodyguard (alleged to be also part of the drug network) (Jenkins 2017).

There is thus the fear factor to consider. Challenging Duterte has proven to be a great risk for the careers (even the lives) of politicians.

In local governments, support could very well be considered a "supermajority" as well—once the proposed bill to postpone the barangay elections and to have the president appoint all barangay officials is approved. If and when this is done, Duterte would have had all important gatekeepers—from all branches of government— covered (Cepeda 2017).

Duterte's populism, therefore, is a product of populist rhetoric combined with popular mobilization and mainstream political-institutional support. Duterte may have won the election by directly appealing to the people without the tempering or mediation of political institutions like political parties or movements, but in his administration, he has had to rely on political institutions. A populist rejection of pluralist institutions and values does not necessarily mean the abolition of such institutions—but merely their capture by the populist leader.

Dissent Under Duterte

Dissent under Duterte has been minimal because Duterte has successfully presented himself as the embodiment of dissent against the people's enemies. The framing of Duterte as "the alternative" is the reason why the few dissenters who have challenged him have not been able to generate mass support. These dissenters—mostly coming from the Liberal Party—represent the "old system" that the president is supposedly out to transform. Lumping all dissenters as part of the Liberal Party or the "yellows" has been an effective means to deflect the validity of issues raised by dissenters.

The president and his administration also package all criticism against his policies as a demolition job by the "yellows." Thus, Duterte is continuously able to present himself as *the* alternative to elitist rule.

Moreover, Duterte often deals with criticism and manages dissent in a dismissive and macho way. It is not surprising that the staunchest opposition to Duterte's governance, especially his war on drugs, come from women: Senator Leila de Lima and Vice President Leni Robredo. On many occasions, Duterte has already exhibited his views toward women: they are always his subordinates and never his equals. The president's sexism/misogyny was in full view when he publicly supported the slut-shaming of de Lima during the Senate and House investigations of the senator's alleged links to drug syndicates.

The president is notorious for his sexist jokes and demeaning remarks about women. His allies downplay this as merely being a part of his character. The president's spokespersons—including his spokes*women*—often present the president's sexism as harmless and insignificant. For example, during a government-led celebration of International Women's day, a female government official claimed that "we voted for a President . . . not for a priest . . . [or] for a saint" and that the president's catcalling of women was a "relative" issue that depends "on the person who will be hurt" (Salaverria 2017). A former female senator, now a Duterte ally in Congress, has also dismissed the president's sexism as "a boy's thing" (Spot.ph 2017).

President Duterte declared Vice President Robredo as his enemy when the latter gave critical remarks against the war on drugs in her message to a United Nations meeting on extra-judicial killings (*The Straits Times* 2017). The relationship between the two elected officials has been strained since the beginning of their terms. The president, early on, had said that he could not consider the vice-president for any Cabinet appointment. Duterte reasoned that he did not want "to hurt the feelings" of Ferdinand "Bongbong" Marcos Jr., the son of former dictator Ferdinand Marcos, whom Robredo defeated in the elections for the vice-presidency (Gonzales 2016). Although the president eventually reneged on his refusal to appoint Robredo and appointed her as head of a government housing agency, tensions reached a new peak when the president, through a mere text message sent by a Cabinet member, asked the vice-president to refrain from attending Cabinet meetings. In reaction to being barred from Cabinet meetings, Robredo resigned from the housing portfolio and from the Cabinet (Cupin 2016).

After her resignation from the Cabinet, Robredo positioned herself as an opposition figure against some of the administration's policies, especially regarding extra-judicial killings, the war on drugs, and human rights. Calls on Robredo to accept a role akin to a "figurehead" of a "united opposition" against President Duterte ramped up, with some preferring that she also cut her ties with the Liberal Party. Robredo has refused to do both, refusing to let go of her Liberal Party ties while also taking a less extreme position compared to her other party-mates or other figures in the opposition. She has been criticizing the administration on the issues of human rights, extra-judicial killings, and the Marcos burial while abstaining from calling on the president to resign or be impeached.

The relationship between the president and the vice-president is further complicated by actions of the president's supporters and allies. Robredo has had to contend with the electoral protest filed against her by Bongbong Marcos. Duterte and Marcos supporters alike have used this electoral protest to assail Robredo's legitimacy as vice-president. Prominent pro-Duterte personalities, in fact, organized a Palit Bise (Replace the Vice) rally in Luneta, calling for her impeachment or resignation (Pasion 2017). Duterte supporters have accused the vice-president of being behind the impeachment move against the president, despite the fact that it was the Magdalo Party in the House of Representatives—the party allied with Sonny Trillanes, a staunch anti-Duterte senator—that filed an impeachment case. Robredo has repeatedly denied her involvement in this impeachment initiative and President Duterte has publicly declared that he believes Robredo's denial (De Jesus 2017).

At this point, it remains to be seen if the allies of the president—most especially Bongbong Marcos and his supporters—will be successful in their efforts to unseat the vice-president and weaken her legitimacy and popularity. It is becoming clear, however, that Robredo will not be "the" opposition leader that some quarters, especially the Liberal Party, has been hoping for. Moreover, as long as Robredo continues to associate herself with the Liberal Party—the members of which have moved en masse to the Duterte camp—her worthiness as a leader that can unify the opposition will always be questioned.

Dissent is also absent because the traditional but non-institutional organized opposition—the Communist Left composed of the Communist Party of the Philippines, the National Democratic Front, and the New People's Army (CPP-NDF-NPA)—has set one foot in and one foot out of the Duterte administration. An erstwhile opposition force to all recent governments, the Left's alliance with President Duterte has been visible as evidenced by the former's acceptance of offers of Cabinet appointments and cooperation in peace talks.

The Catholic Church hierarchy has also been less visible in this administration. The Church has launched some mobilizations against the death penalty but these expressions of protest have been few and far between.

Some sectoral movements have been taking center stage in engaging Duterte. Organized labor, for example, has been unified in its rejection of the win-win solution being proposed by the Department of Labor and Employment. Human Rights groups, including alternative lawyers' groups, have renewed their efforts in the wake of the extra-judicial killings. Some urban poor movements have also been attempting to mobilize against Oplan Tokhang. Women's groups have also mobilized against the misogynistic views of government as in the case of the slut-shaming of Senator de Lima. On issues such as the Marcos burial and the death penalty law, youth mobilization has been apparent.

The protests and engagements have evidently not risen to the level of popular dissent. Despite these protests, Duterte still commands a 70–80 percent popularity rating and his campaign against criminality has garnered an 84 percent approval rating. As explained above, the populist rhetoric and its attendant popular mobilization has been systematically sustained and in fact institutionalized through legislative measures. That level of mobilization and institutionalization is hard to match. Still, the protests matter because they represent a challenge to Duterte—amidst the apparent hegemony of Duterte and his politics of fear. They represent the existence of a counter-narrative to the dominant "Duterte can do no wrong" narrative.

Aside from these pockets of dissent, there is also growing international dissent. However, because Duterte's local-national support is consolidated, it has been easy for the Duterte camp to dismiss dissent from international players such as the United Nations, EU, Amnesty International, Human Rights Watch as "foreign intervention" or an encroachment on Philippine sovereignty. In the absence of massive, popular domestic dissent, international dissent merely comes across as dissonant.

Vacuum Without a Name

Given the conditions that gave rise and sustenance to Duterte's populism, the opposition that is needed is one that will reject both the authoritarianism of populism and the elitism of pluralism. This is, of course, easier said than done, not only because Duterte's base is cohesive but also because this vacuum—that space in between populism and pluralism—has yet to have a name. Because it has no name, it is very difficult to fill.

There used to be a name for this space: socialism or the Left. The Philippine Left was at the forefront of the struggle against authoritarianism (Marcos) and the "class struggle" against the oligarchs and the bourgeoisie. The Left, however, has obviously failed to capture the imagination of "the people" and instead has developed quite negative public images: threatening, opportunistic, fragmented.

The image of being threatening was, to a very great extent, a product of Marcos's "red scare" tactics in the 1970s and 1980s. It has been reinforced, however, by the Left's own coercive practices such as the New People's Army exacting revolutionary taxes and permits to campaign. The opportunistic image, meanwhile, is projected every time Left groups establish alliances with politicians that in their own rhetoric they abhor. The Left's fragmentation also becomes obvious when the public sees the various Left groups active in varying factions of the elite—especially during elections—and bickering with each other over which faction is worthier of support.

The Left thus may not be in the best position to fill the vacuum in the present juncture. Currently, the Left has been projected as being divided between the "anti-Duterte" Left (Akbayan, which was allied with the Aquino regime) and the "pro-Duterte" Left (the CPP-NPA-NDF and the Makabayan group). Thus, whatever these Leftists advocate are easily dismissed as suspect, i.e., as either for or against Duterte. Organizations are never monolithic, however, and dynamics within these organizations are likely to be more complex than the simplistic pro-anti-Duterte framing. There might also be contention within these groups regarding their organizations' positioning vis-a-vis the Duterte presidency. Said contention must be welcomed if only to foster public conversations about what's wrong with either pure populism or pure pluralism or why Leftists must not merely resemble mainstream players of both sides.

Because no other group aside from the Left has traditionally occupied the anti-authoritarian, anti-elite space, it will probably take a while for the current vacuum to be named, even longer to fill. Perhaps, all this marks a post-ideological stage where grand narratives are no longer useful in shaping political discourse and action. Another "ism" is not likely to be invented anytime soon.

Naming, however, is still possible. The space in between populism and pluralism can be reimagined as policies and practices that (real, not mythical) people can debate yet agree on. Thus, the vacuum can be occupied by names such as "security of tenure," "rehabilitation," "environmental protection," "federalism without political dynasties," "parliamentarism with real and inclusive political parties," "economic rights as human rights," "gender equality," "LGBT rights," "troll-free internet," participatory local development," "participatory governance," "transparency," and "accountability."

The opposition the nation needs now is one that will educate various publics about what can replace the policies and practices that have been undemocratic and elitist, policies and practices that have been detrimental to the development of "the people." Populism, after all, is a "language" and as such presents a form of politicization. The task at hand is to influence the content and direction of the politicization that is currently occurring.

The pro- and anti-Duterte sides, however, have been so polarized and radicalized that discussions on policies can be undermined simply through the Dutertard vs. Yellowtard labeling. The usual, popular mouthpieces of the elites, thus, cannot and should not lead the opposition against Duterte. New faces and social forces must emerge for transformative public conversations to flourish.

References

Abao, Carmel Veloso. 2016. "Engaging Duterte, Engaging Ourselves." *Rappler*, 16 July. http://www.rappler.com/thought-leaders/139850 -engaging-duterte-engaging-ourselves.

Agoncillo, Jodee. 2015. "Groups Still Push Duterte to Run for President in 2016 Elections." *Inquirer.net*, 26 September. http://newsinfo. inquirer.net/725621/groups-still-push-duterte-to-run-for-pres ident-in-2016-elections.

Braun, Joseph P. 2011. "Populism and Human Rights in Theory and Practice: Chavez's Venezuela and Fujimori's Peru." MA thesis, University of Nebraska-Lincoln.

Cepeda, Mara. 2017. "Barbers Files Bill Postponing Barangay Elections for 3 Years." *Rappler*, 27 March. http://www.rappler.com/ nation/165390 -barbers-bill-postpone-october-2017-elections.

Cupin, Bea. 2016. "Robredo to Resign from Duterte Cabinet." *Rappler*, 4 December. http://www.rappler.com/nation/154503-vice-president- leni-robredo-resign-duterte-cabinet-hudcc.

CNN Philippines Staff. 2015. "Communist Rebels to Declare Unilateral Ceasefire Before March Ends." *CNN Philippines*, 26 September. http://cnnphilippines.com/news/2017/03/25/communist-party-of- the-philippines-ceasefire-duterte.html.

Cruz, RG. 2017. "Deputy Speakers Who Oppose Death Penalty to be Replaced: Alvarez" *ABS-CBN News*, 8 February. http://news.abs-cbn. com/news/02/08/17/deputy-speakers-who-oppose-death-penalty- to-be-replaced-alvarez.

De Jesus, Julliane Love. 2017. "Duterte Assures Robredo Impeachment Against Her Won't Prosper." *Inquirer.net*, 28 March. http://newsinfo.inquirer.net/884573/duterte-assures-robredo-impeachment-against -her-wont-prosper.

Espejo, Paulina Ochoa. 2015. "Power to Whom? The People between Procedure and Populism." In *The Promise and Perils of Populism: Global Perspectives*, ed. Carlos de la Torre. Lexington, KY: The University Press of Kentucky.

Fonbuena, Carmela. 2016. "New 'Party' Kilusang Pagbabago Formed to Protect Duterte." *Rappler*, 5 December. http://www.rappler.com/newsbreak/in-depth/153167-kilusang-pagbabago-duterte-evasco.

Gonzales, Yuji Vincent. 2016. "Duterte: Bongbong Could Be Our New VP." *Inquirer.net*, 20 October. http://newsinfo.inquirer.net/828171/duterte-bongbong-marcos-could-be-our-new-vp.

Jansen, Robert. 2015. "Populism and Human Rights in Theory and Practice: Chavez's Venezuela and Fujimori's Peru." In *The Promise and Perils of Populism: Global Perspectives*, ed. Carlos de la Torre. Lexington, KY: The University Press of Kentucky.

Jenkins, Nash. 2017. "Exclusive: Inside the Cell of Leila de Lima, Duterte's 'First Political Prisoner.'" *Time*, 25 February. http://time.com/4682886/leila-de-lima-manila-philippines-duterte/.

Judis, John D. 2016. *The Populist Explosion: How the Great Recession Transformed American and European Politics.* New York: Columbia Global Reports.

Pasion, Patty. 2017. "Robredo Urged to 'Stop Shaming' Duterte." *Rappler*, 2 April. http://www.rappler.com/nation/165907-palit-bise -rally-robredo-stop-shaming-duterte.

"Philippines to Reaffirm EU Ties After Duterte Criticism." 2017. *ABS-CBN News*, 30 March. http://news.abs-cbn.com/news/03/30/17/philip pines-to-reaffirm-eu-ties-after-duterte-criticism

"Philippine Vice-President Leni Robredo Slams Drug War." 2017. *The Straits Times*, 15 March. http://www.straitstimes.com/asia/se-asia/philippine-vice-president-leni-robredo-slams-drug-war.

Rappler. 2017. "Duterte's Fight vs Criminality Gets 84% Approval Rating." *Rappler*, 13 January. http://www.rappler.com/nation/158214-performance-ratings-duterte-pulse-asia-survey-december-201684%approvalrating-survey.

Romero, Alexis. 2016. "Duterte Secures 'Supermajority' in House." *Philstar.com*, 8 June. http://www.philstar.com/headlines/2016/06/08/1590856/duterte -secures-super-majority-house.

Salaverria, Leila. 2017. "Forgive Duterte's Sexist Remarks, Palace Tells Women." *Inquirer.net*, 1 April. http://newsinfo.inquirer.net/885531/forgive-dutertes-sexist-remarks-palace-tells-women.

Spot.ph. 2017. "These Mind-boggling Statements by Pia Cayetano Are from a Talk About Empowering Girls." *Spot.ph*, 20 March. http://www.spot.ph/newsfeatures/the-latest-news-features/69645/pia-cayetano-sexism-quotes-a00001-20170320.

EPILOGUE
DUTERTISMO BEYOND DUTERTE

Nicole Curato

There is a question I am often asked by foreign media: "When do you think President Duterte's popularity will drop?"

The premises behind the question are as revealing as the question itself. It presupposes that the decline in Duterte's popularity is inevitable. It assumes that there are readily conceivable factors that can spell the demise of the strongman's appeal. The fact that this question is being asked reflects the curiosity, if not bewilderment, of those observing from a distance—why would a murderous president continue to enjoy eighty percent trust rating a year into his presidency in spite of global condemnation against his human rights record?

In this book, we have tried to make sense of President Duterte's rise to power beyond President Duterte. The roster of contributors is curated to surface a range of perspectives, whether it is using the lens of gender, generations, geography, security, or citizenship, among others. The chapters took a critical rather than a celebratory tone, for part of the analytical challenge is to lay bare the structures of power that emerge in the Duterte regime.

There are many lessons we can draw from the first six months of Duterte's rule. As the chapters suggest, the regime's legitimacy is underpinned by a complex web of negotiated relationships with the state's coercive apparatus, concessions to elite rule, adaptability to changing media landscapes, as well as resonance of Duterte's rhetoric to the sentiments of a frustrated public.

Despots are never one-dimensional actors. Duterte is more than the mass murderer he is often portrayed. For his supporters, he is also a compassionate leader who brought home distressed Filipinos working in Saudi Arabia. He is also a loyal commander-in-chief who dutifully visits wounded soldiers in military camps. He is the president who invites militant protesters for a chat after his national address instead of ordering a violent dispersal. And yes, he is a dangerous man who considers murder a national policy.

What underpins his popularity is the public's willingness to disregard the latter in favor of his other qualities. This is not fanaticism but a product of the constant weighing of anxieties, aspirations, and values by citizens in relation to what the man in charge can deliver. What we see is a nation making complex judgments amidst complex realities. And it is precisely these judgments that are worth debating, not dismissing.

There is nothing exotic about the Philippine case. Realities in the Philippines are increasingly becoming a feature of nations facing constant crises. All over the world, we see communities living double lives where cultures of denial provide the comfort required for daily survival. It is necessary for many to shelve troubling information, whether it is about melting polar ice caps, starving children, or refugees fleeing from war. To understand the seeming lack of outrage in the Philippines is to understand the very same conditions that normalize apathy and oppression elsewhere.

As we learn more about the character of the Duterte regime, there are more questions that demand critical conversations. The imposition of Martial Law in Mindanao tests the strength of the Philippines' democratic institutions, whether the co-equal branches of government are willing and able to monitor and correct the executive's abuses, if need be. The air strikes in Marawi showcase what the state is willing to do to confront terrorists, but it also puts into sharp focus how the state responds to humanitarian crises and engages in the politics of rebuilding.

Finally, how the public responds to the President's failed promises is worth observing. A year into Duterte's presidency, roads, trains, and airports are still congested. Oppressive labor practices still prevail. Breadwinners continue to look overseas for better opportunities. Terrorist organizations continue to thrive. Bodies, meanwhile, are being shoved in pairs into unmarked graves. The promised end to the drugs, corruption, and crime within three to six months has long been abandoned. All these as the public continue to pin hopes on the strongman.

Instead of asking when will Duterte's popularity drop, perhaps we should first ask, how can the world pay better attention? To effectively condemn, it is first important to listen.

ABOUT THE CONTRIBUTORS

Carmel Veloso Abao is an instructor of Political Science at the Ateneo de Manila University and a PhD candidate in Development Studies at the De La Salle University. She specializes in social movement studies and international political economy. Before joining the academe, she was involved in a number of social movements in the country—as a labor organizer for Workers' College (now defunct), as deputy director of the Institute for Popular Democracy (IPD), and as the founding national secretary general of Akbayan (Citizens' Action Party).

Patricio N. Abinales is professor at the Asian Studies Program, School of Pacific and Asian Studies, University of Hawaii-Manoa. His latest publications include the second expanded edition of the book *State and Society in the Philippines* (Rowman and Littlefield, 2017), which he co-authored with his late wife, Donna J. Amoroso. He is currently writing a small book on martial law and an introduction to the "Modern Philippines" for American high school seniors.

Jesse Angelo L. Altez (@AngeloAltez) is a writer for the Basic Education Assistance for Muslim Mindanao-Autonomous Region in Muslim Mindanao, a development project funded by the Australian Aid. He's a regular contributor to the *Philippine Daily Inquirer* where he tackles issues relevant to Mindanao.

Cleve Kevin Robert V. Arguelles (@CleveArguelles) is assistant professor and chair of political science at the University of the Philippines Manila. He specializes in political participation, populism, and democracy. He completed his BA and MA Political Science at the University of the Philippines in Manila and Central European University in Budapest, respectively. His thesis, "Grounding Populism: Perspectives from the Populist Publics," was awarded the 2017 Best MA Thesis in Political Science at CEU Budapest.

Walden Bello is an international adjunct professor of Sociology at the State University of New York at Binghamton. He is the author of over twenty books, the latest of which are *State of Fragmentation: The Philippines in Transition* (Quezon City: Focus on the Global South, 2014), *Capitalism's Last Stand?* (London: Zed Books, 2013), and *Food Wars* (London: Verso, 2009). He served in the House of Representatives of the Republic of the Philippines from 2009 to 2015 and made the only resignation on principle in the history of the Congress of the Philippines.

Jason Vincent A. Cabañes is a lecturer in International Communication and deputy director of Research and Innovation at the School of Media and Communication, University of Leeds. He currently co-leads (with Cheryll Soriano) the Newton Tech4Dev Network's research stream on the lives of digital laborers in the Philippines. His most recent works have been published in top-tier journals such as *New Media and Society*, *Media, Culture, and Society*, *Visual Studies*, and *South East Asia Research*.

Kloyde A. Caday (@KloydeCaday) is a faculty member of the Department of English Language and Literature at the University of Southern Mindanao in Kabacan, Cotabato. He earned his Master of

Arts in English at Ateneo de Davao University. His research interests include sociolinguistics and Mindanao literature.

Lisandro E. Claudio (@leloyclaudio) is associate professor of History at the De La Salle University. His latest book is *Liberalism and the Postcolony: Thinking the State in 20th-Century Philippines* (National University of Singapore, Kyoto, and Ateneo de Manila University, 2017).

Jayeel S. Cornelio (@jayeel_cornelio) is the director of the Development Studies Program at the Ateneo de Manila University. He is co-writing (with Filomeno Aguilar Jr., Jowel Canuday, and Lisandro Claudio) a monograph based on Vote of the Poor 2016, a study funded by the Institute of Philippine Culture. He has also written extensively on religion. His first monograph is *Being Catholic in the Contemporary Philippines: Young People Reinterpreting Religion* (Routledge, 2016). In 2017, The National Academy of Science and Technology has recognized him the Outstanding Young Scientist in the field of sociology.

Sheila S. Coronel (@SheilaCoronel) is the dean of Academic Affairs of the Columbia Journalism School and the Toni Stabile Professor of Professional Practice in Investigative Journalism. She was founding director of the Philippine Center for Investigative Journalism and has received numerous prizes for work on the Philippines. Her most recent work on Duterte has been published in various outlets, including *The Atlantic.*

Nicole Curato (@NicoleCurato) holds the Australian Research Council's Discovery Early Career Research Award Fellowship at the Centre for Deliberative Democracy and Global Governance at the University of Canberra. Her work on the Philippines has been published in academic journals, including *Current Sociology, International Political Science Review,* and *Journal of Contemporary Asia,* among others. She is the associate editor of *Political Studies* and has edited Special Issues for journals, including *Critical Asian Studies* and *Philippine Sociological Review.*

John Andrew G. Evangelista is an instructor of Sociology at the University of the Philippines-Diliman where he is also completing his Master's degree in Sociology. He obtained his Bachelor's degree in the Social Sciences at the University of the Philippines-Baguio. His research interests include social movements, gender and sexuality studies, and popular culture.

Ronald D. Holmes is the president of Pulse Asia Research, Inc. He is an assistant professor of Political Science at the De La Salle University and a PhD candidate at the Australian National University. His dissertation examines the political economy of pork barreling in the Philippines after 1986.

Jayson S. Lamchek completed his PhD on the law and politics of human rights at the Australian National University in 2016. After graduating from the University of the Philippines College of Law in 1999, he joined the Public Interest Law Center as an associate for more than six years. He has also lived and studied in Japan and Europe as a Monbusho and Erasmus Mundus scholar. He is currently working on a book manuscript based on his dissertation, to be published by Cambridge University Press in 2018.

Anna Cristina Pertierra is a senior lecturer in Cultural and Social Analysis at Western Sydney University. Her research examines everyday media and consumption practices, drawing from ethnographic research in the Philippines, Mexico, and Cuba. Her recent books include *Media Anthropology for the Digital Age* (Polity, 2017) and *Locating Television: Zones of Consumption* (with Graeme Turner, Routledge, 2013).

Nathan Gilbert Quimpo, a long-time political activist before turning to an academic career, is an associate professor of Political Science and International Relations at the University of Tsukuba, Japan. He has taught at the University of the Philippines, University of Amsterdam, and Sophia University (Tokyo). He is the author of *Contested Democracy and the Left in the Philippines after Marcos* (Yale University Southeast Asia Studies, 2008), co-authored *Subversive Lives: A Family Memoir of the Marcos Years* (Anvil, 2012), and published in *Comparative Politics, Pacific Review, Asian Survey, Critical Asian Studies, Journal of Asian Security and International Affairs,* and *Southeast Asian Affairs.*

Emerson M. Sanchez (@SanchezEmersonM) is a PhD candidate at the Centre for Deliberative Democracy and Global Governance at the University of Canberra. He is the recipient of Australia's Endeavor Postgraduate Scholarship in 2014. He was an instructor of Communication at the University of the Philippines-Manila and a policy researcher for various organizations. He has conducted research on natural resource politics, social movements, and peace-building in the Philippines.

Julio C. Teehankee (@jteehankee) is a full professor of Political Science and International Studies at De La Salle University where he served as the dean of the College of Liberal Arts from 2013 to 2017. He is the executive secretary of the Asian Political and International Studies Association—the regional professional organization of scholars in political science, international relations, and allied disciplines. He is also the president of the Philippine Political Science Association. He completed his postdoctoral studies at the Graduate Schools of Law and Politics at the University of Tokyo, Japan and obtained his PhD in Development Studies from De La Salle University. He is co-authoring a book on the Philippine presidency with Mark R. Thompson of the City University of Hong Kong.

Adele Webb (@adelehwebb) is a PhD candidate in Politics at the University of Sydney's School of Social and Political Sciences, and a member of the Sydney Democracy Network. She specializes in the fields of political sociology and political theory. Her doctoral research uses a historical study of democratization and the middle classes in the Philippines to consider the relationship between democracy and ambivalence. She has written on Philippine politics for the Australian media, including The ABC and The Conversation, with a large public reach. Previously, she worked in international justice advocacy and was director of NGO Jubilee Australia.

INDEX